A GUIDE TO SANDWICH GLASS
PRESSED TABLEWARE

RAYMOND E. BARLOW
JOAN E. KAISER

PHOTOGRAPHS BY
  FORWARD'S COLOR PRODUCTIONS, INC.
  LEN LORETTE
  HUGO G. POISSON

EDITED BY LLOYD C. NICKERSON

Schiffer Publishing Ltd

77 Lower Valley Road, Atglen, PA 19310

BARLOW-KAISER PUBLISHING COMPANY, INC.

OTHER BOOKS BY RAYMOND E. BARLOW AND JOAN E. KAISER

The Glass Industry in Sandwich Volume 1
The Glass Industry in Sandwich Volume 2
The Glass Industry in Sandwich Volume 3
The Glass Industry in Sandwich Volume 4
A Guide to Sandwich Glass Blown Tableware, Pressed Cup Plates and Salts
A Guide to Sandwich Glass Whale Oil Lamps and Accessories
A Guide to Sandwich Glass Kerosene Lamps and Accessories
A Guide to Sandwich Glass Vases, Colognes and Stoppers
A Guide to Sandwich Glass Witch Balls, Containers and Toys
A Guide to Sandwich Glass Candlesticks, Late Blown and Threaded Ware
Barlow-Kaiser Sandwich Glass Price Guide

A GUIDE TO SANDWICH GLASS
PRESSED TABLEWARE
First Edition

Copyright © 1993 by Raymond E. Barlow and Joan E. Kaiser

All correspondence and inquiries should be directed to

Barlow-Kaiser Publishing Company, Inc.
P.O. Box 265
Windham, NH 03087

in conjunction with

Schiffer Publishing Ltd.
77 Lower Valley Road, Rt. 372
Atglen, PA 19310

This book may be purchased from the publisher.

Try your bookstore first.

First Printing

Library of Congress Catalog Number 93-84876
International Standard Book Number 0-88740-552-5

Front cover: Photo 1126 Open work fruit basket on foot, c. 1845. *Courtesy of The Bennington Museum, Bennington, Vermont.*
Back cover: Photo 1041 Acanthus Leaf and Shield sugar on foot, c. 1845. Photo 1077 Double Peacock Eye (Peacock Feather) dish, c. 1840. Photo 1136 Worcester tumblers, c. 1860. Photo 1144 Mirror (Punty, Concave) bowl on foot, c. 1860.

INTRODUCTION

A book that will guide you when you are in the process of buying, selling or appraising Sandwich glass is the most important tool you can own. This book is one of a series of guide books that describes in detail every type of glass that was produced in Sandwich, Massachusetts. All of its photos are taken from those that appear in Volume 1 of *The Glass Industry in Sandwich*, a larger book by the same authors. The identification numbers are the same as those in the larger edition, which allows easy cross-reference. (Guide books with photos from Volumes 2, 3 and 4 are available.)

The photos from the large edition, Volume 1, have been divided into two smaller guides. This guide contains the complete chapter on pressed tableware, which includes the Lacy glass so closely associated with the term *Sandwich glass*. Another guide contains chapters on free-blown and blown molded tableware, pressed cup plates, and open and shaker salts.

The extensive categorization and illustration of Sandwich glass will make this guide valuable for field use. The prices in this guide reflect the market at the time of publication.

WHAT IS SANDWICH GLASS?

It is simple to define Sandwich glass. It was all glass that was produced within Sandwich, Massachusetts, a town on Cape Cod that was founded in 1637.

Glass production came to Sandwich in 1825, when Deming Jarves built and operated an enterprise that became world famous. He called it the Sandwich Glass Manufactory. It was incorporated as the Boston and Sandwich Glass Company in 1826. During the sixty-three years it was active, the factory produced an average of 100,000 pounds of glass per week. Yet this production was only *part* of the glass that should be attributed to Sandwich factories.

In 1859, the Cape Cod Glass Works was established and began to manufacture glass. For ten years, this second factory produced 75,000 pounds of finished glassware each week in competition with the Boston and Sandwich Glass Company. When this company closed, production once again started up in 1883 under the name of the Vasa Murrhina Art Glass Company. Because of manufacturing difficulties, very little of their spangle and spatter glass reached the market. However, the pieces that can be documented should be given Sandwich attribution.

There were several later attempts to manufacture glass in Sandwich after the closing of the Boston and Sandwich Glass Company factory in 1888. In that year, a group of glassworkers built a small glass works and called themselves the Sandwich Co-operative Glass Company. This venture lasted only three years, but its products are recognized as Sandwich glass.

Still another company, the Electrical Glass Corporation, started production in 1890, followed by the Boston and Sandwich Glass Company II, the Boston and Sandwich Glass Company III, and the Sandwich Glass Company. The Alton Manufacturing Company was the last to produce glass on this site. Its most notable product resembled Tiffany glass and was called Trevaise. Like its predecessors, the Alton Manufacturing Company was short-lived, and, in 1908, glass was no longer manufactured in Sandwich. *But the glass made by all of these small companies is recognized as Sandwich glass because of its geographical source.*

There were several other companies in Sandwich that worked on glass but did not make it. They cut it, etched it, engraved it, decorated it, and assembled it. The glass that they worked on, called *blanks*, was brought to Sandwich from factories in Pennsylvania. Regardless of what was done to the surface of this Pennsylvania product, *it cannot be called Sandwich glass*. Only glass that has been shaped while hot can be attributed to a particular factory.

This book deals only with the glass that was manufactured in Sandwich and is therefore entitled to be called Sandwich glass.

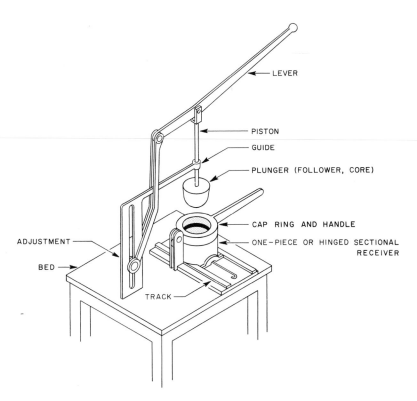

Fig. 7 Lever-operated pressing machine after an illustration in English glassmaker Apsley Pellat's *Curiosities of Glass Making* published in 1849. The plunger and receiver with cap ring could have been used to press a Lacy sugar or slop bowl with a patterned rim. With so few points of adjustment, the plunger attached to the piston of such a machine often entered the receiver at an angle, resulting in an object that was thick on one side.

Screw-operated pressing machine described by Frederick T. Irwin, author of *The Story of Sandwich Glass*, as a "press used in shaping glass at Sandwich, Massachusetts". Irwin's original manuscript and related work product were incorporated into the Barlow-Kaiser collection of documents.

or screw mechanism was operated, allowing the plunger to descend into the mold, displacing the glass and forcing it as it cooled to conform to the shape and pattern of the mold. The plunger was lifted, the mold slid back to the edge of the bed and the hardened article removed.

If the piece was complete, a *sticker-up boy*, or *taker-in boy*, transferred the piece to a pan at the annealing leer. If incomplete, the article was attached by its bottom to a small gob of hot glass on the end of a *punt*, or *pontil rod*. Holding the rod, a glassworker thrust the article into a small hole built into the furnace called a *glory hole*. The reheated article was rendered ductile for final forming with hand tools and/or joining to another unit by means of a hand-formed disk of hot glass called a *merese* or *wafer*. (A pontil mark on any pressed object indicates hand work after removal from its mold.) It was placed on a leer pan, which was a chain-driven metal tray that traveled through the tunnel of an annealing leer. The annealing leer was a long oven heated at the furnace end by wood. Finished articles were evenly heated and allowed to cool slowly as they reached the other end. This tempered the glass and removed stress.

Glass in a molten, molasses-like consistency flows downward like water and can be moved around to fill all crevices available to it. Therefore, seams of molds in which glass was pressed must be tighter than seams of molds in which less fluid bubbles of glass were blown. It took years of experimentation to determine where seams should be located and how sections should be hinged to conceal those places where the glass inevitably seeped into all of the cracks, crevices and openings that occurred in molds. The problem was confounded by the necessity of venting molds here and there. Despite its many imperfections, pressed glass was routinely advertised along with blown glass by firms such as I. H. and E. G. Parker of Boston in 1822.[6]

Jarves left the New England Glass Company in 1824, but the development of molds for pressing small items continued. His successor Henry Whitney, together with machinist Enoch Robinson, patented a machine for pressing door knobs on November 4, 1826. (According to existing Patent Office records, their patent was filed second to that of John P. Bakewell of Pittsburgh, Pennsylvania.)[7] Jarves' income during his first two years in Sandwich was derived from the sale of articles that were free-blown and blown into molds. But during this two-year period, he and his Boston mold makers continued to improve on previous pressing mold construction, and by March 1827 they were ready to introduce pressed articles to market.

The Boston and Sandwich Glass Company sloar book, the weekly account book in which articles made by each group of glassmakers were itemized, first recorded the commercial pressing of glass the week of March 24, 1827. The shop of Reverend Benjamin Haines made twelve "round scallop pressed salts". The mold was passed to Michael Doyle's group and later in the week "round scallop pressed salts" were listed as part of their production. Both Haines' and Doyle's attempts were successful. The sloar book (now preserved at the Ford Archives and Tannahill Research Library, Henry Ford Museum, The Edison Institute, Dearborn, Michigan) shows that pressing increased as molds and machinery became available. Numerous toy plates less than 3" in diameter (see photo 3342) and cup plates (see Chapter 8 in this volume) were pressed in April. By May, they were manufactured by the hundreds.

They were crude at best and when compared with work done by skilled glass blowers, they were saleable only as seconds.[8] With no prototypes on which to base manufacture, machines and molds were one-of-a-kind. Plates were pressed upside down. The patterns to be stamped into their bottoms were on the plunger.[9] Patterned plungers with too much play descended too little and too far and sometimes at an angle. The glass itself, having been melted in a furnace fueled by wood, cooled before it received a sharp impression. If these and other problems were solved, rewards would be forthcoming from the production of articles that previously had been crafted only in metal and wood.

Strong documentation proves that in 1827 and 1828 great strides were taken in this new direction. Molds were devised in which larger pieces of tableware could be pressed.[10] As described in Chapter 2, a rudimentary tumbler was pressed in an Eye and Scale pattern mold which needed too much finish work to be saleable. (A similar pattern can be seen on a lamp in photo 2070.) It took some time to perfect the pressing of cylindrical holloware. Unlike flat plates and shallow nappies that were pressed upside down in a single-section mold that was easy to cast, tumblers were pressed right side up. The pattern had to be on the inner wall of the lower part of the mold rather than on the plunger. If there was depth to the pattern, a complex sectional mold was required for removal of the tumbler. Because the sections expanded and contracted when the mold was necessarily heated and cooled, hinges eventually loosened. The sloppy fit of sections of a once-tight mold created unattractive seam marks and fins on the finished tumbler, interfering with the visual attractiveness of the pattern. Such defects had to be machined off in the cutting shop, an added expense. A method had to be found to keep the rim even in thickness. If the unpatterned plunger entered the mold at an angle, the tumbler was uncomfortable to drink from as well as unsightly.

Jarves put his Eye and Scale tumbler, which he described as "the first tumbler made by machinery in this or any other country", aside as he concentrated on improving production of shallow articles with patterns of minute figures and stippling today referred to as *Lacy*. He further improved this method to increase production volume and simplify the making of molds. He proposed to make Lacy glass in two steps; the first to give pattern and the second to give form. First, the inside surface of the lower unit of the mold was designed to be circular and flat to the very edge. This was the part that was placed on the track of the pressing machine which Jarves called a *receiver*. The patterned plunger was also flat. When the plunger, which Jarves called the *mold* because it was the unit with the pattern, descended into the lower receiver unit and made contact with the hot glass, it pressed a flat disk of glass with the figural and stippling pattern molded into the upper surface. Next, the warm, flexible, patterned sheet of glass was removed from the receiver and was turned over, placing the patterned surface underneath. The next step was to shape the

flat sheet by placing it in another circular metal receiver that had the required form of the finished dish or nappie. The sheet of glass came into contact with the concave upper surface of the second receiver and settled, or "slumped", into the configuration. If the sheet cooled too quickly, a convex unpatterned follower forced the sheet to conform to the lines of the receiver.

Jarves was granted a patent on December 1, 1828, for his "mix and match" system of integrated plungers, receivers, receiver/formers and followers. (The abstract of the patent No. 5290X as published in *Journal of the Franklin Institute* can be found in Chapter 3.) Kirk J. Nelson, curator of the Sandwich Glass Museum, analyzed Jarves' wording of the patent and presented his findings in an article entitled "Early Pressing Technology in Sandwich" that appeared in the 1990 issue of the museum's annual journal *The Acorn*. Nelson deduced that one characteristic of an article made by slumping flat glass into a curved receiver/former is that the thickness of the rim assumed "a very pronounced outward slant", its angle determined by how much the flat sheet with a perpendicular rim was bent upward to form the sidewall of the required dish or nappie. A group of Lacy patterned plates, dishes and nappies exhibit this characteristic. Those appearing in this volume are Shield and Pine Tree, Heart and Lyre and Heart and Rosette. Their rims are slanted, their unpatterned upper surface has wrinkles from an excess of material that resulted when glass already formed flat was reshaped concave.

Deming Jarves envisioned a smooth factory operation of glassmakers stamping out patterned sheets with little down time to adjust and replace mold parts on machinery beds and pistons. He saw lined up at the annealing leers numerous items in the same pattern completed by workers who had assembled together a group of plate, dish and nappie receiver/formers and simply turned over the flat sheets into them. However, he continued to have down time because he did not anticipate the percentage of objects that became warped. Correspondence between Jarves in Boston and his brother-in-law and factory Superintendent William Stutson illustrated some of their concerns.

On January 7, 1829, Jarves wrote to Stutson claiming that Heart pattern articles bulged in the center.[11]

> The 5 & 6 & 7 in. heart patt last sent up. About ⅓ of the quantity will not set steady, but rests on the center like a pivot. This must be corrected and no more come up with that fault by placing a button about ¼ inch thick in the center of the receiver.

A ¼" thick button placed in the hot glass receiver on the pressing machine would have no affect on preventing a warp. However, a button centered in the receiver/former under cooled glass might. Jarves commented about receivers and lamp plates in his January 23, 1829, letter to Stutson. He explained a former request for plates by saying he had meant to order dishes.

> T'is very possible that I might call the 20 doz. Harp 9 inch plates instead of dishes. But, on reflection, you must have perceived that I meant dishes, as you cannot with that mold make plates even with receivers and I was not ignorant that you had many, but I think it almost impossible that I requested you to make 12 Lamp Plates in same mold.....There is some mistake.

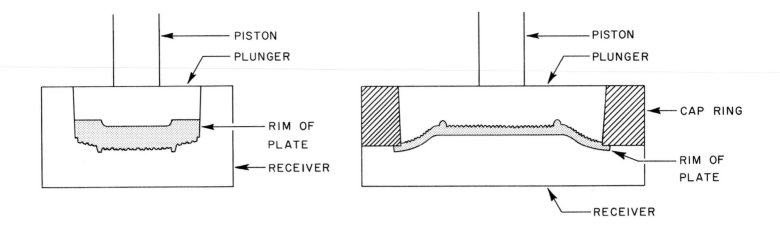

Fig. 8   Cross sections of molds in which glass was pressed showing the advantages of a cap ring, or cover plate. The mold on the left was for a Diamond Check (Checkered Diamond) toy plate as shown in photo 3343. It consisted of a plunger and a patterned receiver. The plunger was the diameter of the finished plate. Thickness was controlled only by the amount of glass dropped into the receiver. This plate was pressed right side up, but similar molds were designed to press plates upside down. The mold on the right was for a Lacy cup plate. It was one of several types that combined a patterned plunger, a receiver and a cap ring. The plate was pressed upside down, the receiver forming the smooth upper surface of the plate. The rim of the plate was formed by glass forced into a cavity between the receiver and cap ring. The cavity maintained the configuration of the rim whether or not the amount of glass dropped into the receiver varied or the plunger entered at an angle. However, the cavity was subject to underfill.

Jarves went on to say that Stutson should not destroy a dish receiver by turning it down (in the machine shop) into a plate receiver and offered this solution.

.....for the Lamp Plate, I think the dish receiver could be filled up even with clay or plaster & dried hard or sheet iron & give it the sweep wanted, instead of turning down a new receiver.

And again an admonishment about warped nappies:

Many of our Heart patt Nappies are returned as they do not set flat, but turn around on a center. The maker must have more care about them.

The comments about lamp plates are particularly intriguing. Coupled with Jarves' instructions in a January 5, 1829, letter, they led authors Barlow and Kaiser to the conclusion that 9" diameter plates in the Harp and other patterns were placed under lamps to prevent fuel from staining table linens and destroying furniture finish. On January 5:

I sent you a plunger for the dish mold you have had that had the fluted bottom. I wish one dozen made of it, to be slightly concave like a Grecian Lamp Plate, which can be done by putting a false bottom in the receiver.

The degree to which Jarves' slumping method was refined becomes unimportant in light of the invention of a *cover plate* or *cap ring* which took place certainly before Jarves perfected a method of pressing a handled piece for which he was issued a patent on May 30, 1830. The cap ring was a circular section of a pressing mold that encompassed the rim of an article. It controlled form (plain, scalloped, pointed), pattern (ribbed, beaded) and thickness. The lack of a cap ring likely had prevented Jarves from mass producing his Eye and Scale tumbler in 1827. Numerous competing glass companies had

people working diligently with mold makers to forward the pressing process, but it was Phineas C. Dummer who was granted a patent for what is believed to be such a cap ring on October 16, 1827. Dummer and his business partners operated the Jersey Glass Company in Jersey City, New Jersey. As summarized in *Journal of the Franklin Institute*, his patent was "On the construction and use of moulds with a core, for pressing glass into various forms: called Dummer's scallop, or coverplate". By controlling the thickness of the rim, like items appeared to be identical even when the sidewall and bottom varied. The concept of a cap ring was the catalyst that made the pressing of glass viable. Here was another mold piece that was interchangeable, allowing one pattern to be pressed with several rim configurations. Numerous improvements quickly followed that rendered Jarves' slumping method obsolete. Kirk Nelson's revealing research cleared the way to logical interpretations of the scant documentation available to us 160 years after the fact.

The evolution of Jarves' patented two-step pressing method coupled with his correspondence serve as an example of the dependency of the Boston and Sandwich Glass Company factory, located in Sandwich, Massachusetts, on mold makers and metal founders situated elsewhere. During the formative years of the pressing industry, Jarves worked closely with Enoch S. Dillaway, who was first listed in the 1827 Boston Directory as a brass founder on Salt Lane. He moved a number of times over the years, but records show that he remained close to Jarves' enterprises.[12] Three letters call attention to the Jarves-Dillaway business relationship. On September 19, 1827, clerk William T. Mayo at the Boston office informed Jarves, who was in Sandwich, "Dillaway is unwell and works slowly on the molds". Said Mayo to Jarves on November 23, 1827, "Hadley and Dillaway have had castings from Hooper's charged to the company".[13] Mayo informed William Stutson on July 11, 1829, "Dillaway is about making a fruit basket mold open work…"

These documents, however, do not prove that Jarves worked with Dillaway exclusively. In an 1829 ledger of Boston and Sandwich Glass Company miscellaneous accounts, D. & J. O'Hagear (sic) were paid for castings and moldings. Of course, we cannot differentiate between metalwork required for glass production and castings for items such as furnace grates or engine parts needed for the ordinary maintenance of factory machinery. Subsequent documents, although scant, prove that relying on outside labor for mold making purposes continued to be the practice of all glass factories in Sandwich.

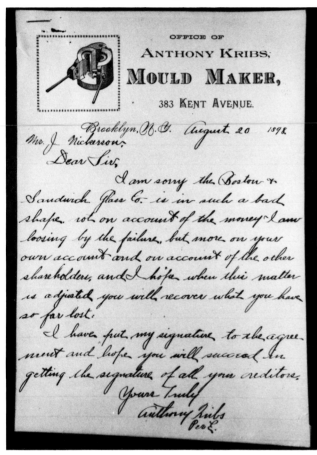

On November 16, 1896, Brooklyn, New York, mold maker Anthony Kribs billed Albert Vaughn Johnston's Boston and Sandwich Glass Company II for a variety of molds and matching wooden patterns. This letter from Kribs dated August 20, 1898, shows him to be a creditor when the Sandwich factory failed early in 1897 (see Chapter 4 in Volume 4). The Kribs documents prove that Sandwich glass companies had business dealings with mold makers far from the Boston area. *Courtesy, Sandwich Glass Museum, Sandwich Historical Society*

Mold maker Anthony Kribs' advertisement as it appeared in the May 10, 1888, issue of *Crockery and Glass Journal*.

According to another article written by Kirk J. Nelson for *The Acorn* dated 1990 entitled "The New England Glass Co. vs George W. Robinson, Machinist", the Boston and Sandwich Glass Company did not employ mold makers in the early 1830's. George Whitefield Robinson was a machinist who terminated his employment at the New England Glass Company before his contract expired. When the glass company sued him, Robinson's attorneys called on William Stutson, superintendent at the Sandwich factory, to testify that the loss of Robinson's services at the East Cambridge works would not substantially affect production and that Robinson's job description of overseeing the maintenance and hanging of pressing molds could be taken over by any qualified machinist. In a deposition taken of Stutson on January 22, 1834, Stutson stated that at Sandwich he had never employed any person to make molds to press glass and had no difficulty in obtaining them when wanted. In fact, a document in a private collection indicates that Robinson maintained a working relationship with the Boston and Sandwich Glass Company. On September 3, 1836, agent Jarves and factory bookkeeper Charles Southack authorized a $250 payment to Robinson. In 1847, Deming Jarves, William Stutson and associates established an iron foundry in North Sandwich (see Chapter 7 in Volume 3). A July 1, 1851, bill to the Boston and Sandwich Glass Company included a mold casting, mold hinges and a deck light mold. But even though owned by Jarves, the Manomet Iron Company was a separate entity.

In the very late years, invoices and statements dated 1896 record the purchase of molds by the Boston and Sandwich Glass Company II from Philadelphia, Pennsylvania, mold maker William J. Wilkinson and Brooklyn, New York, mold maker Anthony Kribs. The Kribs statement included an August 3 invoice for one octagon cracker jar mold and "making model for same". In a December 22, 1881, advertisement run by Kribs in *Crockery Journal*, he claimed "All glass manufacturers use my molds". An accompanying article had this to say about Kribs.

> The glass molds are sold to glassmakers in Brooklyn and all through New Jersey, Pennsylvania, Massachusetts and elsewhere. Pittsburgh makes particularly large demands. Mr. Kribs receives designs from his customers and makes and finishes the patterns in wood or plaster-of-Paris, as the case may be.

Such documented examples establish several important facts. Molds in which Sandwich glass was pressed or blown, whether designed by the mind of a glass factory employee or mold factory employee, were ultimately purchased from a commercial mold making factory. The commercial mold maker, after designing the mold and how it should hinge, had the option of casting it at his own facility if he had the capability or sending it to an outside foundry. After casting, a mold of the required pattern and its accompanying wooden model was shipped to the glass factory and was paid for by the glass company. The glass company now owned and placed into inventory that particular mold. Unless the pattern itself was under patent (Editor's note: Most were not. Patents during the early years were for improvements of mold mechanisms.), the commercial mold maker was free to sell identical glass mold castings to as many other glass companies as he could. This was his living and his right. He also had the right to sell similar molds to factories that made articles in other mediums such as clay or silver.

This should put to rest undocumented claims—legends perpetuated out of habit by writer after writer—that identical articles were made in several glass factories because glass-workers moved from factory to factory "and took their molds with them". Molds were not owned by employees. They were owned by glass companies and stayed in their possession until they were sold by choice or as the result of bankruptcy.[14]

When deponent William Stutson was asked about the degree of skill needed to press glass, he replied that the beauty and finish of the finished product depended on the quality of the molds rather than the skill of the presser. A mechanic was required to "keep the moulds in order", but a common laborer could be taught in one to four weeks to man a pressing machine. To stockholders of the Boston and Sandwich Glass Company, the pressing of glass represented increased profits. Stutson used employees as glass pressers who had previously been yard men and blacksmiths. They did not command the pay of a master gaffer who had apprenticed for years to learn the art of blowing and manipulating glass into usable articles. The receiver and plunger shaped the glass and the most difficult task to be learned by a man in a pressing shop was that of estimating the amount of hot glass to be inserted into a given mold. Unless an article required hand tooling after removal from the mold, an object that once required a skilled gaffer, a servitor, a foot maker and two boys eighteen minutes to make was ready to be placed in the annealing leer in less than one minute. As the men in a pressing shop became skilled in their specific jobs, the time necessary to complete an item dropped significantly and glass became available to the ordinary household at a price that a blue collar worker could afford. At the time Stutson made his statements for the Robinson trial in 1834, the Boston and Sandwich Glass Company had from sixty to seventy machines for pressing glass. "The ware made by these moulds are salts, dishes, plates, lamps, lamp feet, window lights (window panes), deck lights, wafer boxes (for wafers used in sealing letters), sands (containers that sprinkled sand to dry ink), inks, and a variety of other articles."

Stutson's deposition was taken at the height of what was to become known to collectors as the *Lacy period*. Patterns evolved into complicated combinations of rosettes, floral and grape vines, medallions enclosing fine diamond point, scrolls and peacock tails. Remaining surfaces were stippled so that light reflected back into the eyes of the beholder, creating a delightful silvery sheen. The term *Lacy* was adopted because many of the plates resembled lace doilies so necessary to protect table linens and upholstered furniture from lighting fuel and food spills. Based on Deming Jarves' January 23, 1829, reference to nine inch lamp plates, the authors suggest that lace patterns were deliberately adapted to glass plates because their primary use may have been as replacements for doilies—a sort of "glass doily" that functioned as an underplate for lamps and slop bowls and as a charger under dinner plates. Perhaps smaller plates were used under smaller lamps. We offer this not as a conclusion, but a possibility that may be documented in years to come.

When Ruth Webb Lee wrote her book *Sandwich Glass*, she pictured numerous Lacy patterns pressed into a variety of objects. This was her interest in Sandwich production and she researched it as thoroughly as was possible in 1939. A skillful writer, she preserved for future historians a wealth of knowledge for which we are forever grateful. But because she concentrated so heavily on what was in truth a minor portion of Boston and Sandwich Glass Company production, she left the impression that Lacy glass was the Sandwich glass industry's major accomplishment. At the same time Lee was engaged in research, George McKearin and his daughter Helen prepared for the publication of *American Glass* in 1941. The McKearins presented a more balanced overview of glassmaking in the United States, a compilation that led to collectors' awareness of the industry's magnitude and the enormity of production that took place in Sandwich alone. It was astonishing to realize that an isolated village on Cape Cod was responsible for vast quantities of glass manufactured successfully for generation after generation. This book clearly described the changes in production methods that increased factory output and reduced costs so as to stay competitive in the market. Although the McKearins, too, had special glass interests, they were fair in their assessment that, while pressed glass became a major portion of American flint glass house production, pressed glass with Lacy patterns was only one of several styles that were phased in and out according to the need to make imperfect products appear brilliant.

By the 1840's, busy Lacy patterns that completely covered the surface were no longer required. A changeover from wood to coal as furnace fuel produced glass that was more workable, so quality control improved. A financial panic in 1837 made the price of molds with intricate patterns prohibitive. The discovery of excellent grades of glass sand in western Massachusetts that could be transported by rail to Sandwich resulted in a finished product that was less brittle, but with a soft transparency that did not have to be hidden beneath millions of handmade dots. (The history of the Massachusetts glass sand industry is told in Chapter 10 of Volume 2.) By 1850, in the authors' opinion, most Lacy production was curtailed except for special orders pressed in molds that were retained for that purpose. Proof of this is found in the study of lamps appearing in Volume 2. Production of kerosene lamps began at the Boston and Sandwich Glass Company soon after 1850. Not one Sandwich Lacy lamp designed for kerosene has ever been found, so it is reasonable to conclude that the production of new molds with intricate Lacy patterns had been discontinued and in their place evolved bold patterns such as Worcester, Bull's Eye (Lawrence) and Cable and reeded patterns like Bellflower (R. L.) and Hamilton (Cape Cod) that were both quick to mold and pleasing in final form.

Deming Jarves with his son John left the Boston and Sandwich Glass Company in 1858 and erected a new factory nearby. Operated by John W. Jarves and Company as the Cape Cod Glass Works, its primary output was commercially designed pressed patterns that were available to all glass factories that purchased the molds. A study of their *List of Glass Ware*, printed after Jarves reorganized as the Cape Cod Glass Company in 1864 and reprinted in its entirety on pages 108–110 in Volume 3, does not reveal a pattern that was original to the works or that was not also manufactured at the Boston and Sandwich Glass Company factory. During the years of the Civil War, both Sandwich factories as well as all flint glass works scattered throughout the country relied heavily on the manufacture of kerosene lamps. Sales of tableware, long the backbone of the industry, decreased. Mold makers, however, continued to follow trends and produced new patterns that, judging from the forms still available on the antiques market, sold readily when the war was over.

A major change in American glassmaking technology came with the development of glass formulas using ingredients that were less expensive than those required for the making of high quality pressed ware. Until the early 1860's, flint glass was made from formulas that included metallic red lead derived from pig lead oxygenated in a specially constructed furnace. Credit is usually given to William L. Leighton, Sr., for developing an improved formula that included lime and soda instead of lead. In the winter of 1864, Leighton, formerly employed by the New England Glass Company and now working at J. H. Hobbs, Brockunier and Company in Wheeling, West Virginia, substituted inexpensive bicarbonate of soda (baking soda) for the carbonate of soda and soda ash of older non-lead recipies.[15] But Leighton was not alone in non-lead formula experiments. Pittsburgh, Pennsylvania, historian George H. Thurston writing in 1888 stated that John Adams of Pittsburgh's Adams, Macklin and Company experimented in the early 1850's with a view toward making tableware with lime as a substitute for lead. In his book *Allegheny County's Hundred Years*, Thurston claimed Adams was successful within a few years.[16] A document at The Rakow Library of The Corning Museum of Glass, Corning, New York, shows that by May 18, 1864, similar formulas were in use at Jarves' Cape Cod works. The five-year-old factory was visited that day by Thomas Gaffield, a member of the firm of Tuttle, Gaffield and Company, operators of the Boston Crystal Glass Works. Gaffield and the superintendent of his glass house had come to inspect a new furnace. He recorded the following in his notebook.

Mr. Waterman showed us about the works, which are not kept in very neat order. They make and use oyster shell lime. Mr. Neale was not favorably impressed with the management of the works. No lead is used here.....

Gaffield's words were perhaps unfair in view of the fact that he visited the Cape Cod works at a most inopportune time. The Civil War had taken away young glassmakers, and management was undergoing major reorganization due to the deaths of two people for which Jarves had established the works, his son John and his daughter Mary who was the wife of Henry Frederick Higginson, the man in charge of the Cape Cod Glass Works' Boston office. Gaffield's observation about lime formulas, however, is extremely interesting in that it proves widespread use at the time Leighton supposedly perfected them.

When lime-soda formulas were refined to the point where pressed glass carried an acceptable level of strength and polish and could compete for its share of the market, most flint glass factories in the United States converted to its manufacture. As the cost of each batch of glass decreased, so did the retail price of the finished product.

At first the Boston and Sandwich Glass Company refused to lower its standards. It was not until 1873,[17] four years after the Cape Cod Glass Company closed, that they finally changed to non-flint formulas in an attempt to retain a share of the pressed tableware and lamp market. The Sandwich works entered this market when other companies already had ten years of experience pressing and fire polishing lime-soda articles. Sandwich employees found the inexpensive formulas difficult to work with. Although barytes were added to improve the polish,[18] the glass lacked brilliance and character. The famous resonant ring of early flint glass was gone. To make available a commercially satisfactory product, it again

became necessary to change back, as others had done over the last decade, to patterns that covered up the lack of shine. The period from 1863 to 1873 was transitional throughout the glass industry. It can be truly said that Sandwich did not fare well because of the failure to modernize their plant and to accept the competitive formulas for glassmakers.

The new styles of this transitional era are represented by such patterns as Beaded Acorn Medallion, Powder and Shot (Horn of Plenty), and Loop and Dart. While large areas of glass pieces remained unpatterned due to mold making costs, shallow ornaments and stylized flora were interspersed with contrasting, grayish, granular, pebbly bands. The pebbly surface on the glass was first the result of very shallow stipples similar to those of early Lacy glass, but placed closely together to hide the glass rather than to reflect the light. The shallow stippling evolved into a sandy finish caused by etching the surface of the mold.

As does every manufacturer operating within a free enterprise system, the Boston and Sandwich Glass Company had been faced with competition from equally successful rivals. It had held its own when sharing the market with glass houses in eastern states. The eastern houses were separated by the Allegheny Mountains from Pittsburgh, Pennsylvania, houses that supplied cities along the Allegheny, Ohio and Mississippi Rivers. As the United States expanded west, a high concentration of glass companies came to life in the Pennsylvania and Ohio area, where fuel was abundant and inexpensive. When railroads were built and goods were transported to inland cities, previously two distinct markets separated by mountains merged into one serviced by East and Midwest houses. By the early 1870's, keen competition once again forced the Boston and Sandwich Glass Company to limit pressed tableware production. The factory turned its attention to thinly blown glass articles that were threaded, cut, engraved, etched and covered with Overshot.

By 1885, the Pittsburgh area alone gave employment to 25,000 men and boys. Pittsburgh glass companies aggressively extended their market by opening sales rooms in Boston, and for the Boston and Sandwich Glass Company it was "no contest". Pressed tableware could be manufactured in Pittsburgh, shipped to Boston and sold at lower prices than lesser quality articles manufactured in Sandwich and shipped to Boston. Other than the pressing of inks, pomades, match boxes and sponge cups, the pressing era was over.[19] The Boston and Sandwich Glass Company closed January 1, 1888, and their molds were sold in 1889 to Boston china and glass distributor Jones, McDuffee and Stratton. The owners of private molds asked to have them sent to other companies.

Several attempts were made to reopen both Sandwich factories, the Cape Cod and the Boston and Sandwich. These short-lived, highly speculative ventures pressed some glass, but production was limited. Glass was pressed for the last time by the Alton Manufacturing Company operating at the Boston and Sandwich site. Their relative success lasted only several weeks into the first part of 1908. The figural and novelty items pressed by Alton are the latest that can be documented as Sandwich glass.

The molds acquired by Jones, McDuffee and Stratton were dispersed to other glass houses, where some were filled until styles became outdated. Wooden patterns distributed throughout the industry became the basis for the making of new molds. Here are excerpts from an article entitled *Sandwich*

Models from the March 1927 issue of *The Magazine ANTIQUES* about leftover wooden patterns.

In due course, these models came into possession of the late James E. Johnston, of Sandwich, who turned them over to Colonel A. H. Heisey, founder of the firm of A. H. Heisey & Company, glass manufacturers, of Newark, Ohio. The extensive interest in old Sandwich patterns led recently to investigation of the entire cache. As a result, the contents of three of the original barrels were found intact.....The Sandwich models.....are now being utilized by the Heisey Company as a basis for careful modern reproductions, some of which are not easily differentiated from original specimens.

The list that follows are pressed patterns documented as Sandwich without question. It was compiled from glass company records such as lists written by factory personnel, printed lists of articles for sale, identification of discarded fragments dug from factory sites, and independent research by the authors.

Albion
Arch
Arched Grape
Argus
Armorial
Ashburton
Barberry
Beaded Acorn Medallion
Beaded Circle
Beaded Grape Medallion
Beaded Medallion (Beaded Mirror)
Bellflower (R. L.), single vine
Bigler (Flute and Split)
Blackberry
Bleeding Heart (Floral)
Block
Block with Thumbprint
Bradford Blackberry (Bradford Grape)
Buckle, with and without band
Bull's Eye (Lawrence)
Bull's Eye and Fleur-de-lys
Bull's Eye and Rosette
Cable
Cable with Ring
Chrysanthemum Leaf
Colonial
Comet
Crystal
Diamond Point (Mitre Diamond)
Diamond Point (Sharp Diamond)
Diamond Point with Panels (Hinoto)
Diamond Quilted with Bull's Eye Border
Diamond Thumbprint (Diamond and Concave)
Dickenson
Divided Heart
Drapery
Early Moon and Star (Star and Punty, Star and Concave)
Excelsior (New England)
Fine Rib (Reeded)
Flowered Oval (Flower Medallion)
Flat Diamond

Flat Diamond and Panel
Flute, and variants
Flute with Diamond Border
Four Printie Block
Frosted Leaf
Gooseberry
Gothic
Grape and Festoon, clear and stippled background
Grape Band Variant
Greek Key (Greek Border)
Hamilton (Cape Cod)
Hamilton with Leaf (Rose Leaf)
Hamilton with Frosted Leaf (Rose Leaf)
Honeycomb (New York, Utica, Vernon)
Horn of Plenty (Comet)
Huber
Inverted Fern
Inverted Heart
Leaf
Leaf and Dart
Lincoln Drape, no tassel
Loop (Leaf), and variants
Loop and Dart
Loop and Dart with Diamond Ornament
Loop and Dart with Round Ornament
Lyre (Harp)
Magnet and Grape with Frosted Leaf
Magnet and Grape with Stippled Leaf
Mirror (Punty, Concave)
Morning Glory
Mount Vernon
Mount Washington
New England Pineapple (Pineapple, Loop and Jewel)
Old Colony
Old Dominion
Open Rose (Cabbage Rose)
Paneled Fern (Hammond)
Paneled Waffle
Paneled Wheat
Patch Diamond
Petal and Loop
Pillar
Plume, with variants
Powder and Shot (Horn of Plenty)
Pressed Leaf (New Pressed Leaf)
Prism
Prism and Crescent
Prism and Diamond Point
Prism Panel
Punty and Ellipse (Monroe)
Raised Diamond
Ribbed Acorn (Acorn)
Ribbed Grape (Mount Vernon)
Ribbed Ivy
Ribbed Palm (Sprig)
Ripple
Sandwich Loop (Gaines)
Sandwich Star (Quarter Diamond)
Sawtooth (Mitre Diamond)
Scalloped Lines (Scalloped Band)
Smocking
Snowflake

Star and Punty
Stippled Band
Stippled Fuchsia
Stippled Star
St. Lawrence
Strawberry
Sunk Diamond
Three Printie Block
Tree of Life
Tulip
Utica
Waffle
Waffle and Thumbprint (Palace)
Washington
Worcester
Zouave

THESE SIMPLE HINTS WILL HELP YOU IDENTIFY SANDWICH PRESSED TABLEWARE

When glass is pressed into a mold, its inner surface does not follow the contour of the pattern but is smooth. Mold marks are distinct and may have fins caused by excess glass that seeped between mold sections.

On footed articles, look for the hand-formed wafer of glass by which separately pressed units were joined.

Study those individual units of articles made by joining them with a wafer so you will recognize them when found in different combinations.

Sandwich Lacy patterns lack unity. Non-related elements were combined to fill available space with little regard to overall design merit.

French Lacy patterns are well thought out with elements in proportion to each other, resulting in a satisfying total pattern.

Study the depth of Lacy patterns. Sandwich patterns are shallow and French patterns are molded in deep relief.

Pittsburgh Lacy patterns have large bull's eyes, beads and circles.

All Sandwich Lacy glass is flint glass that is fluorescent blue under both short wave and long wave black lights.

Lacy adult size handled cups and matching saucers, and tumblers and goblets were not Sandwich products.

Study the Sandwich three-petaled lily which, as far as is known, was only used at Sandwich.

Study the *List of Glass Ware Manufactured by Cape Cod Glass Company* reprinted in its entirety on pages 108–110 in Volume 3.

You will not find two colors blended together such as Amberina or color fading to clear such as Rubina on pressed tableware. Neither will you see opalescent rims. Sandwich items in two colors were manufactured by pressing separate units in solid colors and attaching them with wafers.

Look carefully for the monogram, or "logo", on reproductions that were made for museum gift shops; it is sometimes well hidden within the pattern. Examine for the place where a "logo" may have been removed. Be aware, however, that glass houses manufacturing reproductions for museums have been known to replace a mold section with one that has no monogram so they can feed new glass into the antiques market at the expense of the museum that paid for the mold.

UNITED STATES PATENT OFFICE.

HIRAM DILLAWAY, OF SANDWICH, MASSACHUSETTS.

IMPROVED GLASS-PRESS.

Specification forming part of Letters Patent No. **57,296**, dated August 21, 1866.

To all whom it may concern:

Be it known that I, HIRAM DILLAWAY, of Sandwich, in the county of Barnstable and State of Massachusetts, have invented new and useful Improvements in Glass-Presses; and I do hereby declare that the following is a full, clear, and exact description thereof, which will enable others skilled in the art to make and use the same, reference being had to the accompanying drawings, forming part of this specification.

The present invention consists, first, in a novel arrangement of parts for operating and moving the plunger or follower and obtaining the requisite degree of pressure upon the glass within the mold; second, in so arranging the mold that it can be moved into or out of the line of movement of the plunger or follower, the mechanism employed to accomplish which is susceptible of adjustment to accommodate the various sizes of molds; third, in so arranging the plunger or follower that when such portion of the same as is to cover the mold is over and upon it, it will be there tightly and firmly held while the plunger or follower is acting upon the inside of the mold—a result of great importance.

Having thus in general terms stated the principal features of the present invention, I will now proceed to describe the same in detail, together with other minor improvements involved in the press, reference being had to the accompanying plates of drawings, in which—

Figure 1, Plate 1, is an elevation of the rear side of a glass-press constructed according to my invention; Fig. 2, Plate 1, an elevation of one side of the same; Fig. 3, Plate 2, a vertical section taken in the plane of the line x x, Fig. 1, Plate 1; Fig. 4, Plate 2, a horizontal section taken in the plane of the line y y, Fig. 1, Plate 1; and Fig. 5, Plate 3, a horizontal section taken in the plane of the line z z, Fig. 1, Plate 1.

Similar letters of reference indicate like parts.

A in the drawings represents the table or bed-plate of the press, which, at each corner, is supported or rests upon the upper ends of posts B, that, at their lower ends, are connected together and braced by horizontal bars C, and also set or mounted on wheels or rollers D, for convenience in moving the press about from place to place.

To the upper side of the table are fixed two parallel upright posts or rods, E E, that are connected together by a cross bar or head, F, near their upper ends, G, a vertical screw spindle or shaft passing loosely through the center of the fixed cross-head F, and also through cross-heads H and I, one above and the other below the fixed cross-head F, arranged to move up and down upon the uprights E E, hereinbefore referred to.

The upper cross-head, H, is confined or held on the spindle G between two screw-nuts, J J, one above and the other below the cross-head, by means of which the position of the said cross-head upon the spindle can be adjusted at pleasure.

The lower cross-head, I, rests upon the projecting flange K of the spindle, to which flange it is secured by bolting, riveting, or in any other proper manner.

The lower end, L, of the spindle G forms the plunger or follower for the mold, and is to be made of such shape as may be necessary for the mold used.

M is a horizontal head-plate on spindle G, which is held between two screw-nuts, N N, one above and the other below the plate. From each of the four corners of this plate M parallel vertical rods o extend, which rods are of equal length, two upon each side of the cross-heads, with the upper ends of those rods upon the same side of the cross-heads secured together by cross-bars P.

The outer ends of each of the cross-bars P are connected, through vertical rods Q, with the cross head or plate R, placed below the cross-head I, which plate R is set over the plunger end of the spindle G, and plays upon the fixed uprights of the bed-plate.

Between the head-plate R and the cross-bars P on the rods Q spiral springs R² are placed, on which springs the cross-bars rest, they being held upon the said rods by means of screw-nuts S.

To each end of the upper vertical sliding cross-head, H, similar connecting-rods T T are hung, that, extending downward upon each side of the press, are hung at their lower curved ends, U U, to one end of crank-arms V V of a common horizontal shaft, W, hung in vertical elongated or slotted bearings W of parallel standards X, secured to the under side of bed-plate A at their upper ends, and at their lower ends to a common horizontal connecting-bar or brace, S. On each of the outer ends of the bar or brace S is hung a similar bent arm or rod, Z, that at their upper ends are hung to the opposite ends of the crank-arms V, hereinabove referred to, at which the connecting-rods T were hung.

To one end of the horizontal shaft W a vertical lever arm or handle, A², is secured, by depressing or raising which, through the rods connecting said shaft W with the upper sliding cross-head, H, said cross-head, together with the screw-spindle on which it is placed and all the other parts connected therewith, as hereinbefore explained, are consequently lowered or raised, as the case may be, and thereby the plunger or follower of said spindle made to enter or to be withdrawn from the mold B² used, which is placed upon the upper side of the bed-plate A of the press in proper position therefor, this mold being arranged in a novel manner, as will be hereinafter described, so that it can be slid into position for the plunger to enter it, or out of line with the movement of the plunger, for the purpose of removing the article molded in it.

From the above description of the connecting parts between the operating-lever A² and the plunger or follower for the mold, and the manner in which they are arranged and combined, it is plain to be seen that when the cross head or plate R has been brought to bear upon the top of the mold, on which it comes to a rest or stop, by then continuing to depress the operating-lever the plunger can be made to still further enter the mold, passing through the said plate R, by such movement of the plunger, is firmly held, through the compression of the spiral springs R², by the cross-arms P, moving upon the guide-rods O, thereby preventing all possibility of the cover or plate R rising from the mold as the plunger acts in it, the importance of which is obvious.

The mold B² is provided with a handle, A⁴, for convenience in removing it from the press. The mold is placed upon a plate, B⁴, that is arranged to slide upon a dovetail tenon or strip, C⁴, secured to the upper side of the table or bed-plate A. To the rear side of the sliding plate B⁴ is hung the inner end of a short connecting-rod, D⁴, to the outer end of which is hung, by its swiveled nut E⁴, the lower end of a vertical inclined connecting-bar, F⁴, that is hung upon a fulcrum, G⁴, of the stationary projecting arm H⁴ of the upper part of the press, and at its upper end is pivoted to one end of a short connecting arm or link, I⁴, arranged to slide in the horizontal groove J⁴ of the upright K⁴ of the press. To the other end of the link is hung a vertical connecting-rod, L⁴, in the lower end of which turns the horizontal shaft W, hereinbefore referred to.

The rod L⁴ passes through the band M⁴ fixed to one side of a slide-bar, N⁴, arranged to move or slide in the ends of standards O⁴, secured to one side of the bed-plate A.

From the lower side of the slide-bar N⁴ extends a bent or curved arm, P⁴, which, by its straight portion O⁴, is secured in the slide-bar N⁴ by means of nuts R⁴, so that it can be adjusted to project more or less by its curved end.

S⁴ is an arm secured to horizontal crank-shaft W, and notched at T⁴, which arm, as the said shaft W revolves and rises in its elongated bearings, abuts against the downward-projecting lug U⁴ of the slide-bar N⁴ and carries such bar along with it, and through the connecting parts described slides the mold out from under the plunger, when, depressing the lever-handle A², the said arm S⁴ then acts upon the shoulder or corner V⁴ of the curved arm P⁴, and again sliding the slide-bar, but in an opposite direction to that above explained, moves the mold under the plunger and in position for being operated upon by it.

The outward and inward movement of the mold above described is to be arranged so as to occur at the proper times with reference to the upward and downward movement of the plunger or follower.

To enable the handle or lever A² to be changed in position upon the shaft W, to which it is secured, I employ a ratchet-clutch, X⁴, as plainly shown in the several figures of the drawings, whereby, as is obvious, the desired result can be secured.

Having thus described my invention, I claim as new and desire to secure by Letters Patent—

1. The plunger or follower L, hung on a sliding head or frame moving upon guides E E and connected, through rods U, with crank-arms of a shaft, W, arranged in slotted bearings, to the opposite ends of which crank-arms rods z are connected at one end, and at their other hung upon fixed pivots X, substantially as and for the purpose specified.

2. The mold B⁴, arranged and connected with the shaft for operating the plunger in such a manner as to be moved under and away from the line of movement of the plunger, substantially as and for the purpose described.

3. The head-plates M and R, rods O and Q, cross-bars P, springs R², when all arranged and connected together and to the plunger so as to operate substantially as and for the purpose set forth.

The above specification of my invention signed by me this 30th day of April, 1866.

HIRAM DILLAWAY.

Witnesses:
CHS. W. LAPHAM,
LUTHER DRAKE.

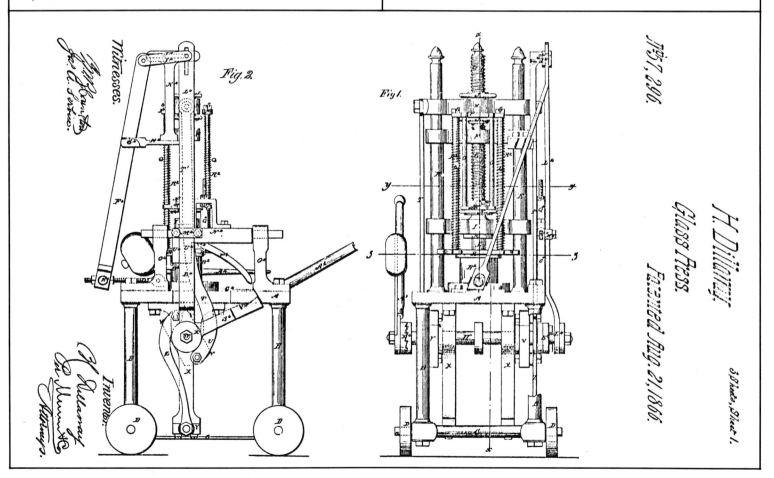

Fig. 2.

Fig. 1.

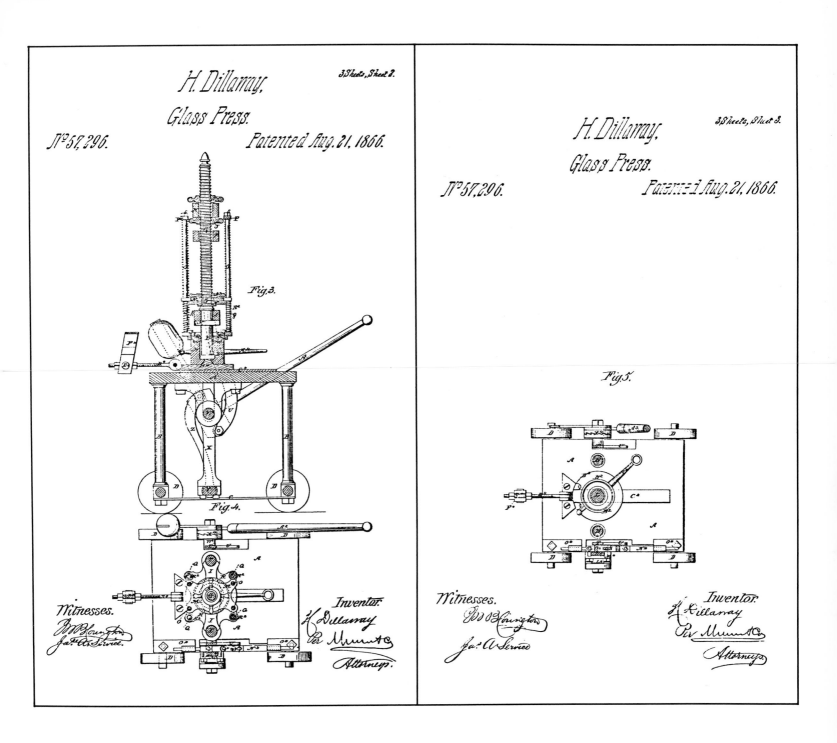

H. Dillaway,

Glass Press.

Nº 57,296.   Patented Aug. 21, 1866.

3 Sheets, Sheet 2.

Fig. 3.

Fig. 4.

Witnesses.

Inventor.
H. Dillaway
Per Munn & Co
Attorneys.

H. Dillaway,

Glass Press.

Nº 57,296.   Patented Aug. 21, 1866.

3 Sheets, Sheet 3.

Fig. 5.

Witnesses.

Inventor.
H. Dillaway
Per Munn & Co
Attorneys.

Machinist Hiram Dillaway's patent No. 57,296 for an improved screw-operated pressing machine, dated August 21, 1866.

United States Patent Office.

HIRAM DILLAWAY, OF SANDWICH, MASSACHUSETTS.

Letters Patent No. 63,325, dated October 1, 1867.

IMPROVEMENTS IN GLASS-WARE PRESSES.

The Schedule referred to in these Letters Patent and making part of the same.

TO ALL WHOM IT MAY CONCERN:

Be it known that I, HIRAM DILLAWAY, of Sandwich, in the county of Barnstable, and State of Massachusetts, have invented an Improvement in Presses for Forming Glass-Ware; and I do hereby declare that the following, taken in connection with the drawings which accompany and form part of this specification, is a description of my invention sufficient to enable those skilled in the art to practise it.

The invention relates particularly to the construction or arrangement of mechanism of presses for forming glass-ware in moulds, and the improvement consists in the disposition of a pair of segment-gears in relation to each other, and to gear-pinions, into which they alternately mesh, and to the actuating shaft and lever, and to the plunger and its connections, the segment-gears being placed, one on the shaft which carries the working handle or lever, and the other on the shaft, or an arm or crank upon which the plunger is connected, each segment being so disposed that the teeth of one or the other always mesh into the teeth of a smaller gear upon the opposite shaft, the arrangement being such that during the first part of the downward movement of the plunger, while its work is light, (or before it reaches the mould,) the segment on the driving-shaft meshes into the gear or pinion on the plunger-shaft, and of course effects a correspondingly rapid descent of the plunger, while, as the plunger reaches the mould, and its descent is resisted by the contents thereof, the driving-segment runs out of connection with its pinion, and the pinion on the driving-shaft simultaneously runs into connection with the segment on the plunger-shaft, the same power thereby effecting the descent of the plunger, but at a slower speed, the segment-gears upon the plunger-shaft being made adjustable with reference to the position of the plunger, so that the change from quick speed and light pressure to slow speed, at a point where the resistance increases, may be regulated as circumstances may render desirable.

The invention also consists in the peculiar method of effecting the descent of the plunger, which comes down upon the top of the mould in such manner that after the follower is carried down against the mould it is held rigidly in position, or is kept from springing upwards, while the pressure upon the glass in the mould continues or is being effected.

The drawings represent a press embodying my invention. A shows a side elevation and B an end elevation of the same. C is a vertical cross-section, taken in line with the plunger.

a denotes the frame of the press; *b*, the bed or table, upon which the mould *c* rests, said mould being centred beneath the plunger *d* by stops *e*, or other suitable means. Said plunger *d* is bolted to a cross-head, *f*, sliding upon vertical rods or ways *g*, said cross-head being connected to another cross-head, *f'*, by an adjusting-screw, *h*, the cross-head *f* being raised or lowered by said screw and nuts *i*, to adjust the position of the plunger with reference to the particular mould to be used. The upper cross-head is connected to arms *k*, projecting from the ends of a shaft, *l*, by connecting-rods *m*. This shaft bears a segment-gear, *n*, (concentric with the axis of the shaft,) and a pinion, *o*, said gear and pinion being respectively opposite and alternately meshing into a corresponding gear, *p*, and a pinion, *q*, on a driving-shaft, *r*, which latter shaft is actuated by a long hand-lever, *s*. When the plunger is at its highest position, the teeth of the driving-shaft segment are in connection with the teeth of the plunger-shaft pinion, as seen at A. If the lever is now drawn down, the segment-teeth work upon the pinion-teeth of the plunger-shaft, the difference in the radii of the two gears causing the quick descent of the plunger during the first part of its downward movement. As the last tooth of the driving-segment leaves the pinion, the first tooth of the plunger-shaft segment comes into connection with the driving-shaft pinion, the segment being then driven by the pinion, and effecting the completion of the descent of the plunger with the full power exerted by the short arm of the lever (namely, the radius of the driving-pinion) upon the segment.

Now, in order to effect this change from driving-segment to driving-pinion, at different points in the course of descent of the piston or plunger as may be desirable, according to the size of the mould or the degree of pressure necessary to be exerted, I make the plunger-shaft segment adjustable in position upon the shaft, and relatively to the arms *k*, so that the change from the driving-segment operating the pinion to the driving-pinion operating the segment may be made to occur at any position of the arms *k* within their limit of motion. For this purpose I make the plunger-shaft pinion and segment (which are integral) movable upon the shaft, and upon or near the face of the pinion I make clutch-teeth *t*, clutching into teeth *u* on the shaft. At the opposite face of the segment I cut a screw-thread on the shaft, and place on this thread a nut, *v*. By turning back this

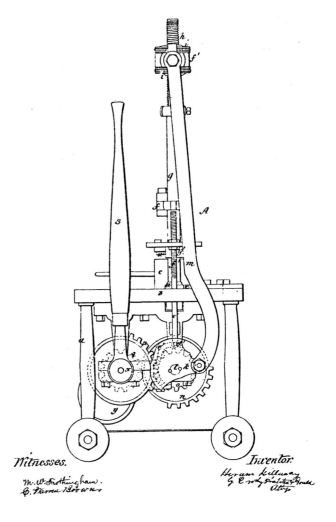

Witnesses.

M. W. Frothingham.
B. Varne Browns

Inventor.

Hiram Dillaway
G. Crosby Fielhold Ellicott
Atty

---

2   63,325

nut the gears may be slipped back upon the shaft, disconnecting the clutch-teeth, and the gears may then be turned upon the shaft until the segment-teeth are brought to the required position relatively to the position of the arms *k*, this change being preferably made when the piston is at its height, and with the lever *s* (at the start) in upright position. The lever will be moved in making the change; but in order that it may be in vertical position at all times when the plunger is at its height, it may be connected to the driving-shaft by a clutch, *w*, and a nut, *x*, which will permit the inclination of the handle relatively to the segment-teeth to be changed as may be desirable. To carry the plunger up, a weight, *y*, may be hung upon an arm on the shaft *l*, and this weight may be made adjustable in position, in accordance with the positions of the gears, by a clutch, *z*.

The follower is shown at *a'*, fixed on the under surface of a cross-head or plate, *b'*. This plate or the follower is generally made to move downward with the plunger until it reaches the mould, and to be cushioned against springs, to allow the plunger to descend after the follower strikes the mould. This is objectionable, in that under a great pressure from the glass in the mould, the follower yields, (by compressing the springs,) and leaves the pressed article imperfect in shape. To remedy this, I separate the follower from the plunger, and impart its movement directly from the shaft *l*, as follows: At each end of the shaft is a cam or cam-groove, *c'*, in which a pin, *d'*, plays, this pin projecting from the foot of a vertical rod, *e'*, the follower-plate being mounted on the upper ends of the two rods *e'*. Each cam-groove is inclined towards its shaft at one end, and is concentric with the shaft at the opposite end. As the shaft turns, the irregular part of the cam draws down the rods and follower until the follower closes over the top of the mould. The concentric parts of the cams then slide over the cam-pins, and the rods and follower are thereby held in stationary position. To regulate the stop of the follower, the rods *e'* have screw-threads *f'* upon their upper ends, upon which nuts *g'* work, and the position of the follower-plate is determined and adjusted by these screws and their nuts, as will be readily understood.

I claim the combination of the driving-segment gear and pinion, with the respective pinion and segment-gear with which each alternately connects, when arranged to operate to produce the descent of the plunger or piston, substantially as shown and described.

I also claim combining the follower with mechanism which not only effects its descent, but holds it stationary upon the mould during the continued descent of the plunger, substantially as described.

HIRAM DILLAWAY.

Witnesses:
F. G. NEWCOMB,
CHARLES B. HALL.

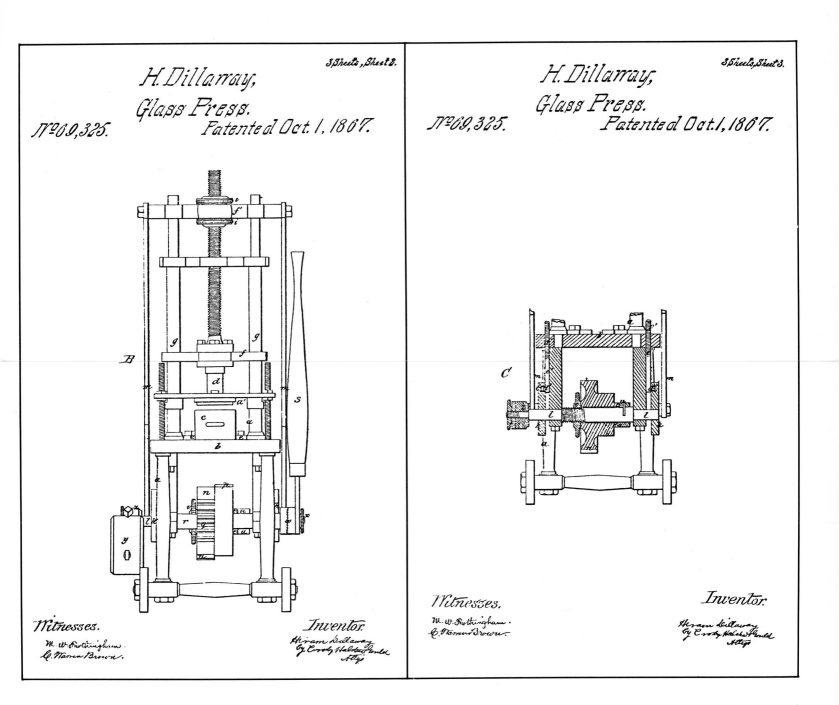

Machinist Hiram Dillaway's patent No. 69,325 for an improved screw-operated pressing machine, dated October 1, 1867.

NOTES TO CHAPTER 6

1. As stated by Deming Jarves in *Reminiscences of Glass-making*.

2. As noted by Apsley Pellatt in *Curiosities of Glass Making*, "Various slabs of coloured Glass, of small sizes, were pressed into metallic dies by the ancients, as proved by the specimens of embossed and intagliated Glass, of various patterns, in the British Museum; but no machinery was used by them in producing any completely hollow vessel or utensil, at one operation."

3. According to Boston and Sandwich Glass Company Superintendent William Stutson in a deposition taken on behalf of George W. Robinson, "The art of pressing was introduced into this country in the year 1817".

4. The New England Glass Company offered for sale at auction on October 16, 1819, "Prest Castor Bottles", "Prest Pocket Flasks" and "Prest Seragon Liquor Bottles". The advertisement appeared in the October 4 issue of the *Boston Commercial Gazette*.

5. The following was excerpted from *Reminiscences of Glass-making* by Deming Jarves. "Soon after the introduction of the (glassmaking) business into this country, a very great improvement in the mode of manufacture was introduced. Pellatt, in his admirable work on glass, alludes to the American invention in only a few words, and passes it by as of but slight importance; but it has brought about a very great change, and is destined to exert a still greater; in fact, it revolutionized the whole system of the flint-glass manufacture, simply by mould machines for the pressing of glass into any form.....The writer has in his possession the first tumbler made by machinery in this or any other country. Great improvement has of course taken place in the machinery....."

6. Parker advertised in the Plymouth, Massachusetts, newspaper *Old Colony Memorial and Plymouth County Advertiser* on September 7, 1822.

7. United States Patent Office records are by no means complete. The office was destroyed by fire on December 15, 1836. Not all patents were resubmitted and some that were are buried deep in the Archives and are irretrievable. We have examined American pressed salts that appear to have been made prior to Jarves' venture in Sandwich in 1825. The salts, the New England Glass Company ad and the Parker ad clearly show we cannot rely on patent records alone to establish a sequence of events.

8. Factory policy was that a worker was reprimanded if more than 10 percent of his output had to be sold as seconds. In early years under Jarves, he might be expected to pay for the loss to the company if his workmanship was a continuous problem and of course he could be fired. As quality improved over the years, so did the quality of the seconds. Many pieces in collections today were originally auctioned at trade sales as seconds. In unsaleable condition, items were taken home for the worker's household use.

9. On June 28, 1828, Jarves wrote to Superintendent Stutson, "Be careful no one gets a clay impression from the new dish moulds. Better take the plunger away." Jarves' instructions were clarified by Kirk Nelson's interpretation that the pattern was on the plunger.

10. Pressed glass is referred to as *press-moulded* in England, an apt description and more accurate than the American term. The authors wish it was in use here. It is so sensible when you consider that glass blown into a mold is called *blown molded*. See *English 19th Century Press-Moulded Glass* by Colin R. Lattimore.

11. A selected group of factory correspondence was published in 1984 by the Sandwich Historical Society in the book *Your Obdt. Servt., Deming Jarves*, edited by then Sandwich Glass Museum Director Barbara Bishop and Historian Martha Hassell. Additional letters have since been acquired by the Sandwich Glass Museum.

12. According to Boston City Directories, Enoch S. Dillaway's place of business was 30 Market in 1828, 30 Cornhill in 1829 and 4 Noyes Place from 1830 to 1836, all in Boston proper. He relocated by 1837 to 4th Street between B Street and C Street in South Boston not far from Thomas Cains' Phoenix Glass Works, where he was listed as a machinist. Admittedly, Dillaway probably designed molds for factories other than those with which Jarves was affiliated, but the fact is Dillaway changed his place of business during the time his services should have been least needed—during the 1837 financial crisis—to a convenient location near the site of Jarves' new Mount Washington Glass Manufactory. We believe extended research would show that Hiram Dillaway, a machinist who eventually became head of the Boston and Sandwich Glass Company machine shop, was related to Enoch S. Dillaway. As documented on page 145 of Volume 3, family papers record that Hiram Dillaway came to Sandwich from the Mount Washington Glass Manufactory. Boston and Sandwich Glass Company payroll records first listed Hiram in Sandwich in December 17–29, 1838. In 1853, according to the Boston City Directory, Enoch S. Dillaway was back in Boston listed as a mold maker at 51 Federal Street, the address of the Boston and Sandwich Glass Company since 1845. In 1859, after Deming Jarves and the Boston and Sandwich Glass Company severed their relationship, Enoch S. Dillaway moved to 26 Federal Street, the Boston and Sandwich Glass Company's new headquarters. His son Enoch S. Dillaway, Jr., also a mold maker, continued to run the 51 Federal Street office.

13. Isaac Hadley was listed as a brass founder working at Enoch S. Dillaway's 1828 and 1829 addresses. In 1830 and 1831, he was still listed as a brass founder, but his place of employment was not given. Henry N. Hooper first appeared in the 1826 Boston Directory as an agent for the Boston Copper Company on Batterymarch. He was listed as "successor to late Boston Copper Co." in 1830. In 1833, Hooper and associates W. Blake and Thomas Richardson were listed as Henry N. Hooper and Company, copper dealers on Batterymarch. The business relocated to 24 Commercial the following year, where it remained for a number of years. They cast the factory bell for the Boston and Sandwich Glass Company building erected in 1833. Henry N. Hooper and Company was also listed under *Bell Founders*, *Brass Foundries* and *Lamp Makers* in various directories.

14. There is proof that companies borrowed molds from time to time, but individuals had no access to them.

15. *The New England Glass Company 1818–1888* published by The Toledo Museum of Art listed five formulas from a notebook kept by John H. Leighton. One entered in the late 1840's was labeled "to make flint glass without lead". It contained sand, pearlash, soda, lime, borax, arsenic and manganese.

16. As related in *Pittsburgh Glass 1797–1891* by Lowell Innes, page 44.

17. William Germain Dooley, in an article entitled "Recollections of Sandwich Glass by a Veteran Who Worked on It" published in the June 1951 issue of *Hobbies*, interviewed an elderly glassmaker who told Dooley, "The earliest pressed glass at Sandwich had lead in it.....Use of lead was discontinued for litharge, though the glass still contained some from the broken lead glass in the cullet. Later pressed glass used the cheaper ingredient, lime, which does not take a polish.....This was just beginning to be used in 1873 when I came to Sandwich." Lead glass continued to be used for blown glass.

18. Again quoting the Boston and Sandwich Glass Company glassworker interviewed by William Germain Dooley. According to Noah Webster's *An American Dictionary of the English Language*, barytes is sulphate of baryta, generally called *heavy-spar*. Baryta is a metallic substance called *barium* or *barytum*. It is an oxide which when combined with sulphuric acid forms sulphate of baryta, or *heavy-spar*.

19. An American Flint Glass Workers Union Local No. 16 list of items produced at the Boston and Sandwich Glass Company between 1879 and 1883 was comprised primarily of blown tableware and lighting equipment. The list of pressed ware was short and a notation indicated that it was "work made by spare hands" to fill their time.

1001 PRESSED DIAMOND CHECK (CHECKERED DIAMOND) PLATES

(a) Completely molded
(b) Incomplete 1" H. x 6" Dia. 1828–1832

Diamond Check and *Checkered Diamond* were descriptions used interchangeably in Boston and Sandwich Glass Company correspondence. In a letter to William Stutson dated October 17, 1827, Deming Jarves referred to "Check'd diamond Cup Plates", using a symbol for the word *diamond*. On January 30, 1828, Boston clerk William T. Mayo wrote a letter to Stutson that included an order of William Allison for "diamond check Cup plates", again using the diamond symbol. Diamond Checks are small squares quartered into four tiny squares, or checkers. It is one of the earliest patterns pressed at Sandwich. The pattern of checkers appears as an allover pattern covering the center to the table-rest. The undulating chain on the border is comprised of Diamond Check placed end to end. These elements are molded beneath the plate, the upper surface unpatterned except for a chain of tiny beads near the serrated rim. (Do not mistake the tiny quartered squares for stippling that covers the background on pressed Lacy pieces.) Plate A is a complete one that was purchased. Plate B was dug from the Boston and Sandwich Glass Company factory site, thrown out because it was unsaleable. Not enough hot glass was placed in the mold to fill all of its crevices when the plunger forced it into shape. Finding an article discarded because it was made in an underfilled mold is, in the authors' opinion, absolute proof of origin.

1002 PRESSED DIAMOND CHECK (CHECKERED DIAMOND) AND FAN PLATES

(a, b) 1" H. x 6" Dia.
(c) ¾" H. x 5¾" Dia. 1828–1832

Plates A and B are alike, shown together so that you realize the depth of color of plate B. The overall pattern fills the center, which is surrounded by twenty fans at the rim. These patterns are molded beneath the plate. A single chain of beads around the rim is molded into the upper surface. The center of plate C is quartered, two quarters having the Diamond Check pattern and two having rays radiating from an eight-pointed star. Five-pointed stars alternate with fans on the rim. Early pressed plates can be ½" thick and may be thicker on one side than on the other. This was a common occurrence because the first molds used for pressing were one piece, completely open at the top to allow entrance of a plunger that was the diameter of the finished object. When the plunger entered the mold at an angle, the thickness varied. Unusual characteristics such as this add to the value of a piece.

1003 PRESSED DIAMOND CHECK (CHECKERED DIAMOND) AND FAN PLATE

1½" H. x 9" Dia. 1828–1832

This large plate was not designed to be a dinner plate, but a serving plate used in conjunction with a set of china. In 1947, Francis (Bill) Wynn of Sandwich was digging near the location of an early furnace. He uncovered numerous fragments of this pattern, one of which is shown on the right. Some were pale blue and amethyst. All of the plates and fragments examined by the authors are very thick and are uncomfortably heavy to handle. Diamond Check completely covers the center. The border is a combination of twenty-seven eight-petaled rosettes alternating with bull's eyes. Fans radiate from the bull's eyes. Note that the fans are relatively the same size regardless of the diameter of the plate; larger plates have more fans. A matching cup plate was made.

1004 PRESSED DIAMOND CHECK (CHECKERED DIAMOND) AND SHEAF PLATE

¾" H. x 5⅛" Dia. 1828–1832

The many variants of Diamond Check attest to its acceptance in the market. This unusual example is one of the mysteries that one frequently discovers in old glass. Two concentric rings were inscribed into the patterned center of the mold, creating an unpatterned band. The procedure appears to have been an afterthought that would provide a change in pattern at little expense. Subtle changes in mold making never fail to fascinate the glass scholar. Look for them when searching for glass; unusual characteristics give depth to your collection as well as increased value. The table rest is plain and there is no pattern on the flat inside wall. The border is composed of eighteen sheaves of wheat molded beneath and a chain of tiny ovals on the upper surface of the rim.

1005 PRESSED SHIELD AND PINE TREE NAPPIE

1" H. x 6" Dia. 1828–1830

This elaborate pattern of trees alternating with shields was designed before the invention of the cap ring and before stippling was adapted to cover the surface of pressed flint glass that was dull in comparison to flint glass that was blown. (Plates pressed in a mold with a cap ring have a circular mold seam visible inside the rim.) The beaded circle in the center was an early device that helped conceal crude workmanship in the area that might be attached to a stem as it appears in the photo that follows. Eight petals radiating from the center create the effect of a daisy. Shields alternating with pinwheel rosettes and small blossoms complete the central pattern to the rope table rest. Overlapping leaves that nestle snugly against the table rest point toward the rim. The border of ten trees alternating with ten shields extends to the beaded rim, not possible if the mold had a cap ring. A similar plate with widely spaced blossoms instead of leaves is not believed to be Sandwich, but may have been a product of the New England Glass Company of East Cambridge, Massachusetts. The New England works listed a tree pattern in an undated early catalog.

1006 PRESSED SHIELD AND PINE TREE

(a) Plate ¾" H. x 6" Dia.
(b) Nappie on foot 4" H. x 6" Dia. 1828–1830

This photo deserves careful study. Close inspection of the rims of both plate A and nappie B reveals that they were shaped into different forms by the "slumping" method explained by Deming Jarves in his patent No. 5290X dated December 1, 1828. Each piece was pressed into flat, patterned sheets and after removal from the flat mold were placed in plate-shaped and nappie-shaped receivers. This resulted in the edge of the rim of plate A being almost vertical, while the edge of the rim of nappie B is slanted at a 45 degree angle. Kirk J. Nelson, glass curator of the Sandwich Glass Museum, presented a thorough study of Jarves' pressing method in the 1990 issue of *The Acorn*. The nappie's flat sidewall gives it the form of a pan. It was attached to its knopped stem and hand-formed foot by a wafer of glass under the beaded circle in its center. Jarves' procedure was used intensively for a short period of time. The advent of the cap ring rendered it obsolete.

1007 PRESSED HEART AND LYRE (HARP) DISH

1⅞" H. x 9" Dia. 1828–1830

There is ample proof that the Boston and Sandwich Glass Company spent much time and thought perfecting Heart plates, dishes and nappies during this brief period. Note that the edge of the scalloped rim is visible, showing that the plate was pressed in a flat mold and after removal was slumped into a dish-shaped receiver. (A similar Heart and Lyre piece at The Bennington Museum, small and with a leaf central pattern, has the production flaw of a bulging center that required a button to be placed in the receiver.) A flurry of correspondence between Deming Jarves and William Stutson caused by Stutson's confusion over Jarves' instructions draws our attention to the slumping of Harp into dessert dishes, dining plates and lamp plates. On January 19, 1829, Jarves requested "20 doz of the Harp patt 9 inch Plates, weight & kind required for dessert dishes". (Whether dessert was placed in these dishes or they were underplates for smaller china dishes is not clear.) In a letter to Stutson on January 23, 1829, Jarves clarified his request by admitting he erred in calling the dishes "plates" when plates couldn't be made with a particular plunger and receiver combination and there was no receiver/former at the factory for slumping the glass into the shape of a plate. He suggested the dish receiver be filled with clay or plaster so that it could be used as a make-do plate receiver. Again on January 23, "You have made a much handsomer article of the Harp dish than I expected. They must sell in South America for dining plates. They are truly elegant. You cannot make too many of the Harp patt. dishes & plates." The eight-pointed motif in the center of this plate is called *Diamond Star*. Between the stippled points are unpatterned areas surrounded by a ring. An overall pattern of strawberry diamonds extends to the table rest, which is clear and divides the diamond center and the stippled band that covers the wall of the dish. The border has fifteen lyres alternating with hearts. Because of intensive use of this pattern at a time when great strides were made in mold design, variants abound. There can be stippling between the hearts and lyres. Hearts were the perfect element to extend into the scallops of the rim, but this effect is lost when the same pattern was pressed in a mold with a cap ring. *Courtesy, Sandwich Glass Museum, Sandwich Historical Society*

1008 PRESSED HEART AND ROSETTE DISH

2" H. x 10⅞" Dia. 1828–1830

Dishes that were produced by laying them in an unpatterned receiver after they were removed from a flat mold do not have a table rest. The degree of the "slump" varied the diameter of the central portion that would hug the table. This beautiful example has a Heart Medallion center. An eight-pointed star is enclosed by a ring. Eight hearts have diamonds above them connected by semicircles. A ring separates the Heart Medallion from a wide band of stippled diamonds. The border of this large piece has twenty-two stippled hearts alternating with twenty-two eight-pointed rosettes. As you can see in the photo, the stippling in the hearts extends to the rim because a cap ring was not used. *Courtesy, Sandwich Glass Museum, Sandwich Historical Society*

1009 PRESSED HEART AND SHEAF PLATE

¾" H. x 6¼" Dia. 1830–1845

Note the seam mark that surrounds the plate near the rim. We can determine that the plate was pressed after the cap ring improvement by the presence of this seam mark. If you examine several identical plates, you would find that they appear to be reasonably uniform because the rim of each is the same thickness, hiding the fact that the bottoms and walls vary in thickness. The central pattern is composed of four elongated diamonds separated by four stippled triangles. A half-fan or semicircle is above each triangle. This combination of stippled triangle and semicircle resembles an ice cream cone. Keep this in mind and look for variations of the ice cream cone on other Lacy pieces such as the Peacock Eye (Peacock Feather) and Shield tray in photo 1053. Reading from the central pattern to the rim, there is a band of stippling, a band of strawberry diamonds and a border pattern of thirteen stippled hearts that alternate with sheaves of wheat. In reality, what appears to be stippling is often very fine diamond point that softens in the annealing leer. *Courtesy, Sandwich Glass Museum, Sandwich Historical Society*

1010 PRESSED HEART CHILDREN'S LEMONADE

2" H. x 2" Dia. 1830–1835

The Heart series of Lacy ware is worth close study because the construction methods by which they were produced dovetail with Deming Jarves' patents for pressing glass as recorded by the United States Patent Office. On May 28, 1830, Jarves was issued patent No. 6004X for the forming of the handle on a glass cup during the pressing operation instead of attaching a handle after the cup was made. A handle-shaped excavation was to be made in the mold. "The plug, or piston, which is to form the inside of the cup, is made to fit exactly into a rim which forms the top of the mould, so that when it is pressed down none of the fluid glass which has been put into the mould can escape at top, but will, by pressure, be forced into the cavities described." The part of the mold described in the patent as "a rim which forms the top of the mould" we today call a *cap ring*. Jarves' patent therefore proves that the cap ring was in use prior to May 1830. This lemonade with a pattern of three hearts alternating with three fleur-de-lys is believed to be the earliest known example of the Jarves patent. *The Bennington Museum, Bennington, Vermont*

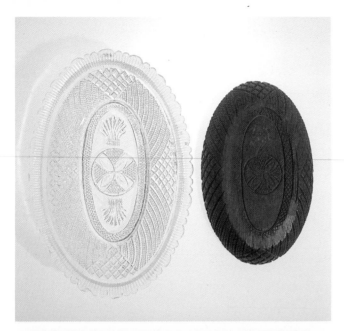

1011 PRESSED SHEAF OF WHEAT DISH

(a) Dish 2" H. x 9½" L. x 6¼" W.

(b) Wooden pattern 1830–1840

This oval dish is distinguished by a central pattern of a circle made up of four leaves in a quatrefoil on a stippled ground and a sheaf of wheat at each end. A triangle of strawberry diamond is centered at the sides and ends. The reeded rim has a large scallop alternating with two small scallops. The wooden pattern on the right is for the same dish in a smaller size. Note that the wooden piece does not include the rim pattern which was part of a cap ring. A variant of this pattern has a rim with diagonal reeding and a plain edge. It has not been documented as Sandwich. However, the Boston and Sandwich Glass Company, which made the dish shown, and another flint glass company, which made the variant, could both have bought their respective molds from the same mold manufacturer. This pattern is not deeply incised into the wooden model and therefore was not deeply incised into the mold. The wooden pattern, the iron mold and therefore the finished pressed glass dish were less expensive to produce than the intricately designed large dish that follows. *Courtesy, Sandwich Glass Museum, Sandwich Historical Society*

1012 PRESSED DIAMOND DISH

2⅝" H. x 12¼" Dia. 1830–1840

The diameter of this dish is the largest we have been able to document as having been made at the Boston and Sandwich Glass Company. Whether it was called a dish, plate or nappie cannot be verified. Very little documentation in the form of paperwork has been preserved for study. The early sloar book ends in March 1828 and, at that time, round, oval, oblong and rectangular dishes were listed. In the very center is a stippled square abutted by four of the curious half-fans or semicircles. These are surrounded by four points alternating with four Gothic Arches. A ring separates the center from a band of stippling that resembles fine diamond point enclosed by a rope table rest. The sidewall is made up of three overall diamond patterns combined in patchwork quilt fashion, a design feature that was used on cut glass in the 1830–1860 period. The entire pattern is tied together by a chain of stippling that follows the form of the scalloped rim. *Courtesy, Sandwich Glass Museum, Sandwich Historical Society*

1013 PRESSED CAPE COD LILY CELERY ON FOOT

7½" H. x 4⅝" Dia. 1830–1840

The Lacy pressed period came into being in the late 1820's and advanced quickly to a point where large, deep molds could be filled with hot glass and the glass could be removed with saleable results. Although there is ample proof that some molds in which holloware was pressed had cap rings, it appears that the mold for this celery did not. The pattern extends uninterrupted to the edge of the scalloped rim. Fragments of the celery were found in light blue, although at present no colored celeries have been recorded in museum or private collections. Clear examples are known having no foot as well. The separately pressed foot with its leaf pattern and knopped standard, also used on other Lacy items, was joined to the celery with a hot disk of glass known as a *wafer*, or *merese*. The celery itself is divided into three bands of pattern roughly equal in width. Reading from the bottom, the lower band begins with veined leaves placed side to side. Rows of unpatterned leaves are above. The center band is made up of what collectors believe are lilies. However, each of the six so-called "lilies" are a combination of two petals of a tulip in which a tiny heart is centered. There is a veined leaf on each side of the tulip blossom, and stippling and ribs above the heart. The upper band repeats the veined leaves from the bottom of the body with another row of veining at the rim. The patterns were molded into the outside of the body and beneath the foot. *Courtesy, Sandwich Glass Museum, Sandwich Historical Society*

1014 PRESSED ACORN PLATES
(a) "WASHINGTON GEORGE" center
(b) Trefoil center
¾" H. x 6" Dia. 1830–1845

Plates A and B carry the same pattern with the exception of their centers and rims. Plate A has a poorly molded portrait of a man facing right encircled by the name "WASHINGTON GEORGE". It may have been made in 1832 to commemorate the 1732 birth of United States General and first President George Washington. The reason for his surname preceding his given name remains a mystery. Plate A is by far the rarest of the two. The center of plate B is quartered into four trefoil. The pattern of acorns, oak leaf clusters and star surrounding the center becomes predominant with the removal of the portrait. Note the difference in the size of the oak leaves. Expect to find variations such as this when studying glass from this era. Handmade molds varied according to the skill and eye of the mold maker. Both rims have beaded scrolls and rosettes. Interchangeable cap rings account for the scallops and points of rim A and the large scallop alternating with two small scallops of rim B. Fragments of both plates were dug at the Sandwich site.

1015 PRESSED ACORN PLATE
¾" H. x 6" Dia. 1830–1845

Throughout the life of the Sandwich glass industry, the acorn was a popular motif. Simple acorn forms and realistic figural acorns with caps were adapted to finials and stoppers. Later patterns of tableware combined acorns in medallions and acorns with ribs. *Acorn* was the name of a ship that transported passengers and glass company freight from Sandwich to Boston (see pages 32–33 in Volume 2). Because of the significance of the acorn motif, this plate was extensively reproduced. When determining authenticity, keep in mind that the five-pointed star on the original plate shown here has two points adjacent to the table rest. A reproduction was made at the Pairpoint Glass Company in Sagamore, Massachusetts, for the Sandwich Glass Museum. It has one point facing the table rest and the star is surrounded by the logo "SGM". The initials "AW" are molded outside the table rest of the reproduction examined by the authors. This is the mark of Alvin White, a Sandwich resident who designed the mold for the museum reproduction. The reproduction has a scallop and point rim whereas the original shown here has one large scallop alternating with two small scallops. Early glass is very rare in color.
Courtesy, Sandwich Glass Museum, Sandwich Historical Society

1016 PRESSED OAK LEAF NAPPIE
1¾" H. x 7¼" Dia. 1830–1845

A *nappie*, also spelled *nappy*, is a shallow bowl. Its sidewall is curved. If the sidewall was flat, the piece was termed a *pan*. There are several variants of the Oak Leaf pattern, all of which have four flat leaves in the center. The nappie in this photo has an eight-petaled beaded rosette in the center, from which the oak leaves radiate. A chain of beads in an unstippled band surrounds the scrolled leaves of the border near the serrated rim. This series of nappies range in diameter from 3" to 9". The serrated rims can vary. The large quantities dug at the factory site indicate prolific production over an extended period. All Sandwich Lacy glass was made at the Boston and Sandwich Glass Company, which was the only factory operating in Sandwich at the time.

1017 PRESSED OAK LEAF NAPPIES
(a) 1¼" H. x 7¾" Dia.
(b) 1¼" H. x 6¼" Dia. 1830–1845

Here are two variants of the Oak Leaf pattern. Both nappies have the same center, a four-petaled blossom surrounded by beads and four trefoil between the oak leaves near the table rest. The four-lobed beaded quatrefoil in nappie A has slender lobes, while that in nappie B has short, full lobes, leaving you with the impression that the center patterns are not the same. This variation was the mold maker's way of adapting the pattern to different diameter centers. This is to be expected in molds that were made by hand. Note the scrolled leaves in the border patterns. Although larger in diameter, nappie A has leaves with fewer serrations on each side. Nappie B has more serrations per leaf.

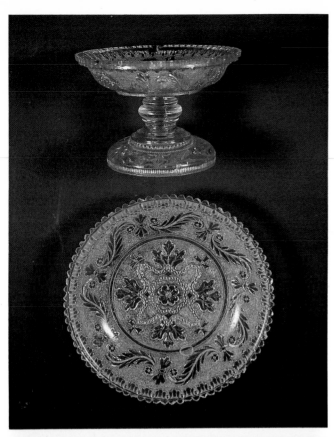

1018 PRESSED OAK LEAF NAPPIES

(a) On foot 3¾" H. x 5¼" Dia.

(b) "Off foot" 1¾" H. x 7¼" Dia. 1830–1845

All of the nappies shown in this chapter were documented without question by at least two methods, one of which is fragments in various stages of completion that were dug from the Boston and Sandwich Glass Company factory site in Sandwich. These fragments are now in private and museum collections. As far as the authors have ascertained, all of the Lacy bases that we have seen attached to known Sandwich nappies carry documented Sandwich patterns. This does not mean that other flint glass factories did not also manufacture them because, during this period, the Boston and Sandwich Glass Company did not employ their own mold makers. This Oak Leaf nappie A appears to be small in diameter in relation to its base, so it is possible that the base was used on several sizes of nappies. The base was pressed in a mold with a patterned plunger. A stippled ring surrounds the standard, outside of which is a chain of beads. An intricate combination of diamonds and ribbed swags complete the base to a reeded band near the rim. The unpatterned, knopped standard was pressed in one piece with the base. The terms *base* and *foot* are interchangeable to collectors.

1019 PRESSED OAK LEAF NAPPIE ON SCROLLED LEAF FOOT

4¼" H. x 9¼" Dia. 1830–1845

The owner of this footed nappie is indeed fortunate because seldom does one encounter a Lacy nappie or bowl with an applied foot that matches the pattern. It was cost prohibitive to manufacture a foot that could be combined with a limited number of upper units, so most lower units had less detail to make mismatching less noticeable. Here is a Lacy nappie with the previously shown Oak Leaf center and Scrolled Leaf border combined with the only Scrolled Leaf foot ever seen by the authors. The combination presents an elegant look that most Lacy pieces lack. It is an example of the surprises that still await an astute buyer.

1020 PRESSED SCROLLED LEAF NAPPIE

¾" H. x 4½" Dia. 1830–1845

The original name of this Lacy pattern is not known. In many instances, patterns were identified by a stock number. Names used today were assigned by independent glass scholars, so they often conflict. Ruth Webb Lee in her book *Sandwich Glass* and George and Helen McKearin in their *American Glass* identified this pattern as *Scrolled Leaf* because of the S-shaped leaves of the border. However, this leaf and blossom border was also used on dishes with Oak Leaf centers. The four-petaled blossom was incorporated into many Sandwich Lacy patterns, another example of the "mix and match" method of providing the consumer an unlimited assortment of table accessories. The term *Lacy*, used to describe pressed pieces with stippled backgrounds, cannot be found in original documents and is a Twentieth Century term. *Stippled*, a descriptive term for tiny dots that reflect the light, is also a collectors' expression. Nineteenth Century French catalogs refer to a *sand background*. The same patterns could be ordered with or without the sand background.

1021 PRESSED PRINCESS FEATHER MEDALLION PLATE

1¾" H. x 8½" Dia. 1830–1845

The name *Princess Feather* is a misnomer. It is an aberration of Prince's-feather, or *Polygonum orientale*, a tall, woody herb with oval leaves. The base of the leaves clasp the stem. On this Lacy pattern, two stems form a medallion. A star against a fine diamond background is centered in each of four medallions. Other stars are between and below the leaves. There are many variants of this medallion and leaf pattern. Stars may be replaced by flowers, leaves replaced by buds. The fine diamond point in the medallions can vary. We know of at least five centers and there are probably more. Take special note of the color of this plate, a pale amethyst. *Courtesy, Sandwich Glass Museum, Sandwich Historical Society*

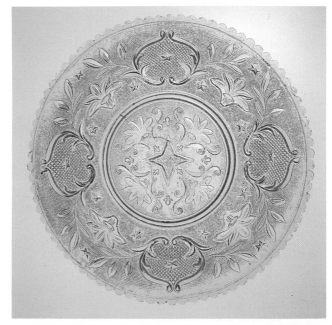

1022 PRESSED PRINCESS FEATHER MEDALLION NAPPIE

2" H. x 10" Dia. 1830–1845

Here is the same medallion as shown in the previous photo, widened by adding circles at the top and bottom where the two stems of the Prince's-feather meet. Rather than a star, this variant has a diamond in the center of each medallion. The diamond motif is repeated in the quartered diamond above the hearts that alternate with the medallions. Note the intricately designed central pattern of the nappie. A tiny quatrefoil surrounded by beads forms the center of a fourteen-petaled rosette. The diamond motif is again repeated. Concentric circles of leaves and beads complete the center to the table rest. The larger the piece, the more time was spent on creating elaborate patterns to hid the defects of early manufacture. When an excellent grade of glass sand became available in the 1840's, stippled Lacy patterns were phased out in favor of patterns that emphasized the brilliance of the glass. See Chapter 10 in Volume 2 for information about the glass sand industry.

1023 PRESSED FLEUR-DE-LYS AND THISTLE NAPPIE

2" H. x 9¼" Dia. 1830–1845

For the purpose of identification, collectors refer to this pattern as *Fleur-de-lys and Thistle*. The prominent fleur-de-lys alternates with Princess Feather Medallion, each medallion having a plain oval in its center. A thistle flanked by two leaves appears in low relief above the fleur-de-lys. The central pattern is made up of a quatrefoil surrounded by concentric circles of tiny beads, stemmed flowers, diagonal leaves and another circle of small beads near the table rest. Stippling and very small beads earmark Lacy glass pressed in molds that were manufactured in the Boston area. With relatively short study, one quickly learns the difference between the diminutive beads in Sandwich molds and the larger bull's eyes, beads and circles molded into Midwestern pieces. Note the small scallops on the rims of this and the preceding nappie.

1024 PRESSED PRINCESS FEATHER MEDALLION NAPPIE ON FOOT

3¾" H. x 5⅞" Dia. 1830–1840

Most nappies made during the Lacy period could be purchased with no foot or on a pressed Lacy foot that varied in pattern. This extremely rare foot was also used as a base for a whale oil lamp with a blown font and a button stem. Unlike most Sandwich pieces, the foot has a pattern that was molded on both surfaces. On the outside, eight ovals alternate with eight darts to form a rim of large scallops and points. On the outside surface of the dome of the base, a band of diamond point surrounds it. Diamonds molded beneath the base account for the complexity of design that reflects light in many directions. As far as the upper unit (nappie) is concerned, the pattern was molded into the surface that would not come into contact with its contents. *Courtesy, Sandwich Glass Museum, Sandwich Historical Society*

1025 PRESSED PRINCESS FEATHER MEDALLION NAPPIE

1¼" H. x 6½" Dia. 1830–1845

The boldness of the Prince's-feather twigs paired to form the four medallions makes this variant most satisfying from a design standpoint. A five-leaved plant between the medallions near the table rest marks each quarter point. (A similar variant has five-pointed stars flanking each plant.) The central pattern can change, but this one is the most common. The five-leaved plant is repeated four times, alternating with four diamonds. Four scrolled brackets add to the beauty of the center. This nappie can be found in at least five sizes with heights varying from 1¼" to 3". Note the difference between fine diamond point in each medallion and stippling that covers the remaining background. Diamond point was the result of fine crosscut lines. Stippling was line after line of tiny dots made by a punch or drill bit.

1026 PRESSED PRINCESS FEATHER MEDALLION NAPPIES

(a) On foot 4" H. x 6½" Dia.

(b) "Off foot" 1⅜" H. x 6½" Dia. 1830–1845

When nappies and bowls were to be produced both with and without a foot, the sloar man differentiated the forms by listing them in the sloar book as being "on foot" and "off foot". This Princess Feather nappie has been found with eleven different bases to date and very likely was combined with others that we have not yet encountered. The Lacy base in this photo was pressed separately. It is hollow beneath and has a pattern of vertical ribs inside the standard. The foot is patterned on both surfaces. Beneath is a pattern of stippled concentric rings made by the plunger. The upper surface has five-leaved ornaments repeated six times on a background of stippled ripples. The nappie and base units were connected by a wafer. Expect the center of the nappie to be distorted because of the heat when the wafer was applied. Fragments of the nappie and the base were dug from the site of the Boston and Sandwich Glass Company.

1027 PRESSED PRINCESS FEATHER MEDALLION NAPPIE ON FOOT

3⅛" H. x 6¼" Dia. 1830–1845

The same nappie shown previously is here combined with a foot that has a pattern of three leaves clustered on a stem that undulates around it. The leaves are on a stippled ground that forms a band on the lower half of the foot. The upper half is unpatterned. The leaves on this unusually attractive foot combine well with the Prince's-feather plant leaves on the nappie, but close inspection reveals that they are not an exact match. The Boston and Sandwich Glass Company also combined this foot with a celery in the pattern known as *Cape Cod Lily*. It is important for the collector to study the separate units independently so that, when different combinations are found, they will be recognized as Sandwich.

1028 PRESSED PRINCESS FEATHER MEDALLION AND BASKET OF FLOWERS DISH

2" H. x 10½" L. x 8½" W. 1830–1845

The center of this dish is rectangular with rounded corners and has a pattern of two shields surrounded by a scroll border. A Princess Feather Medallion is centered in each of the long sides and a Basket of Flowers in each of the four rounded corners. A complicated scroll motif covers each of the short sides. Closely spaced bunches of grapes hanging from a vine complete the border. The undulating rim is scalloped. Each dish in this size and pattern has a lip to accept a cover. We believe that they all had covers when originally purchased. This pattern was duplicated in porcelain by the Royal Meissen factory near Dresden, Germany. Research by Dr. Joachim Kunze published in the German porcelain collectors' journal *Keramos* proved that the Meissen factory referred to such pieces as "porcelain wares in glass patterns". Kunze's article entitled "Meissen Porcelain Designed from Glass Patterns (1831 to 1855)" was translated and published in the Fall 1987 issue of *The Glass Club Bulletin*.

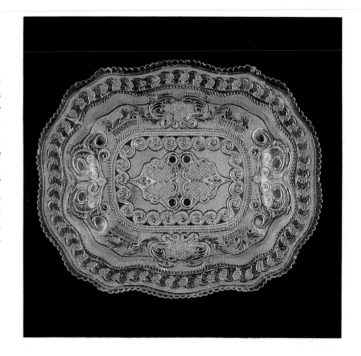

1029 PRESSED PRINCESS FEATHER MEDALLION AND BASKET OF FLOWERS COVERED DISH

(a) Dish 2" H. x 10½" L. x 8½" W.
(b) Cover 3¾" H. x 8½" L. x 6½" W.
(c) Combined size 5½" H. x 10½" L. x 8½" W. 1830–1845

Here is the previous dish with its cover in place. The medallion-like patterns on the sides and ends match the patterns on the dish, but thistles replace the baskets of flowers on the four corners. The bulging center of the cover does not have pattern. Each end of the handle is reeded to match the reeded, or finely ribbed, band that surrounds the cover and dish below its scalloped rim. The center of the handle is a pattern of overlapping, veined leaves. It is interesting to note that the element that appears as veined leaves on this piece appears as hair on the claw foot of the Dahlia nappie in photo 1100. This cover was marketed interchangeably with the similar dish that follows. *Courtesy of The Toledo Museum of Art (Acc. No. 68.33 A&B)*

1030 PRESSED PRINCESS FEATHER MEDALLION COVER FROM ABOVE DISH

(a) Cover

(b) Wooden pattern

Wooden pattern B was a tool used by the mold maker to create the cast iron mold needed to make the glass cover A. It is an exact model of the part of the mold into which the hot glass was dropped. Its surface is smooth as is the upper surface of the glass cover because the Lacy pattern was on the plunger that forced the glass to conform to the shape of the mold. The flat area in the center of the wooden pattern held the wooden pattern for the handle. When the plunger pressed the cover, glass was forced into and filled the handle section of the mold. The pretty pattern showed through clearly when covers were made from transparent flint glass. When made from vivid colors or opaque glass, covers appeared to be unpatterned. *Courtesy, Sandwich Glass Museum, Sandwich Historical Society*

1031 PRESSED PRINCESS FEATHER MEDALLION AND BASKET OF FLOWERS DISH ON LEAF FOOT

6⅛" H. x 10¼" L. x 8½" W. 1840–1845

This footed dish has a pattern that is a variant of the dishes shown previously. The undulating band of grapes on the border was replaced by a band of stippling. Note that this dish also was made with a lip to accept a cover, but for some reason many of the dishes with the stippled border are so warped that a cover does not seat properly. The dish was attached to the pressed Leaf foot by a wafer. The lobed foot was a fairly common one that was combined with a variety of upper units such as the Plaid variant salver in photo 1121, the Leaf nappie on foot in photo 1122 and the Leaf vases in photo 3017. The lobed foot was made in at least two sizes with and without the Leaf pattern. This and the preceding dish were also marketed with a hexagonal base as shown on the open work basket in photo 1126. It can be found in at least three colors: amethyst, canary and blue. *Courtesy of The Toledo Museum of Art (Acc. No. 68.42)*

1032 PRESSED SHIELD, ACANTHUS LEAF AND PRINCESS FEATHER MEDALLION BOWL ON FOOT WITH PRINCESS FEATHER MEDALLION COVER

(a) Bowl 3⅜" H. x 6¼" Dia.

(b) Cover 2⅛" H. x 4¾" Dia.

(c) Combined size 5¼" H. x 6¼" Dia. 1830–1845

This is a deep dish that could have been used for wet sweetmeat which according to Webster's 1847 Dictionary was "fruit preserved with sugar; as peaches, pears, melons, nuts, orange peel, and the like". However, we must not rule out the possibility that it may have held soft cheese such as that made from goat's milk or any of a number of foodstuffs that required protection from insects. Beneath the foot is a pattern of vertical ribs. The bowl was pressed in a mold that had three side sections, each with a different pattern. The section facing out in the photo has an elaborate shield. A second section has a complicated combination of acanthus leaves, scrolls and five tiny rose blossoms. The third side section has the familiar Princess Feather Medallion that is repeated three times around the cover. A Peacock Eye (Peacock Feather) pattern surrounds the bottom of the bowl. The rims of the bowl and cover are laced with bunches of grapes. The cover rests on an inner rim and is an excellent fit. *Courtesy, Sandwich Glass Museum, Sandwich Historical Society*

1033 PRESSED PRINCESS FEATHER AND DIAMOND DISHES
(a) Light green 1¼" H. x 4⅞" Dia.
(b) Olive ¾" H. x 4¾" Dia. 1845–1860

Large amounts of fragments dug at the Boston and Sandwich Glass Company site indicate high production of these shallow dishes in several variants and unusual colors. The Barlow collection of fragments includes dark amber, red amber, blue and shades of green. The center is an eight-petaled blossom on a fine diamond ground that extends in eight points to a wide, smooth table rest. The border has eight Princess Feathers, all bending in the same direction rather than facing each other to form medallions. They alternate with eight diamonds on a ground of shallow stipples. (The fragment above the dishes is an exact match. The lower fragment is a variant with a tiny diamond above each of the eight large ones.) Sixteen large scallops form a wide, smooth rim. The shallow stippling and wide table rest is consistent with European mold features and it is entirely possible that some Sandwich dishes were pressed in imported molds. Jane Shadel Spillman, curator of American glass at The Corning Museum of Glass in Corning, New York, presented a study of like glass in an article entitled "Pressed-glass designs in the United States and Europe" that appeared in the July 1983 issue of *The Magazine ANTIQUES*. According to Spillman, quoting from Hugh Wakefield's *Nineteenth Century British Glass*, "James Stevens, a Birmingham diesinker, is said to have made molds for the United States." A similar pattern is illustrated in a Bohemian catalog thought to date about 1870. At Sandwich, this style of dish represents the latter part of the Lacy period.

1034 PRESSED SCROLLED ACANTHUS LEAF DISH
1" H. x 5" Dia. 1845–1860

Here is another variant of the late Lacy dishes and fragments shown in the previous photo. This blue example has a central pattern of plaid-like squares enclosing eight-pointed stars. A wide, smooth table rest separates the squares from a border of Scrolled Acanthus Leaf placed end to end on a ground of well-executed but shallow stippling. Two large beads near the rim of sixteen smooth scallops repeat the beads at each end of the Scrolled Acanthus Leaf. It is logical to assume that this series of dishes was made in molds that were the product of a single mold making firm. The many colored fragments that were dug at the Boston and Sandwich Glass Company site were concentrated in an area of the dump that was used up to the early 1860's. It is unlikely that the Cape Cod Glass Works, that began to make glass in 1859 (see Chapter 3 in Volume 3), pressed Lacy patterns. A study of the Cape Cod Glass Company's *List of Glass Ware*, reprinted in full on pages 108–110 in Volume 3, does not reveal a pressed pattern that can be construed as having characteristics of Lacy glass.

1035 PRESSED CROSSED CORNUCOPIA DISH
1¼" H. x 8" L. x 3¾" W. 1835–1850

Two Princess Feather Medallions were molded into the oval bottom of this dish, combined with two Crossed Cornucopia that give the dish its name. A rope table rest separates the bottom from four Crossed Cornucopia on the sidewall. The cornucopia is garish and, when combined with the alternating diamond motif, does not represent a pleasing pattern. Yet, the stipples were professionally done. They extend to an evenly scalloped rim.

1036 PRESSED TREFOIL AND CIRCULAR MEDALLION NAPPIE

2⅛" H. x 11" Dia. 1830–1845

The most intricate Lacy patterns were fashioned in the 1830–1835 period, but use of the molds continued into and sometimes beyond the next decade. This large, shallow piece has a central pattern that begins with a quatrefoil with four diamonds between the lobes. Concentric beaded and stippled circles surround it. Sixteen tiny stemmed lilies point toward the center. Sixteen diamonds between the lilies and sixteen half-fans complete the bottom to a patterned table rest. The diamonds are repeated in four trefoil that alternate with circular medallions on the border. The deliberate execution of several sizes of stippling creates a sawtooth motif near a rim composed of one large alternating with two small scallops. This article provides an opportunity to study design elements that were incorporated into the patterns on other pieces. Diamonds and tiny lilies were standard features on toys as shown in Chapter 10 of Volume 3. The circular medallion with bull's eye center is the forerunner of a later pattern known as Buckle. Note also the small leaves near each medallion, a repeat of the handle on the Princess Feather Medallion cover in photo 1029.

1037 PRESSED CROSSED SWORDS

(a) Plate 1¼" H. x 5½" Dia.
(b) Nappie 1" H. x 4½" Dia. 1830–1845

The numerous fragments accumulated by people who dug them from the Boston and Sandwich Glass Company site indicate that the Crossed Swords pattern was made in quantity. There is no historical evidence as to why swords would be used on tableware. We suggest that its manufacture may have coincided with the ascension to the throne of England's Queen Victoria in 1837 or her coronation in 1838. It may have been intended for overseas shipment to England and English colonies. According to Norman W. Webber, author of *Collecting Glass*, pressed Lacy was not made early in England. Glass cooled too quickly to make thin-walled vessels, necessary because England had an excise tax based on weight until 1845. It took several years to solve production problems after the tax was abolished. The transporting of Sandwich glass to India in the 1830's and 1840's is well documented by papers such as a bill of lading to India signed by Deming Jarves and dated March 12, 1844. Both plate A and nappie B have a border pattern of Princess Feather Medallion alternating with hearts. Plate A has a band of herringbone near the evenly serrated, or scalloped, rim. Two small scallops alternate with one large scallop on the rim of nappie B. Study these rim configurations. Pennsylvania glass factories made similar tableware with rims that differed from known Sandwich ones.

1038 PRESSED TULIP AND ACANTHUS LEAF NAPPIE

1⅛" H. x 5⅝" Dia. 1830–1845

The predominant motif in this nappie is the tulip blossom repeated eight times in the center. Four more blossoms appear on the sidewall, each flanked by sprigs of scrolled acanthus leaves. A small four-petaled flower nestles in each of the eight sprigs. The unpatterned ring so evident in the photo is a circular table rest. The nappie was pressed in a well-executed mold that was beautifully stippled. An enormous amount of labor was expended on the pattern of the cap ring, which has a rim configuration of one large scallop alternating with two small ones. Similar Acanthus Leaf patterns were made in France. According to Miriam E. Mucha in an article "Mechanization, French Style Cristaux, Moules en Plain" that appeared in the September 1979 issue of *The Glass Club Bulletin*, a 5⅛" diameter saucer and matching cup were manufactured by Cristalleries de Baccarat in 1842. No pattern name was given for their variant that replaced the tulip on the sidewall with a diamond. Most names assigned to Lacy patterns were suggested by glass scholars and cannot be found in factory documentation.

1039 PRESSED TULIP AND ACANTHUS LEAF NAPPIE ON PLUME FOOT

(a) Nappie on foot 5⅛" H. x 8½" Dia. 1835–1845
(b) Plume and Acorn nappie 1¼" H. x 5⅛" Dia. 1840–1860
This clear Tulip and Acanthus Leaf nappie is shown as the upper unit of a footed nappie. The Plume foot and unpatterned standard was molded in one piece; the standard is open beneath the foot and is hollow to just below the wafer that was applied to fuse the lower unit to the nappie. When a nappie or bowl is attached to its foot with a wafer, the central pattern is sometimes destroyed by the heat at the time of attachment. The pattern may be distorted or melted completely. However, a nappie with its central pattern obliterated was acceptable at the time of manufacture and therefore should be accepted by the collector. This production flaw does not decrease its value. A variant of the Plume foot has a scallop and point rim. Either foot can be combined with a Plume nappie. Plume and Acorn nappie B is pictured to give the reader a better view of the pattern. It was pressed in a different mold with a Plume and Acorn center. Judging from the quantity and colors in which it is found, its production extended into the 1850's, long after production of Lacy nappie A was curtailed.

1040 PRESSED ACANTHUS LEAF AND SHIELD SUGAR ON FOOT

(a) Sugar 3½" H. x 5" Dia.
(b) Cover 2½" H. x 4½" Dia.
(c) Combined size 5¾" H. x 5" Dia. 1835–1850
The acanthus in stylized form has been used as a decorating motif for centuries. In architecture, it is an ornament resembling the foliage or leaves of the acanthus, a genus of plants with prickles. In ancient times, garments were embroidered in acanthine designs. This octagonal sugar has two prominent patterns, one of which is a vertical acanthus leaf on two opposite corners. Scrolls and scrolled leaves surround it. A small lily fills the remaining space on each side of the pattern that covers two sides of the bowl. The other four sides have two scrolled shields enclosing diamonds. The rims of the bowl and foot are smooth. A similar leaf pattern works its way up each of the eight corners of the cover, ending at the bottom of an open rosette, or flower, finial. The rim of the cover has eight straight sides that fit into the eight-sided rim of the bowl, exposing the corners every time the cover was removed and replaced. Most of the covers are damaged at these corners, seriously affecting the value of the combined units. The Acanthus Leaf and Shield was made in several colors including deep emerald green and red-amethyst. Because the molded pattern is on the outside of the cover, the colored sugars are very attractive. When in good condition, they are valued highly.

1041 PRESSED ACANTHUS LEAF AND SHIELD SUGAR ON FOOT

(a) Sugar 4" H. x 5⅛" Dia.
(b) Cover 2⅛" H. x 4½" Dia.
(c) Combined size 5½" H. x 5⅛" Dia. 1838–1850
Here is the Acanthus Leaf and Shield sugar with two major differences. Rather than the smooth-rimmed bowl and foot shown in the previous photo, this fiery opalescent example has scalloped rims. Second, the cover is elaborate in that the eight Acanthus Leaf panels alternate with eight diamond panels. The diamonds do not follow the pattern of the diamond enclosed by the shield on the lower unit, but deviations such as this were common on Lacy tableware. A number of Acanthus Leaf and Shield sugars combined with this cover are known in both clear and color. In color, the bowl and covers are exact matches, proving that they were combined in this manner at the time of manufacture. A matching cream was made with a smooth upper rim and a scalloped foot. For some unknown reason, matching American Lacy sugars and creams do not have matching plates, bowls and nappies. Yet, catalogs of Launay Hautin & Compagnie, distributors of glass made by Cristalleries de Baccarat and Cristalleries de Saint-Louis, illustrated numerous matching pieces available in sets from the French glass houses.

1042 PRESSED ACANTHUS LEAF AND SHIELD CREAM

4½" H. 1835–1850

The pattern on this cream matches that of the previously shown sugar, but the Shield dominates because the Acanthus Leaf is beneath the spout. The Shield is formed by combining several scrolls that enclose three diamonds. A fourth diamond is below center. Although the pressed handle is unusually detailed, it is uncomfortable to hold. It was molded in one piece with the body of the cream as described in Jarves' 1830 patent, but its ornateness dates it five or ten years later than the simple unpatterned handle of the Heart cup or lemonade. When this cream was made, the skill of the mold makers had progressed to the point where a cap ring formed the rim and its elongated spout. The cream can be found in color. The broken pieces in the foreground are fragments that match in pattern dug from the factory site in Sandwich.

1043 PRESSED ACANTHUS LEAF AND EAGLE-HEADED SHIELD SUGAR ON FOOT

(a) Sugar 3¾" H. x 4⅞" Dia.
(b) Cover 2¼" H. x 4½" Dia.
(c) Combined size 5⅝" H. x 4⅞" Dia. 1830–1840

This is one of the most interesting sugars made at the Boston and Sandwich Glass Company. A shield on the lower portion of the bowl supports two eagle heads back to back, their necks crossed. The heads are holding up a basket of fruit, around which are blossoms. Acanthus leaves on the bowl are repeated on the cover, which has a common nipple finial. The rim configuration mimics that of the bowl in photo 1041. The concave sidewall of the bowl, its flat bottom and circular foot are identifying features of sugars manufactured during the second quarter of the Nineteenth Century. Because the sugar is similar to a marked salt manufactured by the Providence Flint Glass Company in Providence, Rhode Island, scholars tentatively attributed it to that works, but no document proves it. South Boston manufacture is equally plausible. Opalescent fragments were found at the Boston and Sandwich site. It was possible for all flint glass factories to have purchased molds for the sugar from the same mold maker, or that the Sandwich works acquired the molds when the shortlived Providence works closed. Any of these early, pressed, patterned, colored sugars are extremely scarce and command top dollar on the antiques market.
Courtesy of The Toledo Museum of Art (Acc. No. 68.57 A&B)

1044 PRESSED EAGLE DISH

1¼" H. x 6" Dia. 1835–1845

The central pattern of this small octagonal dish is an eagle with the American shield on his breast. His head faces right and three arrows in his talon point left. The thirteen five-pointed stars are believed to stand for the thirteen original American states. The Eagle dish was produced in at least three sizes and in several variants with differing borders. Some have a shield on all eight sides and others have four shields alternating with four nectarine blossoms. Variations also occur in the stippled ground, which can extend to the evenly scalloped rim or end in a sawtooth edge. Their historical significance appeals to American collectors. Look for Eagle dishes attached by a wafer to a Lacy foot.

1045 PRESSED THISTLE NAPPIE

1½" H. x 8" Dia. 1835–1850

The thistle is a plant with prickly leaves and white, purple, pink or yellow flowers. Most often, we think of the lavender Scotch thistle, *Onopordum acanthium*. It remains a mystery why two prickly plants, the thistle and the acanthus, were so often used on Lacy Sandwich glass. This nappie has in its very center a single stem with a rose blossom, a bud and three leaves. The rose sprig and two thistles are encircled by rope coils enclosing six-petaled flowers. The table rest has a rope, or cable, pattern. Twelve thistles are on the sidewall, above which are scrolled flowers and sprigs of tiny lilies. Diminutive blossoms such as these worked well on large pieces as shown here and adapted very easily to small salts and toys. The rim has small scallops. Note again the central pattern of coils and flowers. It was attractive when used alone on the drainer that follows.

1046 PRESSED DRAINER

½" H. x 4" Dia. 1835–1850

The term *drainer* was found in a catalog of blown ware manufactured by the Boston and Sandwich Glass Company in the 1870's. Shown in the catalog on page 5 was a "butter and drainer" and "butter, no drainer". We are uncertain whether this glass drainer was inserted into a glass or metal butter dish. In use, the drainer was placed in the dish; there are four feet molded beneath to hold the drainer above the bottom of the dish. Ice was placed on the drainer and pieces of butter on the ice. As the ice melted, it dripped through five holes into the bottom of the dish, keeping the butter from floating in the water. The pattern of coiled rope enclosing twenty six-petaled flowers is identical to that of the above nappie, even to the tiny diamonds between the coils. The rim is smooth. *The Bennington Museum, Bennington, Vermont*

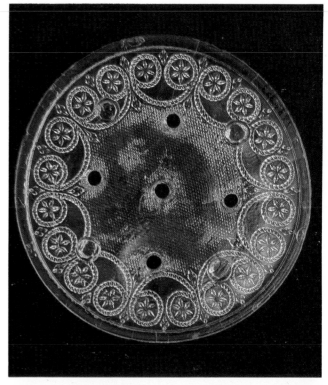

1047 PRESSED DISH WITH OPEN CHAIN BORDER

2" H. x 11⅞" L. x 8½" W. 1830–1840

This most rare dish was made in Sandwich during the height of the Lacy era. Fragments were discovered at the Boston and Sandwich Glass Company site. The mold for the chain border dish was complicated. Many times the glass cooled before it flowed to the center of the handles. Some handles were incomplete and some were left with a line that looks like a crack as seen on the handle to the right. The mold was difficult to open without damaging the open work. The rim was easily broken when bumped by other dishes. The central pattern is a complicated diamond and scroll with lily and rosette, elements of which were small enough to be used on toys as shown in photos 3336–3348. Plumes, "peacock eyes", scrolls and tiny diamonds surround the central pattern, all diverse elements combined into a background of stipples. *Courtesy, Sandwich Glass Museum, Sandwich Historical Society*

1048 PRESSED GOTHIC ARCH AND HEART TUB

(a) Tub 2⅞" H. x 5⅛" Dia.
(b) Cover 2¼" H. x 4⅜" Dia.
(c) Combined size 4¾" H. x 5⅛" Dia. 1830–1835

Tubs were used for butter, which was soft when taken out of a butter churn, and for goat and other soft cheeses. Stippled Gothic Arches surround the lower portion of the body. A band of diamonds placed side to side separates the arches from stippled hearts alternating with eight-petaled rosettes. Lobes of the hearts form the scallops of the rim as they do on early Heart plates, like the one shown in photo 1008. The hearts are not repeated on the cover. An overall pattern of diamonds on the dome and stippled arches on the rim match design elements on the tub. This very attractive early form is extremely scarce. Generally speaking, covers are difficult to find and account for more than half the value of the combined units. If you find an early Lacy cover—or any cover, for that matter—at a reasonable price, buy it. The lower unit will eventually surface. *Courtesy, Sandwich Glass Museum, Sandwich Historical Society*

1049 PRESSED GOTHIC ARCH AND PALM WITH PEACOCK EYE (PEACOCK FEATHER) BOWL ON FOOT

3½" H. x 6" Dia. 1835–1845

The inside surface of this footed bowl is smooth to the outer edge of the rim so that the bowl's contents did not come into contact with the molded pattern. This, and the fact that it did not have a cover, leads the authors to the conclusion that this piece is a slop bowl for food waste such as loose tea leaves. However, it was common for holloware to have duel use, so the bowl could have held loaf sugar. It was common in the 1830's and 1840's for pieces that were to be used together on the table to have the same elements of design, even though their overall patterns were not identical. The Gothic Arch alternating with Palm surrounding the lower part of the bowl is similar to the pattern of the cream that follows. Both pieces have feet with even scallops. Bull's eyes surround the bowl. The tiny nipple in the center of each bull's eye was made by the mold maker's tool that dished out the bull's eyes. Repeated use of the mold caused the tiny indentures to fill with glass that remained when the mold was cleaned. Slop bowls pressed in a well-used mold may not retain this detail. Fifteen hearts above the bull's eyes cannot be seen through the rim because the glass is opaque. Hearts combined with Gothic Arches comprise part of the pattern of the rectangular covered dish with underplate in photo 1051. Possibly the slop bowl, cream and rectangular dish were intended for use at the same setting. At the very least, their respective molds may have come from the same mold manufacturer. *Courtesy of The Toledo Museum of Art (Acc. No. 68.36)*

1050 PRESSED GOTHIC ARCH AND PALM CREAM

4¼" H. 1835–1845

These intricately patterned pieces of holloware were produced by the Boston and Sandwich Glass Company in clear, opalescent and several vibrant colors. This particular example is translucent blue with splotches of white. The Gothic Arch surrounding the lower portion differs from that of the slop bowl, but the alternating Palm carries similar stipples. A chain of beads encircles the center followed by a guilloche band. Quartered diamonds alternating with triangles are on a textured ground that extends to an undulating rim. Other Lacy elements beneath the spout and stippling on the sides of the pressed handle complete the pattern. Note the style of early creams. Protrusions on the handle provided a thumb piece and finger grips. An elongated spout designed for immediate pouring and instant stopping kept the drip minimal. Another cream was made in Sandwich that was similar in Gothic Arch and Palm pattern and stippled handle with protrusions. However, instead of guilloche and band of diamonds and triangles, the upper half has a pattern of Peacock Eye (Peacock Feather). The upper portion of the cream, i.e., chain of beads, guilloche and band of diamonds and triangles, appears on a similar Lacy cream marked "R. B. CURLING & SONS, FORT PITT". The Fort Pitt Glass Works was in Pittsburgh, Pennsylvania. Many American flint glass factories produced Lacy glass. *The Bennington Museum, Bennington, Vermont*

**1051 PRESSED GOTHIC ARCH AND HEART RECTANGULAR DISH
WITH STEPPED COVER AND TRAY**

(a) Dish 2¾" H. x 6½" L. x 4¼" W.
(b) Cover 2¼" H. x 5¾" L. x 3½" W.
(c) Tray 1" H. x 7¼" L. x 4½" W.
(d) Combined size 5⅛" H. x 7¼" L. x 4½" W. 1835–1845
This wonderful three-piece set was made in clear and color with a choice of the stepped cover as shown in this photo or a domed cover as pictured in photo 3245. The cover pattern of Gothic Arches is on the inside, so when the color of the glass is dark or opaque, much of the beauty is lost. The dish has three Gothic Arches on each long side with four stippled hearts below a scallop and point rim. Hearts are repeated on the border pattern of the tray, alternating with stippled six-pointed stars. Its central pattern combines beaded rosettes and, near the table rest, tiny flowers in a band that swags from corner to corner. For detailed study, see photos 3245–3249 where each unit is shown in clear glass. *Courtesy of The Toledo Museum of Art (Acc. No. 68.34 A,B&C)*

1052 PRESSED "U. S. F. CONSTITUTION" TRAY

1⅛" H. x 7⅛" L. x 4½" W. 1833–1845
The bill that approved the construction of the United States Frigate *Constitution* was signed by President George Washington in 1794. She took part in bombardments off Tripoli in 1805 and naval battles during the War of 1812. Nicknamed "Old Ironsides" because of the slight damage incurred during defeat of the British *Guerriere*, the vessel held special interest to the family of last general manager of the Boston and Sandwich Glass Company, Henry Francis Spurr. His grandfather, Zephaniah Spurr, was a Boston wagonmaster who transported guns from the foundry to the ship in Boston Harbor. (See Chapter 2 in Volume 4 for history of the Spurr family.) The *Constitution* was reconditioned in 1833 after a nationwide appeal to preserve her. The publicity may have precipitated the several pieces of tableware that carry her likeness. In dimensions and border pattern, the *Constitution* tray duplicates the underplate of the preceding three-piece set. The Sandwich Glass Museum gift shop has a rectangular tray with a border pattern reproduced in clear and several colors that closely resembles this one. *Courtesy, Sandwich Glass Museum, Sandwich Historical Society*

1053 PEACOCK EYE (PEACOCK FEATHER) AND SHIELD TRAY

1⅛" H. x 8⅜" L. x 4⅝" W. 1835–1845
This rectangular tray is an underplate that was combined with the Lacy Peacock Eye dish shown in photo 3243. The two shields molded beneath the bottom match shields on the dish and its cover. Two cone-shaped, fine diamond point elements in the very center are combined with unpatterned bull's eyes, a device used often on Sandwich Lacy items. A fan in each corner extends from a plain table rest. The border pattern combines the "ice cream cone" motif with alternating unpatterned eyes. The scallop and point rim is one of a limited number of cap ring configurations that can be documented as a product of the Boston and Sandwich Glass Company.

1054 PRESSED GOTHIC ARCH AND PEACOCK EYE (PEACOCK FEATHER) SUGAR ON FOOT

(a) Sugar 3⅝" H. x 5" Dia.
(b) Cover 2⅞" H. x 4⅜" Dia.
(c) Combined size 6¼" H. x 5" Dia. 1830–1845

This sugar carries two famous Sandwich patterns, Gothic Arch around the lower half of the bowl and on the cover with Peacock Eye around the upper portion of the bowl. There is a chain of beads beneath the scalloped rim. The cover with its four large Gothic Arches rests on an inner rim of the bowl. Removal and replacement of the cover caused chipping of the small scallops in early years of use. The chips did not occur when the bowl was removed from the mold in which it was pressed, as some antiques dealers claim. A chipped rim greatly reduces the value of a piece. The cover finial with concentric circles resembles the pressed stoppers in photo 3185. The stippling that identifies these pressed pieces as Lacy was termed *sablée*, or sand, by the French and was referred to as *granulated* by Gustav E. Pazaurek in *Gläser der Empire—und Biedermeierzeit. Courtesy, Sandwich Glass Museum, Sandwich Historical Society*

1055 PRESSED DAISY WITH PEACOCK EYE DISH

1¼" H. x 6½" Dia. 1830–1845

This dish was called "Daisy with Peacock Eye" by Ruth Webb Lee, a glass dealer and scholar who wrote the book *Sandwich Glass*. The drapes or scales that curve out from the table rest to the bull's eyes near the scallop and point rim is a variant of a pattern described as "queue de paon" (end or tail of peacock) in a catalog of Parisian glass distributor Launay Hautin & Compagnie. This dish with its daisy-like center was produced in a number of colors as well as in clear. The clear dish in this photo has a thick double rim, showing that it was pressed in an early mold with a primitive cap ring. The number of fragments dug at the factory site, coupled with known examples in various degrees of refinement, indicate that production took place over an extended period. Its shape and small diameter Daisy center, although pleasing in proportion, would render the dish useless by today's standards. A variant of this pattern was also made in Sandwich. Its drapes or scales extend out straight from the table rest to the bull's eyes. It is also considered an Eye and Scale variant.

1056 PRESSED HEART AND SCALE CREAM

4½" H. 1838–1845

On this familiar Sandwich cream, a pattern of scales dominates. But it is the diamond and two hearts beneath the spout that gave rise to two legends, neither of which can be proven. It has been said that the hearts represented a young man and woman and the diamond symbolized their engagement ring. A second claim was that the hearts and diamond were designed to represent statements made in Abraham Lincoln's eulogy and the number of drapes and columns coincide with the date of his death on April 15, 1865. However, the style and manufacturing method belongs to an earlier era. Note the dip on the right side of the spout. It is only on one side of the spout and was caused when hot glass did not flow into that part of the mold. This is called *underfill*. The authors have seen a clear Heart and Scale cream with this defect in exactly the same location. Clear creams are relatively common but colored ones are scarce.

1057 PRESSED EYE AND SCALE PLATE

¾" H. x 4½" Dia. 1830–1845

Unusually large amounts of fragments carrying this pattern were dug from the Boston and Sandwich Glass Company site. The rays in the center alternate in length. The pointed oval inside the smooth rim resembles an eye and was so named by collectors. Scales that extend to the eyes from a plain table rest are one variation of numerous drape patterns that were in vogue in America and abroad during this time period. Many fragments from the dump site were an inch or more thick with the Eye and Scale pattern pressed into the underside. They were not production errors, but were from large gathers of glass that were placed in the Eye and Scale mold to heat the mold before it was used to press the plates. In 1827, Deming Jarves attempted to press a tumbler in Eye and Scale. The eyes were oval rather than pointed. The tumbler was too crude to be saleable. Similar tumblers known to be French should not be mistaken for Jarves' effort.

1058 PRESSED EYE AND SCALE

(a) Plate ¾" H. x 4½" Dia.

(b) Hand candlestick 3¼" H. x 4½" Dia. 1830–1845

The Eye and Scale plate was one of several that saw double duty as the lower unit of a chamber stick, referred to in the 1870's Boston and Sandwich Glass Company catalog as a "hand candlestick". The hexagonal socket is the same as can be seen on a square base with extended round corners in photo 4016. It was adhered to the Eye and Scale plate by the use of a very thick wafer. This procedure sometimes mutes the pattern in the center of the plate. The applied handle was a simple ring with its tail turned under the rim of the plate to give it strength. These squatty hand candlesticks are extremely rare today. *Courtesy, Sandwich Glass Museum, Sandwich Historical Society*

1059 PRESSED EYE

(a) Plate ¾" H. x 6¼" Dia.

(b) Hand candlestick 3⅝" H. x 6¼" Dia. 1830–1845

This hand candlestick was made the same way as the one in photo 1058, but the gaffer was not as skilled in assembling the units. Note the poor connection between the plate and the socket; overheating narrowed the socket extension. A poorly-shaped ring, set too far into the plate, resulted in an awkward handle. The candlestick has a scar beneath the plate in the center. This is where a pontil rod held the plate when the socket was applied. Do not attempt to attribute glass to a specific factory or assign it to a particular time period because of its color. All flint glass factories had the capability to make any color for which the proper raw materials were available. The pieces shown in this series of books were each documented by at least two of the following methods: family collections of known Sandwich glassworkers, written records, printed catalogs and enough dug fragments with manufacturing defects to prove on-site production. *Courtesy, Sandwich Glass Museum, Sandwich Historical Society*

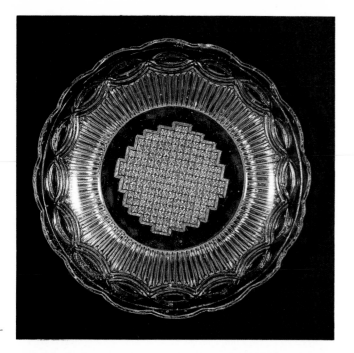

1060 PRESSED RAYED WITH CHAIN BORDER PLATE

¾" H. x 6¼" Dia. 1830–1845

The pattern in the center of this plate is a variant of the Diamond Check (Checkered Diamond), each check quartered diagonally into four triangles. The rayed ribs terminate at inverted scallops and a chain comprised of pointed ovals placed end to end. Note that the scallops of the rim follow the pattern of the chain. The chain was a common element of design that can be found in a number of molds in which glass articles were pressed and blown molded at Sandwich. Other glass houses in the Greater Boston area produced tableware with chain designs by applying threads of glass to blown glass blanks, a technique that cannot be attributed to Sandwich. At the Boston and Sandwich Glass Company site, fragments of this plate were intermingled with fragments of stippled Lacy glass.

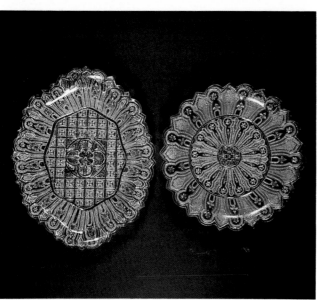

1061 PRESSED HAIRPIN

(a) Dish 1¼" H. x 10" L. x 8" W.

(b) Plate 1½" H. x 8" Dia. 1830–1840

Without question, the pattern known as *Hairpin* is one of the most appealing. It takes its name from the shape of a Nineteenth Century pin that held up large amounts of women's hair in the style of that day. Central to both articles is a leaf-like quatrefoil enclosing a four-petaled blossom. Dish A has an overall background of diamonds in squares. The curved oval border has twenty hairpins that extend to the scallops of the rim. Small six-pointed stars and other diminutive figures are used as fillers. Plate B has thirteen hairpins in its center repeated thirteen times on the border. Note the difference in color between the dish and plate. Although both are considered colorless, dish A has green blemishes from *gall*, the term for impurities that generally rise to the surface of hot glass in the pot. Yet the batch itself was purer than that used to mold plate B. Expect to find this pattern on any number of circular, hexagonal, oval and odd-shaped articles and expect the purchase price to be high for perfect antique pieces. An 8" diameter Hairpin plate with the diamonds in squares center of dish A was reproduced by Duncan and Miller Glass Company of Washington, Pennsylvania. According to Duncan and Miller experts George A. Fogg and Francis C. Maloney, the plate appeared in a 1927 catalog and to date has been found in clear and amber. On the "repro", the border pattern is delineated by small beads, but there is no stippling between the hairpins. The rim has the soft contour of late fire polished articles.

1062 PRESSED HAIRPIN DISH IN FORM OF PEACOCK

1⅜" H. x 9⅜" L. x 8" W. 1830–1840

Here is the beautiful Hairpin pattern adapted to the form generally described as a "shell". However, we show this dish with the diamond square handhold at the bottom to illustrate how closely the entire configuration resembles a peacock. Imagine the diamond squares to be his breast, its sides curving into a long neck and small, plumed head. This odd pattern was unnecessary unless the designer was attempting a peacock, his head centered exactly where it should be in relation to the fanned Hairpin tail. It is interesting to study the forethought that was put into the creation of such pieces as this and the Pipes of Pan dish in photo 1096. Differences in mold making procedures between these articles and other carelessly-executed ones show vast fluctuation in talent. The Hairpin dish was also made in bisqueware by the English firm of I. Hall and Sons. Unfortunately, this wonderful Sandwich glass piece was reproduced for The Metropolitan Museum of Art. The logo "MMA" appears near the rim of the handhold, but is sometimes removed by flea market dealers to deliberately deceive the unwary beginning collector. Take care to examine before purchasing this extremely rare item. *Courtesy, Sandwich Glass Museum, Sandwich Historical Society*

1063 PRESSED PEACOCK EYE (PEACOCK FEATHER) DISH
1¼" H. x 9½" L. x 7¾" W. 1830–1840

This pattern is an early version of the pattern that should properly be named *Peacock Tail*. The peacock, a male peafowl, has a tail that fans out in this manner. Each tail feather of the peacock has an eye-like spot that is shown as one of twenty-four bull's eyes that extends into the beaded, scalloped rim of this dish. A stipple-outlined, unpatterned loop is centered in each feather beneath the eye, a device also seen on the Hairpin dish. The beaded, stippled handle was pressed as part of the dish, molded by the method described by Deming Jarves in his May 28, 1830, patent No. 6004X. Glass flowed into each end of the handle excavation to meet in the middle while hopefully still hot. However, the glass often cooled earlier than planned, leaving some dishes with only two stubs. The handle of the dish in this photo did close, but the glass cooled before the stubs melted into each other completely. Even when well-closed, the center of the handle remained a weak spot that cracked easily when bumped by other dishes. The dish was copied in porcelain by the Meissen factory.

Peacock as illustrated in *Iconographic Encyclopedia of Science, Literature and Art* published in 1851. Note the similarity to the pattern of the dish.

1064 PRESSED PEACOCK EYE (PEACOCK FEATHER) SWEETMEAT ON FOOT
(a) Bowl 3½" H. x 6¼" Dia.
(b) Cover 2½" H. x 4¾" Dia.
(c) Combined size 5" H. x 6¼" Dia. 1830–1845

There are many variants of this pattern which is commonly called *Peacock Eye* and *Peacock Feather*. As you continue to study this chapter, you will understand that it later evolved into a pattern known as *Horn of Plenty*. To date, we have not located a single document from an American flint glass factory or company that referred to any of the three names. Launay Hautin & Compagnie, a French distributor of glass manufactured by Cristalleries de Baccarat and Cristalleries de Saint-Louis, printed catalogs that described similar patterns as *queue de paon*, which translates to "tail of peacock". On this footed bowl in a size usually used for sweetmeat, the tail feathers each have the same type of stipples. The eyes are encircled by a rope ring. Vertical ribs are molded beneath the foot. The rim carries an elaborate grape border. The inside surface of the bowl is smooth so foodstuffs could be easily removed, but the pattern of the cover is on the inside. Do not expect covers to fit well. They often warped from annealing in an unevenly heated leer. Bowls and covers were shipped in separate containers and were matched up by the retailer, so poorly fitted covers are common.

1065 PRESSED PEACOCK EYE (PEACOCK FEATHER) NAPPIE
(a) Nappie 1⅝" H. x 7½" Dia.
(b) Cover 2⅛" H. x 6⅛" Dia.
(c) Combined size 3⅜" H. x 7½" Dia. 1830–1845

Here again is Peacock Eye with the same tail feather repeated around the nappie and its cover. The lower unit is common with its simple circle of stipples inside an evenly scalloped rim. This is the only matching cover the

authors have seen in all their years of research. The open finial with its serrated lobes provides a better grip than common solid finials. The concentric circles surrounding it are on the upper surface. The pattern of Peacock Eye is beneath the cover as is a nipple and a five-pointed star beneath the finial. A reeded band completes the cover to its rim. Occasionally extra covers are sold at auction as part of a well-rounded Sandwich glass collection. Consider their purchase because the addition of a cover skyrockets the value of the nappie. *Courtesy, Sandwich Glass Museum, Sandwich Historical Society*

1066 PRESSED PEACOCK EYE (PEACOCK FEATHER) MUSTARD

(a) Mustard 2" H. x 2¾" Dia.
(b) Cover ¾" H. x 2⅜" Dia.
(c) Combined size 2½" H. x 2¾" Dia. 1830–1845

The feathers beneath the eyes in this variant are covered with alternating stipples and very fine diamond point. A chain of beads surrounds the mustard at the bottom and at the rim just below the seam mark of the cap ring. The mold had three side sections, a cap ring with an inside cover rest and a circular bottom section with a pattern of rayed prisms surrounded by a beaded circle. The convex eyes are plain. The cover, with its inside pattern, matches the bowl, but the eyes are surrounded by stippled circles. The cover has a slot for a mustard spoon, which was usually made of bone or olive wood. The lower unit is readily available and the cover is not impossible to find, considering that many must have broken in use. The unpatterned knob finial is difficult to grasp because there is little room beneath it to accommodate adult fingers. It is interesting that so many Lacy pieces had handles such as this molded in one piece with the body, while it was perfectly acceptable in later years to make pressed glass with applied handles. Some people believe this mustard had an underplate, but the mustard does not seat firmly into any matching plate we have encountered.

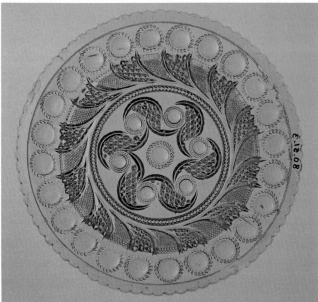

1067 PRESSED PEACOCK EYE (PEACOCK FEATHER) PLATE

⅝" H. x 4⅜" Dia. 1835–1845

This small plate is pale canary in color. The color is visible only on the thickest portions of the plate. The central pattern of beaded bull's eyes, alternating with an S-shaped scrolled eye element, resemble a pattern described in French catalogs as "arabesque and rosette". We mention this only to reiterate that we have not encountered the name *Peacock Eye* or *Peacock Feather* in early Nineteenth Century documents. The rope table rest repeats the diagonal stippling that encircles the center eye. Fine diamonds and stippling alternate on the shallow sidewall. Stippled diminutive rope rings surround eyes on the border. The rim has small even scallops. Colored Lacy glass is extremely rare. In this series of books, we photographed a higher proportion of colored glass than actually exists in the antiques market, so if you are fortunate to encounter early colored glass at reasonable cost, purchase it as a good investment. Be aware that reproductions of this pattern were made over a long period of time, dating back to the 1930's. It was still being copied at the time of this writing on nappies and footed nappies by the Imperial Glass Corporation of Bellaire, Ohio, for The Metropolitan Museum of Art in New York. On the reproduction, the "arabesque" differs in that it is stippled and every other scallop on the rim has three serrations. On these more recent copies, the mark "MMA" is hidden in one of the feathers. Their 1988 catalog shows both forms in clear glass with a 10½" diameter. The reproduction also came in a garish yellow. *Courtesy, Sandwich Glass Museum, Sandwich Historical Society*

1068 PRESSED PEACOCK EYE (PEACOCK FEATHER) NAPPIES

(a) On foot 3⅜" H. x 6" Dia.
(b) "Off foot" 1⅜" H. x 6⅛" Dia. 1830–1845

Compote and *comport* are terms often used by collectors and antiques dealers to describe a nappie or bowl on a high foot. However, both words did not come into general usage until the later quarter of the Nineteenth Century. As related to food and tableware, they do not appear in the 1828 through 1872 Webster's *An American Dictionary of the English Language*. Throughout the same time period, from the 1825 Sandwich Glass Manufactory sloar book to the 1874 catalog, the term *nappie* or *nappy* applies. The nappies in this photo are the same pattern as in the preceding photo. Nappie A was combined with a wafer to a 3⅝" diameter pressed foot with a pattern of diamonds and ribbed swags. Other combinations can be found that heighten the piece to 5". Large nappies may be 9" or 10" diameter and may be connected to a pressed Sandwich Star foot. Study upper and lower units carefully so they can be recognized as Sandwich when combined in different ways.

1069 PRESSED PEACOCK EYE (PEACOCK FEATHER) NAPPIE

1½" H. x 7¼" Dia. 1830–1845

Variants of the Peacock Eye pattern were made in Sandwich, but we cannot limit production to the Boston and Sandwich Glass Company. There were other flint glass works in the area, most notably the New England Glass Company on Miller's River in East Cambridge, Massachusetts. A smaller flint glass works lay to the west that was operated by Patrick Slane, who very well could have been producing the same ware. There were glass factories in South Boston, all competitive, but all manufacturing whatever was popular at the moment. The nappie in this photo has rather large diamonds in the center and two beaded concentric circles around a central bull's eye. Another beaded circle is inside a rim of small scallops. The pattern can be found in several sizes of nappies and in several colors.

1070 PRESSED PEACOCK EYE (PEACOCK FEATHER) PLATE

¾" H. x 5¼" Dia. 1835–1845

This plate can be found in quantity in clear glass, but is extremely rare when silver nitrate was used to stain the amber border. According to Deming Jarves in his book *Reminiscences of Glass-making*, "Twenty-five silver dollars refined will give thirty-seven ounces of nitrate of silver". The star medallion in the center is a combination of an eight-pointed star surrounded by eight diamond squares, the whole enclosed by eight C-scrolls placed side by side. The outer portion of the center is unpatterned to the rope table rest. Stipples alternating with fine diamond point cover the sidewall of the plate to create the feather effect. The eyes are encircled by rope rings. Note that the stain was carefully applied so that the even scallops of the rim remained clear. *Courtesy, Sandwich Glass Museum, Sandwich Historical Society*

1071 PRESSED PEACOCK EYE (PEACOCK FEATHER) AND THISTLE PLATE

1" H. x 8" Dia. 1830–1845

Three thistles alternating with three leaves are in the very center surrounded by stylized leaves on a stippled ground. Again, fine diamonds alternate with stippling on the sidewall, but note the three clear areas, each with a three-petaled lily on a long stem. Originally, this was the mold designer's method of maintaining the proportion of the pattern when three more feathers had to be added for this diameter plate. If stipples and diamonds were alternated, either two or four elements would have had to be incorporated—otherwise two stippled segments or two diamond segments would have been side by side. As far as is known, the lily was used only on Sandwich Lacy pieces. The lilies provide a touch that makes this plate delightful; so delightful that, unfortunately, it was reproduced by the Imperial Glass Corporation for The Metropolitan Museum of Art. If in doubt about its origin, look for the museum logo "MMA" near one lily. The blue Sandwich glass plate shown here has a rope ring and plain ring encircling each eye on the border. There is a small bead between each eye near the evenly scalloped rim. Do not mistake the Peacock Eye for the well-molded, convex beads on Lacy glass from the Pittsburgh, Pennsylvania, area. *Courtesy, Sandwich Glass Museum, Sandwich Historical Society*

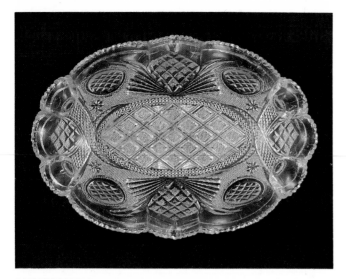

1072 PRESSED CROSSED PEACOCK EYE (PEACOCK FEATHER) DISH

1¾" H. x 6½" L. x 4½" W. 1835–1850

The center of this oval dish is covered with diamond squares up to the rope table rest. At each end of the sidewall, two Peacock Feathers with fine diamond point cross and curve along the table rest, continuing halfway to the shield-like diamond and fan centered on the long side of the dish. Four diamond medallions are enclosed by rope rings. As the manufacture of pressed glass progressed in time, form became as complicated as pattern. The sidewall undulates; a rim of large scallops and points has small serrations. Crossed Peacock Eye (Peacock Feather) pieces are fairly common. Oval and round dishes can be found that have the diamond center shown here as well as the twenty-pointed star in the photo that follows. The diamond square center dish was documented as having also been made in Pittsburgh, Pennsylvania, according to Lowell Innes in his book *Pittsburgh Glass 1797–1891*.

1073 WOODEN PATTERN FOR OVAL DISH

1¾" H. x 7¼" L. x 5¼" Dia. 1835–1850

A form and pattern of tableware originated when a glass company or mold manufacturer asked a designer to sketch and describe on paper the piece of glass to be produced. A mold designer at the mold making facility interpreted the information in wood, creating a full-size model as pictured here. If the glass company and/or mold maker was pleased with the result, a metal mold was made in which the item could be pressed or blown. Some mold makers had their own foundries, others had their molds cast at independent foundries. The finished metal mold accompanied by its wooden counterpart was stored at the glass factory. This wooden pattern served as a model for a larger version of the dish in the previous photo as well as a dish with a like pattern and form but with a twenty-point star bottom. Note the table rest that was segmented to create a bottom with diamond squares. Here is undeniable proof that molds for both variants were purchased from the same mold maker.

1074 PRESSED CROSSED PEACOCK EYE (PEACOCK FEATHER) NAPPIE WITH RAYED CENTER

1" H. x 8½" Dia. 1835–1850

Here is an example of the mold maker changing a pattern slightly to add another mold to his inventory. The pointed ends of the feathers cross but stop short of the plain table rest. The pattern is repeated four times around the sidewall rather than twice as shown previously on the oval dish. The shield-like motif with fans was eliminated, but the diamond medallions remain. The central pattern of stippled and unpatterned pie-shaped slices is a pleasing contrast to the busyness surrounding it. All of these Lacy combinations were produced simultaneously. There is no documentation available to prove which came first within a certain period. Lacy patterns were phased out gradually when a better grade of glass sand was located to produce a brilliant glass requiring no cover-up.

1075 PRESSED CROSSED PEACOCK EYE (PEACOCK FEATHER) WITH RAYED CENTER NAPPIES ON FOOT

(a) 3¾" H. x 5¾" Dia.
(b) 3⅛" H. x 7⅛" Dia. 1835–1850

This pattern is also called *Rayed Peacock Eye* because of the rayed center. Nappie A and the shallow nappie B were both attached by a wafer to the same 3⅝" diameter foot. One would think that either form of nappie could serve the same purpose, yet the slight difference in height meant another piece of pressed Lacy tableware could be offered to the public. As part of our ongoing research, the authors often attempt to use Sandwich glass on the table or elsewhere as it was intended at the time of manufacture. Even though complex patterns were molded on the outer surface, they became embedded with food from being passed from person to person at the dinner table. We do not envy the Nineteenth Century housewife or servant who had to wash the dishes!

1076 PRESSED PEACOCK EYE (PEACOCK FEATHER) DISH

1½" H. x 6¾" Dia. 1835–1850

The number of pieces still available in Peacock Eye variants and the number of fragments dug from the Boston and Sandwich Glass Company factory site indicate prolific production in a period that extended to the end of the Lacy era. This dish has a small diameter center with a diamond point pattern enclosed in a circle of beads. The table rest is almost ¼" high. Two stylized feathers of a peacock's tail come together, joined by a dot near the table rest. Between them is a medallion repeating the central pattern of diamond point and beads. The Peacock Eye and medallion are repeated three times around the dish alternating with large diamonds divided into nine parts. The evenly scalloped rim is flared.

1077 PRESSED DOUBLE PEACOCK EYE (PEACOCK FEATHER) DISH

2" H. x 12¼" L. x 9¼" W. 1835–1850

This is one of the most intricate and beautiful dishes made by the Boston and Sandwich Glass Company during the Lacy period. A bold divided strawberry diamond pattern in the bottom is surrounded by scrolled eyes. The pattern derives its name from the motif on the long side of the dish. Double Peacock Eyes, each pair curved in opposite directions, flank an allover diamond pattern. Divided strawberry diamonds in the end panels that repeat those of the bottom have horizontal chevrons on each side. Double eyes in a figure 8 embrace the curved corner panels. Fans and half-fans complete the dish. The rim is beaded and serrated. The shape of the dish made opening the mold extremely difficult. Expect to find some damage at junctures where the mold was opened. Close scrutiny should determine that the damage occurred before the dish was annealed. This dish was sometimes combined with a pressed triangular scrolled standard and beaded circular base. The base can be seen attached to a whale oil font in photo 2026.

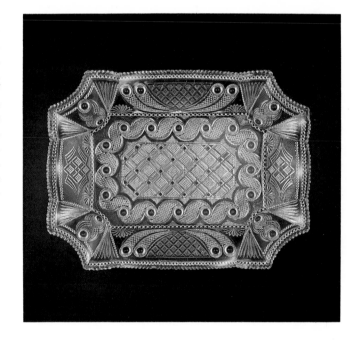

1078 PRESSED PRINCESS FEATHER MEDALLION AND PEACOCK EYE (PEACOCK FEATHER) NAPPIE

2¼" H. x 12" Dia. 1835–1845

This is the largest nappie we have been able to document as Sandwich glass. The central pattern is a thirteen-pointed star surrounded by scrolled "eyes", as called by collectors, or "arabesque", according to French catalogs. Three scrolls are covered with strawberry diamonds that are repeated in a surrounding ring. Four scrolls have diamond point. A lily is to the left and above each eye in the central pattern—matching the long-stemmed lily that is in three of the feathers of the blue plate in photo 1071. A Princess Feather Medallion alternating with four Peacock Feathers is repeated four times around the border. Each set of four feathers has two with strawberry diamonds and two with diamond point. We may never know the original names of these patterns because prior historians who could not document patterns created names based on description. Even when original documentation is found, returning to original names is difficult. The French name for a similar pattern was *queue de paon*, or "tail of peacock", so *Peacock Tail* would have more meaning. Pay particular attention to the rim of one large scallop alternating with two small ones. Because this rim has chips, at first glance it could be mistaken for the previously discussed reproduction that has one large scallop alternating with one large scallop that has three serrations.

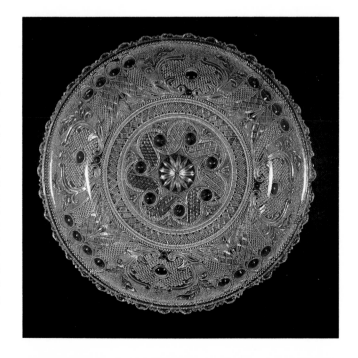

1079 PRESSED FEATHER DISH
1½" H. x 9½" Dia. 1830–1845

The name *Feather* was bestowed upon this pressed pattern by collectors; it should not be mistaken as documented fact. It can be found on several similar forms with the same diameter, but differing in depth. The quatrefoil center emanates from a strange, six-petaled rosette that is inconsistent with its four surrounding brackets. Four elongated hearts with lobes against the brackets point to the table rest. The background is covered with fine stippling. Sixteen curved loops resembling Peacock Feather extend from the table rest. Each has two lobes with a half-fan above. The alternating stippled triangles become part of the zigzag border. Three-lobed fleur-de-lys peek out from the zigzag. The size of the stippling varies to provide contrast and texture. Unlike holloware, such as sugars with vertical mold marks, patterns on flat articles continue unbroken. Well-camouflaged mold marks appear as concentric circles near table rests and rims.

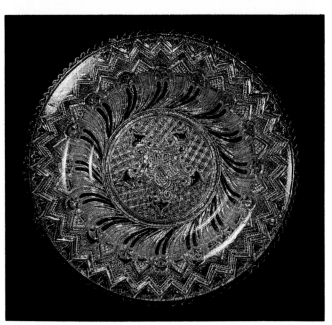

1080 PRESSED FEATHER DISH
1⅝" H. x 10" Dia. 1830–1845

This Feather dish repeats the form of the preceding piece—a nappie center with a broad border. However, the central pattern is a cinquefoil on a diamond background. The cinquefoil is made up of scrolled brackets and arrowheads. Note that many of the rim scallops are missing. The rim is incomplete because the glass cooled too quickly as it flowed into the cap ring. At the time of manufacture, the Boston and Sandwich Glass Company may have included the dish in a package of seconds to be sold at auction. Trade auctions, to which several glass companies invited their largest wholesale buyers, were held regularly in Boston to rid warehouses of such merchandise. Serious students of early manufacturing techniques value articles with production flaws and often pay more for them. However, when purchasing, make sure an incomplete rim is a flaw and not a dealer's unscrupulous attempt to sell a chipped dish that was machined smooth. *Courtesy, Sandwich Glass Museum, Sandwich Historical Society*

1081 PRESSED MULTI-PATTERNED BOWL
4¼" H. x 9⅛" Dia. 1830–1840

The authors wonder if the intricately-patterned mold in which this deep bowl was pressed was a special design for an industrial exhibition at which glass companies were awarded premiums for outstanding contributions to their trade. It was a fine example of how far pressing had advanced in duplicating cut glass designs of its day. In crazy-quilt fashion, numerous elements were combined and tied together somewhat by the overall Strawberry Diamond pattern on the bottom and lower third of the sidewall and half-fans in each of the rim's twenty-two scallops. There are twenty-two cornucopia or feathers that are not divisible by the six patterns they enclose. From left to right, the six sample patterns closest to the viewer are Fine Diamond Point, Herringbone, Reeded, Diamond Check (Checkered Diamond), Scale and Twisted. A similar bowl was exhibited at The Corning Museum of Glass in 1954. The exhibit was curated by James H. Rose, who cataloged it as *The Story of American Pressed Glass of the Lacy Period 1825–1850*. As pictured on the cover, the half-fans in the scallops were replaced by stippling and a chain of beads. The bowl was attached by a wafer to a high Lacy foot. Rose dated the bowl as having been pressed prior to 1830, but our research shows that pressing had not been perfected to this degree by 1830. *The Corning Museum of Glass, Corning, New York*

1082 PRESSED PINEAPPLE AND GOTHIC ARCH DISH

1¾" H. X 10" L. X 7" W. 1830–1845

Inside the table rest, four natural pineapples point inward toward a central cinquefoil with a star center. Each side of the square enclosing the cinquefoil forms the bottom of two opposite Gothic Arches and two crown-like motifs. Gothic Arches on the long and short sides and stylized pineapples on the chamfer of the corners form the major part of the pattern. Pointed leaves and rayed stars soften the lines of the arches. Scales complete the sidewall to a scallop and point rim. Fragments of this rim were dug at the factory site. Invoices dated April and May 1829 of the New England Glass Company in East Cambridge, Massachusetts, listed "Pine Apple" dishes in three sizes. Other than the description, their form and pattern remains undocumented.

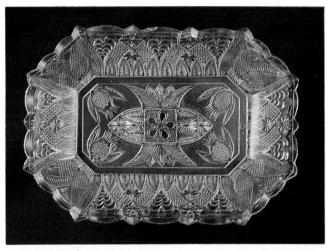

1083 PRESSED LEAF AND GOTHIC ARCH DISH

2" H. x 8¼" L. x 6¼" W. 1835–1845

The authors believe that few patterns were suggested by glass factory personnel. Most originated with the mold making establishment and were not one-of-a-kind. Like molds were sold to any glass company that needed them. The mold designer maximized the design elements to cover the allotted area, so variants can occur from mold to mold for the same or different sizes. On this dish with leaves on each corner, the mold maker used every devise available to vary the texture of each motif. The center has beads and stipples, half-fans and a diamond enclosing a beaded circle on an unpatterned ground. The large leaves on the sidewall are on an unpatterned ground as well. Stippling in the Gothic Arches is larger than the stippling behind the stemmed four-petaled blossoms. The collector should appreciate the talent behind this dish, which is much more attractive than others that were pressed in molds manufactured with no thought for the appearance of the finished product.

1084 PRESSED GOTHIC ARCH SUGAR ON FOOT

(a) Sugar 3¾" H. x 5" Dia.
(b) Cover 2⅛" H. x 4⅜" Dia.
(c) Combined size 5½" H. x 5" Dia. 1840–1850

No other piece of Lacy tableware is known to have been made in as many colors as this Gothic Arch sugar. It must have been well received by the buying public because its availability today attests to its manufacture in quantity. It was made in the years when the earlier complicated Lacy patterns were giving way to simplified versions. The circular foot is plain, but the octagonal bowl has three different Gothic Arch elements. One pointed arch has parallel vertical ribs from top to bottom. A second has ribs that follow the lines of the pointed arch. A third is divided vertically and has an allover pattern of diamond squares. Beads surround each arch and the plain rim. The cover matches in pattern. Its simple unpatterned finial is a common form that continued in use through the 1860's. The eight corners of the cover rim easily chipped from everyday use. Consider the condition of the cover when purchasing, because chips greatly reduce value. Two or three minor flakes are acceptable on colored glass that is this old, but if damage is extensive, wait patiently for another to come along. Removing pressed glass from its mold had been perfected to a point where the procedure was not difficult. A cover chipped at the factory would have been discarded. *Courtesy, Sandwich Glass Museum, Sandwich Historical Society*

1085 PRESSED GOTHIC ARCH DISH

1¼" H. x 4¼" Dia. 1835–1850

This small dish has a large diameter center divided into ten sections. It has no table rest, but lies flat on the table. The rays on the bottom extend onto the sidewall to become part of ten Gothic Arches. Each piece in this pattern is wonderfully proportioned. The lack of stipples adds to its beauty. As mass production methods of glassmaking took priority, bolder patterns were adapted to a wider assortment of pieces, each piece carrying the complete pattern rather than only certain elements as characterized by pattern repetition on Lacy glass. The dishes were not intended to be sold in sets, but the housewife of a low income family could choose matching pieces to beautify her table. For example, this dish might have held an individual portion of berries served from the larger matching dish that follows.

1086 PRESSED GOTHIC ARCH DISH

(a) Dish 1⅝" H. x 7⅜" Dia.

(b) Wooden pattern 1835–1850

To complement the previously shown small Gothic Arch dish, the integrity of the pattern was maintained on this larger one by increasing the number of sections in the center and arches on the sidewall to twelve. Both dishes have a scalloped rim when viewed from above, but when viewed from the side the scallops are inverted. Note that the center of the dish is very clear and the rays are distinct. If the dish had at one time been attached to a foot by a wafer, this center would be distorted and the rays muted. Beneath the center may appear a rough area that looks like an imperfect scar from a pontil rod. (A dish such as the perfect flat one in this photo should not have a pontil mark because there was no reason to hold it by a pontil after it had been taken from the mold.) A defective, incomplete piece has little value, so examine carefully when considering a purchase. The matching wooden pattern is a collectible in itself that commands a strong price in the antiques market. Patterns are generally dark and well-oiled from use. *Courtesy, Sandwich Glass Museum, Sandwich Historical Society*

1087 PRESSED GOTHIC ARCH DISH ON LOOP (LEAF) FOOT

5" H. x 7⅛" Dia. 1840–1850

Two separately pressed units, each with a different bold pattern, were attached to each other by means of the hot, hand-formed disk of glass known as a *merese* or *wafer*. The foot has a pattern of elongated loops pressed into the upper surface. Called *Loop* by collectors, the pattern was listed as *Leaf* in an 1859/1860 catalog of McKee and Brother, flint glass manufacturers in Pittsburgh, Pennsylvania. The upper unit is the dish with rayed center as shown previously, possibly called *Arch* by Boston and Sandwich Glass Company personnel. Its pattern is molded on the outside and the surface on which food was placed is smooth. Loop feet are usually adhered to upper units in the Loop pattern. While not unheard of, combinations of two patterns are relatively rare and command a high price. *Courtesy, Sandwich Glass Museum, Sandwich Historical Society*

1088 PRESSED SHELL PLATE

1" H. x 7¼" Dia. 1835–1850

The central pattern of this twelve-sided, deep plate is composed of a quatrefoil with beads between the lobes, two Princess Feather Medallions with star centers and two beaded ornaments on a stippled ground. Twelve design elements thought to resemble scallop shells alternate with diamonds on the border. The rim is heavily stippled. The large scallops are well rounded. The Shell plate is known to have been made in at least seven sizes, the smallest being a cup plate. There are several variants of Shell documented as Sandwich, but it is possible that other eastern flint glass factories also made them.

1089 PRESSED SHELL PLATE

1" H. x 7¼" Dia. 1835–1850

The Shell pattern photographs clearly enough to afford close scrutiny of minor changes in the molds. At first glance, this plate looks like the previous one. But, starting in the center, we see a seven-petaled rosette rather than the quatrefoil. No stars are centered in the Princess Feather Medallions and the other two ornaments are not beaded. This piece has a rope table rest; the preceding plate has an unpatterned one. A change in the contour of the sidewall necessitated a change in the three-pointed "tail" of each shell. One must look carefully to find the diamonds between the shells. The rim of small scallops is not stippled. Small differences in pattern did not matter to the wholesaler, retailer or buyer because the neophyte glass industry was attempting only to make auxiliary glass dishes to accompany sets of china. In and of themselves, American Lacy glass tableware for the home was intended for miscellaneous purposes.

1090 PRESSED SHIELD AND ACANTHUS LEAF PLATE

1⅝" H. x 9½" Dia. 1835–1845

This is a well-molded, heavy plate with brilliant stipples. In its center, a six-lobed rosette is surrounded by ornamental shields that appear in larger versions on the border. The shields are separated by stylized acanthus leaves climbing up a stippled triangle. Concentric rope rings are on both sides of a plain table rest. Evenly spaced, deep scallops form the rim. It is documented that the Boston and Sandwich Glass Company purchased all molds during this period. Many came from the Boston mold making facility of Enoch Dillaway.

1091 PRESSED NECTARINE AND ACANTHUS LEAF NAPPIE

1½" H. x 5½" Dia. 1835–1845

Little documentation exists to tell us original factory names of patterns. Jarves' early letters indicate that in the 1820's some descriptions were straightforward, such as *Checkered Diamond* and *Harp*, making identification conclusive. Others, such as *Purity*, will never be identified. Regarding the Lacy nappie shown here, Ruth Webb Lee wrote in 1939, "Since it was never known by any name at all, it has been christened Nectarine." A stylized blossom appears on the very center enclosed by a diamond. Stylized leaves extend from arcs that form the sides of the diamond, above which are five-pointed stars on a stippled ground. The four-petaled flower, thought by Lee to resemble a nectarine blossom, is repeated four times on the border, flanked by sprigs of leaves. Each petal has three lobes. Between each floral motif is a stylized acanthus leaf climbing the sides of a curved triangle. Note that in addition to a very fine stippled ground, the mold maker employed larger stipples to delineate the central diamond, border triangles and leaf stalks. The stippled ground extends in a sawtooth edge to the evenly scalloped rim.

1092 PRESSED NECTARINE NAPPIE

¾" H. x 4¼" Dia. 1835–1845

Here is a less stilted version of the Nectarine pattern. The nappie's central pattern is a circle, a beaded circle and a stippled quatrefoil, the whole surrounded by a sixteen-leaf ornament. As in the preceding photo, concentric circles are on the inside and outside of a plain table rest. A stem curving to the right has three naturally-shaped leaves and a nectarine blossom, below which is a beaded bull's eye. The leaves are repeated in groups of five, the outer two ending in scrolls. The two elements are repeated four times around the border. A stippled background extends to sawteeth inside a rim of smooth, even scallops.

1093 PRESSED NECTARINE NAPPIE ON FOOT

4½" H. x 7¼" Dia. 1835–1845

Here is a Nectarine nappie with similar flamboyant blossoms and leaves modified for a larger diameter article. The stem curves to the right, and three leaves were added to fill the allotted space. The five-leaved motif between the nectarine sprigs has a diamond center. The five-leaved pattern on the outside of the pressed foot is effective. The upper and lower units were pressed separately and then fused with a wafer. All Sandwich Lacy nappies with pressed feet were made this way. The nappie was pressed with the pattern on the outer surface, the inside smooth where it came into contact with food.

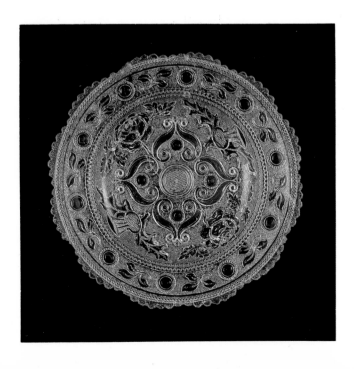

1094 PRESSED ROSE AND THISTLE PLATE

⅞" H. x 5¼" Dia. 1835–1845

This is a lovely, brilliant piece we are sure was pressed in a new mold during a period when production of quality Lacy molds was at its height. Well-defined, sharp stipples cover the center of the plate as well as the scalloped rim. (Patterns pressed in older molds have less detail. Mold surfaces wore from cleaning and oiling. Tiny bits of glass remained in intricate mold surfaces that were oiled over, resulting in a softer finished produce with less depth.) Four sets of scrolls enclosing beaded bull's eyes surround a concentric circle center. The plate does not have a ring table rest, so the two roses and two thistles extend onto the curved wall. Concentric beaded circles separate the blossoms from a border pattern of fourteen beaded bull's eyes alternating with fourteen sprigs of three leaves on a stem. The cap ring for this mold was laboriously cut into twelve large scallops, each divided into seven smaller ones. The combination of a superior mold and a batch of flint glass made during a week when all was going well at the factory resulted in a plate with a silvery sheen.

1095 PRESSED ROSE AND THISTLE NAPPIE

1⅞" H. x 8¼" Dia. 1835–1845

It could be argued forever as to whether this article was listed as a *nappie* or a *deep plate*. Six beaded bull's eyes are in the center. Six fleur-de-lys extend from between them. The whole is surrounded by six C-scrolls placed end to end. The curve of the nappie is made up of alternating roses and thistles. The border pattern is an interesting combination of quatrefoil, beaded bull's eyes and an element resembling a five-lobed leaf with stippled and beaded veins. This combination is repeated six times around the nappie. The rim configuration matches that of the previous Rose and Thistle plate, but to accommodate a larger circumference, each of the twelve large scallops were segmented into nine small ones. Fragments dug at the Boston and Sandwich Glass Company factory site indicate that one larger and two smaller sizes may exist. All dug fragments were colorless, but surprises do happen in the collecting world. Any of the Lacy articles shown could have been made in color.

1096 PRESSED PIPES OF PAN DISH

1⅜" H. x 8" L. x 6⅛" W. 1830–1840

A rare dish made at Sandwich during the Lacy period has a center that depicts the Greek mythological god Pan playing shepherd's pipes. Pan has the head of a man, wings, and the body of a goat. Two facing figures of Pan are connected by scrolls to a center motif of four bunches of grapes. A rose blossom is beneath each figure. The grapes are repeated on one side panel, combined with a wreath and flower-filled cornucopia. (In Greek mythology, a cornucopia is a horn of the goat that suckled Zeus.) On the opposite wall, a crossed spear and oar signify his patronage of fishing and fowling. A scrolled ornament and a large leaf fill the end panels, and a thistle is in each chamfer. Each design element relates in some way to Pan's power as guardian of the bees that pollinate fruit and flower. The dish is heavily stippled to the edge of its scallop and point rim except for the center of the wreath. The overall beauty of this dish makes it one of the finest pieces designed for production at the Boston and Sandwich Glass Company.

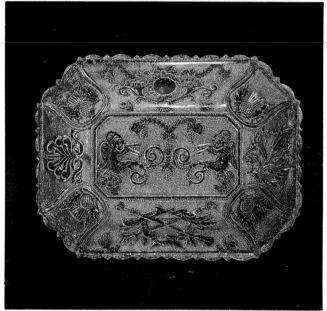

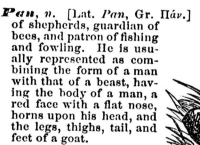

Pan, *n.* [Lat. *Pan*, Gr. Πάν.] (*Myth.*) The god of shepherds, guardian of bees, and patron of fishing and fowling. He is usually represented as combining the form of a man with that of a beast, having the body of a man, a red face with a flat nose, horns upon his head, and the legs, thighs, tail, and feet of a goat.

Pan
(from Dwight's Mythology).

Here is Pan as copied from *Dwight's Mythology* by Webster's *An American Dictionary of the English Language*.

1097 PRESSED GRAPE VINE AND HARP (SATYR) PLATE

½" H. x 4¼" Dia. 1830–1840

Like the above Pan playing pipes, this plate also depicts a *satyr*, as in mythology the half man and half goat figure is called. Here he is shown outstretched over a harp. The fanciful motif is surrounded by a beaded circle and a vine heavy with grapes. Unlike the rope table rest of the Pipes of Pan dish, this one is plain. Four shield-like devices on the border combine leaves and scrolls. They alternate with five-pointed stars. There are no stipples on the rim of even scallops. This plate may have been for an individual serving of grapes taken from the larger Pipes of Pan dish. It is clear that both pieces came from the hand of the same mold maker. Look for whimsical touches that show individuality in design. When identified, they add to the pleasure of collecting.

The satyr is thought of as a rogue in mythology. As illustrated in Webster's 1847 *An English Dictionary of the American Language*, he is playing a lyre. Patterns on glass derived from drawings of mythology and architecture were prevalent during the 1830's and 1840's. They extended into the 1870's as documented by the decorated opal ring shades and vases pictured in the 1874 Boston and Sandwich Glass Company catalog.

1098 PRESSED MEDALLION DISH

1" H. x 5¼" Dia. 1835–1850

On this eight-sided dish, the C-scroll device was used to form the borders of medallions that enclose nectarine blossoms, five-lobed shell-like ornaments, and triangular ornaments made up of leaves and a small six-petaled blossom. Although the center of the dish is stippled in the usual manner, the background in each medallion is rippled. Fanciful fleur-de-lys at each corner near a scalloped, stippled rim gives the dish a personality not found on earlier pieces. There were several reasons why patterns became simplified. With advances in quality control of the glass, there was less need to completely hide defects. And, as the United States approached the financial panic of 1837, cutting the costs of mold making was essential.

1099 PRESSED DAHLIA NAPPIE

2" H. x 9⅜" Dia. 1835–1845

The central pattern is a six-pointed ornament enclosing a six-pointed star on a stippled ground. Unpatterned brackets around the ornament result in the whole resembling a six-petaled blossom. Familiar stippling extends in a sawtooth edge to a rope ring, the table rest and another rope ring. The border pattern is composed of the central motif repeated three times, alternating with a six-pointed element that has a circular, stippled center. The ornaments are flanked by sprigs of leaves, with three each branching toward either side. A stippled ground extends in a sawtooth edge to an evenly scalloped rim. Collectors for years have referred to this pattern as *Dahlia*; however, from the enormous varieties of dahlias raised in the garden of author Barlow, we can find none that relate to any of the ornaments on this nappie.

1100 PRESSED DAHLIA NAPPIE ON TRIANGULAR SCROLLED STANDARD AND HAIRY PAW FOOT BASE

6" H. x 9⅜" Dia., 4½" each side of base
1835–1840

Here is the Dahlia nappie fused with a wafer to a most elaborately detailed base. The base has been found combined with other nappies as well as with a blown Beehive candle socket. Note the chain of beads that runs along the side of the three C-scrolls. Each of the three paws is covered with fur. Interestingly, the design of the fur is the same as makes up the leaves on the handle of the cover in photo 1029. The leaves can be seen on the vertical edges of the base, between the paws. Note the button beneath each paw. If the footed nappie became too hot in the annealing leer, therefore tilting to one side as this one did, only the buttons had to be machined to level the article. *Courtesy, Sandwich Glass Museum, Sandwich Historical Society*

1101 PRESSED BEEHIVE AND THISTLE DISH

1⅜" H. x 9¾" Dia. 1835–1855

The central motif that appears to be a flower is actually six beehives placed side to side, with a bee between each hive. They are surrounded by four five-pointed stars, each star made by combining five diamonds. The stars alternate with thistle blossoms, each flanked by leaves. The border panels have variants of shields, an eight-pointed ornament and a large leaf. A bunch of grapes is on both sides of two of the shields. Acanthus leaves separate the panels at each of the eight corners. As far as is known, the Beehive and Thistle pattern was only used on dishes of this diameter. All documented ones have even scallops on the rim. The rare dish in this photo was stained by silver nitrate. The number of unstained ones in good condition found today and the bushels of matching fragments retrieved from the Boston and Sandwich Glass Company site indicate great popularity. According to Ruth Webb Lee, an entry in William Stutson's notebook shows manufacture of this dish as late as 1859. Due to extended use of the molds, some dishes have shallow stipples and are dull. Watch for bright dishes with clean stipples that give a silvery sheen. There is a difference in value between the two. Light blue dishes were also originally made. Beware of reproductions in several sizes that were manufactured in clear, pink and green tones associated with the Depression era of the Twentieth Century. *Courtesy, Sandwich Glass Museum, Sandwich Historical Society*

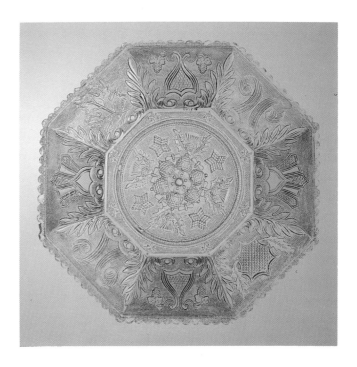

1102 PRESSED PANELED ROSE AND THISTLE DISH

1" H. x 5¼" Dia. 1840–1850

The Rose and Thistle pattern was adapted to this deep octagonal dish which was pressed in a less detailed mold than those used for the Rose and Thistle and octagonal pieces shown previously. A bold sunflower is surrounded by two roses and two thistles, all four blossoms curved to make a flower chain. The rope table rest is circular. From this point outward, the dish has eight sides, each with a bold decorative motif that could stand alone. Two opposite panels have an open rose with leaves, two have an upright thistle with leaf on each side. A four-petaled blossom with sprigs of tiny five-petaled flowers covers two panels and the remaining two have a shell resembling that of a scallop centered between a five-petaled flower and leaves. Although all of these styles historically overlapped, the earlier, stilted, formal patterns slowly gave way to freer, natural patterns. The smooth areas between the patterned panels hint at simplified patterns to come.

1103 PRESSED PANELED ROSE AND THISTLE DISH

1⅞" H. x 9⅜" Dia. 1840–1850

This large, deep, octagonal dish has a stemmed sunflower from which radiate three sprigs of leaves. Two more leaf sprigs are outgrowths of the stem. Four sunflowers appear in the side panels, alternating with the two roses and two thistles that give the pattern its name. The dish is held off the table by a clear rest with a rope ring inside and outside. Due to the octagonal form, we are inclined to believe its use was limited. This may be an unfair judgment based on Twentieth Century practices. As far as is known, all Sandwich octagonal dishes have an evenly scalloped rim. If you find one with a smooth rim, examine for evidence that the rim may have been machined smooth to eliminate chips. *Courtesy, Sandwich Glass Museum, Sandwich Historical Society*

1104 PRESSED DISH

1¾" H. x 8" L. x 6" W. 1835–1845

This dish has no known name. It may originally have had only an inventory number. The tiny flower in the center of the dish is bracketed by beaded scrolls and stylized leaves. Leaves extend into the three-lobed ends of the bottom. A beaded medallion is centered in each long side, from which extend scrolled flowers. The intricacy of the mold made it difficult to remove the dish after pressing, so few old dishes can be found. It was reproduced by the Imperial Glass Corporation of Bellaire, Ohio, for The Metropolitan Museum of Art. Imperial's 1982–1983 catalog states, "These authentic and exclusive reproductions of early American Glass are made to the Metropolitan's high and exacting standards...so superbly recreated by Imperial that each piece must carry the Metropolitan's hallmark....." However, museum logos are often difficult to locate in busy Lacy patterns. Note the leaves that surround the dish near the evenly scalloped rim. On the original in this photo, they are muted at each end—the result of opening the mold. On the 1980's version, the leaves are distinct. Remember also that all Sandwich Lacy articles were made from glass that contained lead.

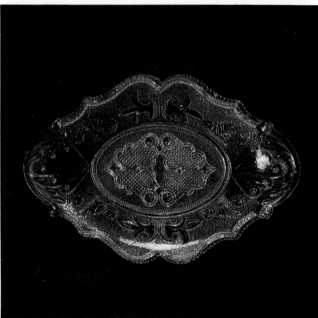

1105 PRESSED SCROLLED ACANTHUS LEAF DISH

1¼" H. x 7¾" L. x 5¼" W. 1835–1850

Note again the C-scroll device that appears with horizontal fleur-de-lys on the long sides of this dish. This and the central pattern of two stippled ornaments distinguish this very rare dish. A five-lobed, shell-like ornament at each end and four scrolled acanthus leaves with flowers complete the pattern. The entire piece has heavy stipples. Even scallops make up the unusually-shaped rim. The dish was found in Boston and Sandwich Glass Company diggings attached by a wafer to a pressed foot. Whether with or without a foot, this Lacy piece is exceedingly rare.

1106 PRESSED BUTTERFLY DISHES

(a) Large 1½" H. x 10" L. x 7" W.

(b) Small 1" H. x 6¾" L. x 4½" W. 1835–1850

This dish is named for the butterfly that occupies a beaded circle in the center. Equally prominent are four pinwheels on the sidewall and two five-lobed ornaments at the ends. The dish was manufactured in three sizes, the large and small shown here, and a medium with dimensions of the previously pictured Scrolled Acanthus Leaf dish. By studying both photos, it is clear that the mold maker had certain standard mold forms in which he inscribed a variety of patterns. These dishes are very heavy for their size; the large one can be ½" thick. Be aware that fragments of the Butterfly dish on an applied foot were found at the factory site. Its rarity would make value substantial.

1107 PRESSED STIPPLED BULL'S EYE NAPPIE

1¼" H. x 6⅞" Dia. 1835–1850

Twelve columns of bull's eyes radiate from the center, extending in five concentric circles to the rim. The bull's eyes in three of the circles enclose fine diamond points that appear as stippling. Fine diamond points comprise the background between each column and the diamonds that extend into the twelve points on the rim. The rim points alternate with twelve large scallops, each divided into five small ones. The bull's eyes of the innermost circle are smooth, as are the eyes of the third circle from the center. This larger circle is the table rest. On occasion, you will find some of these eyes machined and polished to level an otherwise wobbly nappie. The leveling was done at the factory and does not deter from value. Stippled Bull's Eye nappies were made in several sizes in clear and opalescent. They are quite rare.

1108 PRESSED ROMAN ROSETTE (DIAMOND ROSETTE) WITH DAISY CENTER NAPPIE

1¼" H. x 6" Dia. 1835–1845

A pattern that was transitional between early, heavily stippled Lacy patterns and later simplified versions was named by collectors *Diamond Rosette* and *Roman Rosette*. It has a border of large stippled bull's eyes alternating with small unpatterned eyes and a central pattern of a large rosette filled with fine diamond point. The nappie in this photo has the same chain of alternating large stippled and small smooth eyes, but its center is completely different. Here is an eleven-petaled daisy. Although in these Rosette patterns we see a changeover from laboriously inscribed stipples to easily incised fine diamonds, this nappie with daisy center has the detailed rim of earlier pieces. Alternating unpatterned and stippled darts repeat the petal points and diamonds from the center. They extend into the rim scallops.

1109 PRESSED ROMAN ROSETTE (DIAMOND ROSETTE) DISH

¾" H. x 5⅜" Dia. 1835–1850

All through the production years of the Boston and Sandwich Glass Company, more small dishes and nappies were made than anything else. This pattern, called *Roman Rosette* or *Diamond Rosette* because of the rosette in the center, was used on dishes as small as 3" diameter and as large as 10¾" diameter. It had many subtle variants. Note the strange, blurred, diamond pattern in each of the nine lobes of the rosette, giving a quilted effect. The rosette is surrounded by nine diamonds and a border of nine diamond-filled eyes that resemble links of a chain alternating with nine small bull's eyes. Nine diamonds form points on the rim that alternate with large scallops divided into six small scallops. On later Roman Rosette production pieces, the diamonds are removed and the rim is completely scalloped. *Courtesy, Sandwich Glass Museum, Sandwich Historical Society*

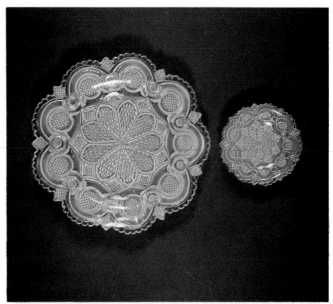

1110 PRESSED ROMAN ROSETTE (DIAMOND ROSETTE) DISHES

(a) Large 1" H. x 7½" Dia.
(b) Small ½" H. x 4½" Dia. 1838–1850

The fine diamonds in the nine-lobed rosette center of these dishes are very distinct in comparison to the pattern on the previously shown amethyst piece. All three dishes carry the chain of nine large patterned bull's eyes alternating with nine unpatterned eyes. Nine diamonds extend into the nine points of the rim. Only the number of rim scallops differ to accommodate different diameter dishes. The large opalescent dish in this photo has each large scallop divided into eight small ones, the medium amethyst dish has six small scallops for each large scallop. Condition of the rim is important when evaluating early glass. Opalescent and pale lavender pieces are fairly common.

1111 PRESSED ROMAN ROSETTE (DIAMOND ROSETTE) DISHES

(a) Deep, on foot 6½" H. x 10¾" Dia.
(b) Shallow 1½" H. x 8½" Dia. 1835–1850

To accommodate the larger diameter of this 3" deep dish on foot, there are eleven links to the chain of alternating large and small bull's eyes. It was joined by a wafer to a matching Roman Rosette foot. All early Sandwich footed dishes, nappies and bowls were pressed in two parts, the foot and the upper unit. After removal from their respective molds, a hot, hand-formed wafer of glass was used as a cementing agent. Look for the wafer beneath the upper unit. It will not have mold marks on it. Shallow dish B is alike in most respects, but the diamonds that form the points on the rim were replaced by eight-pointed stars. Another variant in the collection of The Corning Museum of Glass replaced the rim diamonds with crosses that have four arms equal in length. The Corning Museum dish and the Roman Rosette variants shown in this book are documented Sandwich patterns, but other variants were made in Midwest glass houses.

1112 PRESSED ROMAN ROSETTE (DIAMOND ROSETTE) DISH

⅞" H. x 4⅞" Dia. 1835–1850

A master glass blower took pride in his accomplishments because he alone was responsible for the quality of his finished product. A man who pressed glass had no such joy. He was at the mercy of the mold maker who may or may not have supplied a superior mold. The workmanship on this mold left a lot to be desired. The rays of the nine-pointed star in the center are far from exact. Some of the stippled bull's eyes surrounding the star are circular, some are irregular. The enclosed stipples were set at varied angles. Poor fellow! Every dish he pressed in this mold had the same defects. The outer portion of the mold was executed with less difficulty. The large stippled and small unpatterned eyes were well formed. The nine diamonds that extend to points on the rim alternate with four small scallops. Understand that, even though the authors are critical of the mold, a Roman Rosette dish in this beautiful blue is extremely desirable to a collector. *Courtesy, Sandwich Glass Museum, Sandwich Historical Society*

1113 PRESSED HORN OF PLENTY (COMET)

(a) Nappie 1¾" H. x 6⅛" Dia.
　　Cover 3¼" H. x 5½" Dia.
　　Combined size 4⅝" H. x 6⅛" Dia.
(b) Spoon holder 4½" H. x 3½" Dia. 1850–1870

It is unfortunate that collectors name patterns before original illustrated documentation comes to light. Commonly called *Horn of Plenty*, this one is listed and illustrated in factory catalogs as *Comet*. A "Memo of articles to be made for future sales" at the Cape Cod Glass Company dated November 21, 1867, lists 8" bowls and goblets. The *List of Glass Ware Manufactured by Cape Cod Glass Company* itemizes 3", 4", 5" and 8" diameter nappies in No. 40 Comet. (These documents can be studied on pages 107–110 in Volume 3.) It was also made at the Boston and Sandwich Glass Company. Nappie A is a Sandwich one with a hexagonal finial molded as part of the cover. Very rare, *and probably not Sandwich*, is a similar covered nappie with the head of George Washington for a finial. However, the Washington head cover fits poorly when placed on a documented Sandwich nappie. Spoon holder B has a foot that was pressed as one piece with the body. It was used with matching tableware pieces or with matching lamps as shown in photo 2170. For this reason they are erroneously believed to be spill holders, although listed as spoon holders in factory catalogs. If you find a Horn of Plenty spoon holder without a foot, examine carefully. The foot may have been machined off because it was damaged. If so, the piece has little value. *Courtesy, Sandwich Glass Museum, Sandwich Historical Society*

1114 PRESSED HORN OF PLENTY (COMET) NAPPIE ON WAFFLE FOOT

5¾" H. x 6¼" Dia. 1850–1870

Originally called *Comet*, this pattern evolved from the earlier Peacock Eye (Peacock Feather) when production of intricate Lacy patterns was curtailed. The sixteen circles near the scalloped rim that each formerly depicted an eye in a peacock's feather are now seen as the nucleus of a comet, its long, tapered tail curving toward the bottom of the nappie. The tail can curve in either direction. Every other nucleus is covered with fine diamonds—the alternating ones have bull's eyes. The diamond-covered tails alternate with tails having three punties diminishing in size, but some pieces have four. This nappie did not have a cover. It was adhered by a wafer to a high foot with a lobed standard and a Waffle-patterned base. The pattern is available in a wide variety of tableware pieces in clear glass. An occasional colored piece is found, canary and clambroth (alabaster) being the most common.

1115 PRESSED HORN OF PLENTY (COMET) DISHES

(a) On Horn of Plenty foot 6¼" H. x 10" L. x 7" W.
(b) "Off foot" 1¾" H. x 8⅛" L. x 5¾" W.
1850–1870

Oval dishes are relatively rare, so to find one such as A on a matching foot is most unusual. The comet tails curve in the opposite direction compared to the previously shown footed nappie. Both types were made at Sandwich. Dish B is sometimes found in clambroth (alabaster). Slight variations in pattern and color add to the excitement of collecting, especially when a number of pieces in one pattern are accumulated. Central patterns can vary. Dish B has an overall diamond pattern in the bottom. Some dishes have star bottoms. Unlike the *Comet* pattern shown in photo 1117, this one was not named for a particular comet, but was simply one of several, such as Early Moon and Star (Star and Punty, Star and Concave), that symbolized the heavens.

1116 PRESSED HORN OF PLENTY (COMET) GOBLET

6¼" H. x 3½" Dia. 1850–1870

The private collection of Sandwich glass that descended through the family of Boston and Sandwich Glass Company decorator Annie Mathilda Nye is one of the purest we have studied. With few exceptions, each piece could be traced back to Sandwich glass houses and its attribution can be substantiated by other documentation. The photographing of this collection has been one of our greatest pleasures. This goblet has a heavily gilded rim. It has no wear and may not have been intended for table use, but was taken home as a special gift and held as an example of the Boston and Sandwich Glass Company's or Cape Cod Glass Company's capability. It has a stem with a faceted knop under the bowl and a plain circular foot. When the goblet came out of the mold, the foot was in the form of an inverted nappie. A patent for such a mold was issued to Joseph Magoun of the New England Glass Company on September 25, 1847. The foot was reheated and flattened with hand tools, which is why mold seams are distinct near the stem and muted near the rim. On February 14, 1857, the Boston and Sandwich Glass Company sent John Sise gilded Comet spoon holders for which he was charged $5 per dozen.

1117 PRESSED COMET TUMBLER

3½" H. x 3¼" Dia. 1858–1865

Although the configuration of this tumbler resembles that of an 1840's French pattern described as "arabesques et rosettes", we prefer to believe the knowledgeable antiques dealer who many years ago told author Barlow the origin of this pattern. She adamantly stated it was named for Donati's comet. Giovanni Battista Donati discovered six comets between 1854 and 1864, one of which, first seen on June 2, 1858, bears his name. In October 1858, it attained the brightness of a star of zero magnitude and had a six-million-mile-long tail split into three distinct parts, symbolized on glass by three punties placed diagonally between a large bull's eye that depicts the nucleus. The pattern is repeated three times around the tumbler, each pattern from one piece of a three-section mold. Each vertical mold mark bisects a large diamond. Nine flutes surround the bottom. Its matching water jug weighs over seven pounds when empty. Comet was produced in a limited number of articles and colored pieces are extremely rare.

1118 PRESSED COMET GOBLET

6½" H. x 3⅜" Dia. 1858–1865

The flint Comet goblet shows the unpatterned circle with a center bull's eye that depicts the comet's nucleus. This is the way the luminous mass appeared to the naked eye of the people in Sandwich in the fall of 1858. The tail drops away from the bottom of the circle, showing the counter-clockwise spin of the comet named for Donati. Unlike the tumbler, the three mold sections were designed to hide the vertical seam marks. Beginning on the foot, they ascend vertically to the left side of the large circle, curve with the circle to the right, then ascend vertically to the top of the pattern. The goblet was made in blue. Comet is a product of the Boston and Sandwich Glass Company. If there is doubt as to which Comet pattern was made at the Cape Cod Glass Company, their *List of Glass Ware* laid it to rest. Several sizes of Comet nappies were listed, none of which were made in the pattern shown here. There is no question that the Comet pattern listed was the one referred to today as Horn of Plenty.

The prominence of Donati's comet in the sky of northeastern United States caused the printing of this article in the September 24, 1858, issue of the *Yarmouth Register*, a newspaper published in a neighboring village to Sandwich.

DONATI'S COMET.—The Traveller says that the comet seen in the N. W. in the evening, and again in the morning before sunrise in the N. E, is Donati's, having first been discovered by this astronomer on the 2d of June last. The reason of its being seen now in the evening and again in the morning is that it has now reached a part of its orbit so far North, that in its diurnal revolution it is only about five hours below our horizon, and consequently it is well seen in the West in the evening, and equally well in the East, in the morning, and with the naked eye.

The best view of the comet can be had in the morning, about 3½ or 4 o'clock. The direction of its tail points towards the north polar star. The velocity of the comet, when at its perihelion, is about 150,000 miles per hour. Its distance from the Earth at this time, roughly estimated, is about 87,000,000 miles. Its tail is at least 6,000,000 miles in length.

As this comet is rapidly approaching the earth, it will increase in brightness for a few weeks to come, and will be seen later and later every night. It is rapidly approaching the earth, and during the month of October will be of surprising brilliancy, perhaps more brilliant than any of the present century. It has a period of thirty-one years, and is identical with the comet of '1827, and Charles V.'s comet.

1119 PRESSED SCOTCH PLAID PLATES
(a) Large 1" H. x 8" Dia.
(b) Small ¾" H. x 6½" Dia. 1840–1860

Though the bands of parallel lines intersect to form diamonds rather than squares, this plate is known as *Plaid* or *Scotch Plaid*. At Sandwich, it was made with both types of cap ring as shown here. Plate A has a rim of small, even scallops. Plate B has a smooth, unpatterned rim of sixteen flat sides. As we approach the mid-years of Boston and Sandwich Glass Company production, we see evidence of a greater percentage of glass pressed in molds obtained or copied from outside the Boston area. The Scotch Plaid plate was manufactured in the East and Midwest, possibly, according to Lowell Innes in *Pittsburgh Glass 1787–1891*, at R. B. Curling and Sons' Fort Pitt Glass Works in Pittsburgh, Pennsylvania. A 3¾" high by 9³⁄₁₆" diameter bowl has been recorded that has a sidewall made up of a band of scrolls and lilies and a band of Scotch Plaid.

1120 PRESSED DIVIDED SQUARES (STRAWBERRY DIAMOND) NAPPIE
(a) Nappie 1⅝" H. x 6¼" Dia.
(b) Cover 2⅝" H. x 5¼" Dia.
(c) Combined size 3¾" H. x 6¼" Dia. 1840–1860

This covered nappie in clear glass was pictured by Alice Hulett Metz in her book *Much More Early American Pattern Glass*. At the time of her writing, she had not seen other tableware items in the pattern, as we have not to this day. Nor did she mention color. The name originated with her, but, at a flint glass factory, squares set at a 45 degree angle and divided in this manner were called *Strawberry Diamond*. The center of the nappie has an unpatterned circle from which rays extend to a plain table rest. The large diamonds on the sidewall, when adapted to a curved surface, form gothic arches. Each large diamond encloses inverted fine diamond point. The large diamonds are repeated twelve times around, matching those on the cover. The cover had a plain rim that rests on a ledge inside the undulating rim of the nappie. The pattern is on the outer surface of the nappie. The inside is smooth where it made contact with butter, the usual content of a 6" covered nappie. Yet the pattern is inside the cover and would not be visible if the glass was dark or opaque. The hexagonal finial is bisected by a distinct mold mark. The nappie was poorly smoothed to remove a shallow chip on one convex curve of the rim, so value is somewhat diminished. The *Barlow-Kaiser Sandwich Glass Price Guide* lists prices for perfect pieces.

1121 PRESSED PLAID VARIANT SALVER ON LEAF FOOT

7" H. x 13⅞" Dia. 1840–1860

According to Webster's 1847 *An American Dictionary of the English Language*, a *salver* is "A piece of plate with a foot, or a waiter on which any thing is presented." Glass salvers were used in two ways. Two or more were stacked to form a pyramid on which individual servings of desserts were placed. Singly, they held cakes and confections that were protected by a glass cover 1" less in diameter. This salver is the largest we have seen that can be attributed to Sandwich. It has a 5⅝" diameter Leaf foot that was attached with a wafer. We have seen a smaller one that is 5⅝" high by 10⅛" diameter, so watch for it in other sizes. The pattern is pressed beneath the plate, which has a slightly upturned rim to hold a cover.

1122 PRESSED LEAF NAPPIE ON LEAF FOOT

5¾" H. x 8⅜" Dia. 1840–1860

Both the foot and nappie in the Leaf pattern are very thick and brilliant. The nappie was pressed separately with the pattern of nine large leaves beneath. The end of each leaf curves upward and its thickness forms a sawtooth rim of nine scallops. The matching 4½" diameter foot has eight leaves that form eight lobes around the bottom. These Leaf units were used to form the vases in photo 3017, the bowl reheated and re-formed into upright sections that resemble ferns to surround a bouquet. The foot can be found on many Lacy dishes in clear and color. The vases were also made in color, but we have not yet encountered a colored nappie.

1123 PRESSED LEAF NAPPIE ON FOOT

3" H. x 8" Dia. 1840–1860

Observe how, by simply applying a different foot, an entirely different article was manufactured. The upper unit has a pattern of nine distinct leaves that swirl upward to form a sawtooth rim. The circular foot, or base (the terms are interchangeable), has no pattern. Because it is so simple, it complements the nappie. The method of attaching units of glass together by means of a wafer was not exclusive to Sandwich. It was standard procedure in early American flint glass houses. The Sandwich Glass Manufactory, Boston and Sandwich Glass Company, Cape Cod Glass Works and Cape Cod Glass Company used several styles of wafers which are illustrated on page 43 of Volume 2.

1124 PRESSED OPEN WORK "DISH OR RATHER PLATE"

2⅜" H. x 10" Dia. 1829–1850

According to Boston and Sandwich Glass Company correspondence, this style of molding was known as *open work*. A letter dated July 11, 1829, written by Boston store clerk William T. Mayo to Sandwich Superintendent William Stutson referred to Boston brass founder and mold maker Enoch S. Dillaway's design for such a mold. "Dillaway is about making a fruit basket mold open work similar to this dish or rather plate and must know how it works before he proceeds." This crudely-fashioned article could have been produced as early as 1829. Its large diameter center has rays that extend almost to the table rest. The open work sidewall was reheated and shaped after removal from the mold; therefore, the form varies from dish to dish. Because of the reheating, the points on the rim were blunted. Open work dishes and baskets have numerous stress and annealing lines. It takes careful scrutiny to determine that the lines are factory defects and not cracks. *Courtesy, Sandwich Glass Museum, Sandwich Historical Society*

1125 PRESSED OPEN WORK FRUIT BASKET ON FOOT
6¼" H. x 9¼" Dia. 1840–1855

William T. Mayo's letter clearly documents the form of this piece as a basket, even though it was made of glass rather than wood. The open side provided ventilation to keep fruit from rotting. The flat bottom of the basket has a star molded in its upper surface. The vertical staves extend to broad points at the rim. The broad points alternate with small points that bridge the open spaces between the staves. The glass basket was attached by a wafer to an octagonal base usually found on a Tulip vase as shown in photos 3021–3022. You should have no difficulty in examining colorless baskets for damage. However, be cautious in determining that annealed defects are just that and not cracks. You may encounter this flat-bottomed basket without a foot or on a foot in a combination not previously recorded. If the basket unit and the foot unit are documented Sandwich forms, the combined units can be accepted as Sandwich. *The Bennington Museum, Bennington, Vermont*

1126 PRESSED OPEN WORK FRUIT BASKET ON FOOT
8" H. x 8⅝" Dia. 1840–1855

This Sandwich glass fruit basket was mounted on a pressed hexagonal foot normally used on a Four-Printie Block whale oil lamp as pictured in photo 2104, a Circle and Ellipse lamp as shown in photo 2114, a pillar-molded vase as shown in photo 3020 and the Tulip vase in photo 3023. The foot was pressed as one unit to its knop standard. The wafer that joins the standard to the conical bottom of the basket is visible. The star making up the pattern of the bottom is visible in the side view but is less distinct when seen through the basket from above. Beside giving the attractive basket added height, the conical bottom was an improvement, serving as a drain to keep moisture from accumulating around the fruit. There are sixteen vertical staves and a rim of thirty-two even points. Often one or more of the staves are cracked and value reduced by at least 75 percent. The damage may be difficult to detect in dark glass without the aid of a strong light. A small flashlight and a portable black light are helpful at antiques shows and auction galleries. *The Bennington Museum, Bennington, Vermont*

1127 PRESSED SUNBURST (STAR BOTTOM) NAPPIE
⅞" H. x 4⅛" Dia. 1830–1840

The sunburst was a decorative treatment that was in style throughout the lifetime of the Boston and Sandwich Glass Company. It appeared on blown molded pieces as early as 1825. It remained in use long after the Civil War, molded into pressed glass and cut into the bottoms and feet of blown articles that were cataloged by the company in the early 1870's. On these early pressed pieces, the pattern was varied by changing the number of rays and the number of concentric circles in the bull's eye center and the border. This nappie has a single circle in the center, from which radiate sixteen rays. Concentric rings extend to the scallop and point rim that was made by the use of a mold with a cap ring. The pattern is beneath the nappie and the upper surface is smooth for easy cleaning. Prices in *Barlow-Kaiser Sandwich Glass Price Guide* are for perfect pieces. The value of this nappie decreases about two-thirds because of the damage that took away several scallops and points.

1128 PRESSED SUNBURST (STAR BOTTOM) NAPPIE
1" H. x 4" Dia. 1830–1840

The sunburst, or star, has a bull's eye made up of three concentric circles and nineteen rays. A single ring makes up the table rest, a double ring is on the sidewall and a triple ring surrounds the border near a scallop and point rim. This nappie is an example of an almost perfect piece with only minor roughage on one or two small rim points. A scallop on the right is incomplete because the mold was either underfilled, or the glass cooled too rapidly as it made its way into the cap ring. When purchasing, examine rims carefully. It is easy to differentiate between chips caused by damage and underfill caused by a manufacturing fault. The surface of the glass in the underfilled area has the smoothness of the rest of the article—proof that the article was incomplete before it was annealed. In pricing, consider it a perfect piece.

1129 PRESSED SUNBURST (STAR BOTTOM) PLATES
(a) 1⅛" H. x 6½" Dia.
(b) ¾" H. x 5" Dia. 1830–1840

This series of plates and nappies range in size from small cup plate to large serving plate. Plate A has a sunburst center with twenty long and twenty short rays and concentric rings to the scalloped rim. Plate B has a sunburst center with twenty-six rays that are equal in length. Alternating large and small scallops form the rims of both pieces. They were also made with smooth rims. This was accomplished by pressing in a mold that had interchangeable cap rings. The cap ring was a way of controlling the thickness of the rim; it was cast to the depth and form of the rim, leaving a smaller opening in the top of the mold for a smaller diameter plunger. At the site of the glass factory, fragments of this plain ware were intermingled with fragments of Lacy ware, proving that both styles were produced simultaneously.

1130 PRESSED SUNBURST (STAR BOTTOM) RECTANGULAR DISH
1½" H. x 6" L. 1840–1850

Rectangular, oval and oddly-shaped articles were listed as "dishes" in flint glass company catalogs. They could have held relish, applesauce or any food item we might put in them today. This form of a simple rectangular dish with a chamfer of 45 degrees at each corner is more often found in a small size that was used as an open salt. It is quite scarce in larger sizes, especially colored. There are twenty-eight rays around a central dot and horizontal ribs on the sidewall and rim. The rim is scalloped. A green one in the Kaiser collection is 12¼" long. Numerous fragments from the dig site attest to Sandwich manufacture.

1131 PRESSED BULL'S EYE AND ROSETTE TUMBLER
2¾" H. 1835–1845

This pattern is difficult to find because it was produced in limited quantity. The hexagonal bottom of the tumbler was created by six flutes that extend one-third up the sidewall. Three large rosettes alternating with three bull's eyes complete the upper portion. The element known as a rosette in this pattern closely resembles the sunburst of contemporary blown molded patterns pictured previously. The pattern stops short of the circular rim. Keep this in mind when examining drinking vessels at time of purchase. If the pattern is molded to the rim, either the article is not a drinking vessel or the rim was "cut down" because it was damaged. The mold in which the tumbler was pressed was crudely made, indicating early vintage. Some equally crude early Bull's Eye and Rosette goblets have a thick, short stem. Goblets with a faceted knop stem date into the 1850's as do lamp fonts.

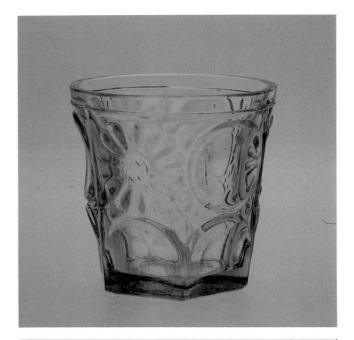

1132 PRESSED FLUTE
(a) Goblet 5¾" H. x 4⅞" Dia.
(b) Toy tumbler 2½" H. x 2¼" Dia. 1840–1875

A *flute* is a panel with an arched top. Most Flute patterns were manufactured for use in taverns and hotels and may not have matching pieces of tableware other than decanters and other drinking vessels. They were designated by the number of flutes that surrounded each article, i.e., "6 Flute" as shown here, "9 Flute", "10 Flute". In goblets alone, there were enormous variations in the form of the bowl, which was combined with numerous stem configurations. A large percentage of flint glass company profits were derived from the sale of glassware for commercial establishments. A particular Flute item cannot be reliably attributed to a specific factory unless it is accompanied by strong documentation. Both pieces in this photo were badly distorted in the making. The stem of goblet A was twisted and tumbler B leans at an angle. These manufacturing characteristics did not prevent them from being usable items. Tumbler B has a pattern of concentric circles on the bottom and sufficient roughage on the circular mold seam to scratch the surface of a table. It holds ½ gill (¼ cup) of liquid. *Goblet A: Courtesy, Sandwich Glass Museum, Sandwich Historical Society*

1133 PRESSED FLUTE WINE COOLER ON ELONGATED LOOP FOOT
10½" H. x 8⅝" Dia. 1860–1870

The extremely rare wine cooler was one of the most beautiful forms made by the Boston and Sandwich Glass Company. It was manufactured by pressing two units as usual, but the upper unit was the complex form identified by Benjamin Haines as *ogee*. The Elongated Loop foot is 5" in diameter. It was applied with a wafer to the lower section of the cooler. The wide upper portion of the cooler has a pattern of simple flutes. The sunken, cylindrical center is paneled. It was designed to be only wide enough to accept a wine bottle standing upright. Ice was packed around the bottle. As the ice melted, cold water dripped around the bottom of the bottle to keep it chilled. The rim of the Flute wine cooler flares out slightly and is scalloped. Whether in clear glass or color, its scarcity will demand a high price.

1134 PRESSED ASHBURTON WINE

4⅝" H. x 2⅝" Dia. 1840–1875

Ashburton is the original name used by all of the glass works that manufactured it. It is a simple pattern of flutes around the lower portion that in this instance extend down the hexagonal stem to a circular step on the foot. A second row of flutes is half-dropped, or staggered, around the upper portion of the sidewall. (If the flutes are directly above each other, the pattern is not Ashburton.) This wine was easily removed from a two piece mold with vertical seams that continued through the center of two upper flutes. On some molds, side sections were designed to hide mold marks by having them follow the edges of flutes. There are numerous variants produced over a long period. The Boston and Sandwich Glass Company pressed a wide range of tableware pieces as did the New England Glass Company of East Cambridge, Massachusetts. A catalog of the New England works printed in 1869 illustrated forty pieces and called the flared-rimmed stemware "flanged". On July 13, 1859, soon after the Cape Cod Glass Works opened, it sent inferior "Ashburton goblets" and "Ashburton hotel goblets" to Boston to be sold at auction. The coloring ingredient of blue glass was cobalt. Peacock blue was derived from the addition of copper. If the proportion of copper oxide to cobalt was increased it became peacock green as shown here. On occasion the flutes were polished and the piece marketed as *Cut Ashburton*.

1135 PRESSED ASHBURTON SUGAR

(a) Sugar 4½" H. x 4⅝" Dia.
(b) Cover 3" H. x 5" Dia.
(c) Combined size 7⅜" H. x 5" Dia. 1840–1875

Numerous documents attest to Boston and Sandwich Glass Company manufacture of Ashburton. It was listed by Edward Haines in his workbook dated January 11, 1847, on an invoice to J. P. Lund dated March 21, 1855, and in a notebook begun by William Stutson in 1859 and presented to George Lafayette Fessenden in 1865. (Fessenden's years as factory superintendent are related in Volume 3 on pages 24–44.) This canary sugar carries its original cover although it fits loosely. The bowl was made in two sizes, so it is possible that the cover was designed to fit both. The underside of the cover rim is ¾" wide. The overhang also allowed for changes in the diameter of the bowl due to warping in the annealing leer. A matching footed cream was made. It has an applied handle. Ashburton items were listed in a catalog from the Mount Washington Glass Works in New Bedford, Massachusetts. *Courtesy, Sandwich Glass Museum, Sandwich Historical Society*

1136 PRESSED WORCESTER TUMBLERS

(a) Large 4¼" H. x 3⅝" Dia.
(b) Small 3⅝" H. x 3¼" Dia. 1840–1875

Most glass factories that made Ashburton also had molds in which to press Worcester. Footed tumblers have been attributed to Pennsylvania and Massachusetts glass houses and chances are they were manufactured in New York houses as well. Two rows of flutes surround the tumbler, each flute one above the other. It was made in a two-section mold that included the foot, with no attempt made to minimize the mold mark. The large blue tumbler was acquired from a long-time collector who only purchased glass with known connections to Sandwich glassworker families. In addition to the blue and green shown here, we are aware of amber and clear. Worcester was listed in William Stutson's memo book, which he compiled between 1859 and 1865. A Boston and Sandwich Glass Company list of molds that appears to date from the mid-1860's, reprinted by Frank W. Chipman in *Romance of Old Sandwich Glass*, included two sets of Worcester tumbler molds. A similar pattern also made at Sandwich has a diamond between the flutes. It is known as *Excelsior*, but was listed as *California* in the New England Glass Company's 1869 catalog.

1137 PRESSED ARGUS SPOON HOLDER

4¾" H. x 3⅝" Dia. 1840–1860

It is likely that glass scholars named this pattern *Argus* in error. According to Webster's 1847 dictionary, *Argus* was "A fabulous being of antiquity, said to have had a hundred eyes." As a pattern, Argus is more accurately depicted in a McKee and Brother catalog on an ale having many concave ovals. On this Sandwich piece, the bottom and upper rows have large flutes one above the other. They are separated by a center row of short flutes or horizontal, elongated ovals that are staggered. Simple patterns such as this followed the financial panic of 1837. Molds were less expensive and could be opened in one minute or less, cutting labor costs. Although manufactured in a number of pieces, Argus is seen less often than Ashburton. This spoon holder was made at Sandwich with a foot, as shown here, and without. Study the location of the elongated ovals, then consider the variant that follows. *Courtesy, Sandwich Glass Museum, Sandwich Historical Society*

1138 PRESSED ARGUS VARIANT TUMBLER

3¾" H. x 2¾" Dia. 1840–1860

Here is another of the flute patterns that were popular in the mid-1800's. Today it is considered a variant of Argus, but at the time of production may have had another title. Beginning at the bottom, a chain of horizontal ovals placed side to side surrounds the tumbler. A row of large flutes surrounds the center. These flutes are staggered. The row at the top matches the bottom chain of ovals. The pattern is so simple that it could be overlooked at a flea market or in an antiques shop, but makes a nice addition to a tumbler collection. If it is made of flint glass, bring it home.

1139 PRESSED BIGLER (FLUTE AND SPLIT) GOBLET

6" H. x 3¼" Dia. 1840–1870

The pattern known as *Bigler* is made up of flutes separated by a V-groove. Holloware such as sugars, creams and stemmed pieces have two flutes, one above the other, separated by a groove that is continuous from top to bottom. While not as common as Flute and Ashburton, it is still possible to attain Bigler tableware and lamps in clear glass, although colored pieces are rare. Patterns with simple, bold elements became popular when the quality of the glass improved to the point that its lack of brilliance did not have to be hidden beneath a myriad of the tiny lilies, scrolls and strawberry diamonds that characterized the Lacy period. Furnaces that were converted from wood to coal, plus the availability of superior glass sand, contributed to this advancement. Although the Bigler pattern is an early one, the goblet dates later. A method for molding a foot in one piece with a goblet was perfected by 1847. *Courtesy, Sandwich Glass Museum, Sandwich Historical Society*

1140 PRESSED BIGLER (FLUTE AND SPLIT) NAPPIE
4" Dia. 1840–1870

McKee and Brothers of Pittsburgh, Pennsylvania, illustrated only Bigler tumblers in their 1864 and 1868 catalogs, possibly named for a prominent Pennsylvania family. The accompanying price lists itemized *Bigler Flute*. Political figure William Bigler became governor of Pennsylvania in 1852. Collectors are confused by slight deviations in pattern due to changes in mold design to conform to different articles. The best advice the authors can give is to tell you to study individual elements in each pattern and do not be distracted by form. Confusion was compounded by line drawings in McKearin's *American Glass* of two whale oil lamp fonts differing in form but carrying the same pattern. As shown in Barlow-Kaiser photo 2097, a cylindrical font is called *Thumbprint and Arch* and a tapered font is *Bigler*. Boston and Sandwich Glass Company documents referred to a "flute and split" tumbler mold and the Cape Cod Glass Company's *List of Glass Ware* included "No. 205 Flute and split" tumblers, lemonades (handled tumblers) and 3" diameter nappies. This amethyst 4" diameter nappie has a star bottom and eight flutes alternating with eight splits or grooves. The rim is plain.

1141 PRESSED BIGLER (FLUTE AND SPLIT) NAPPIE ON LOOP (LEAF) FOOT
5½" H. x 7¼" Dia. 1850–1870

This is a wonderful piece when standing alone and a magnificent addition to a collection of Bigler or Loop pattern glass. The pattern of seven loops on the circular foot was called *Leaf* by Pennsylvania houses. At the Boston and Sandwich Glass Company it was commonly fused to a Petal, or "6 Ball", candle socket to make the popular Petal and Loop candlestick as shown in photo 4032. A hand-formed wafer, by which the 4⅜" diameter foot was fused to the nappie, can be seen above the hexagonal knop standard. The nappie bottom slopes gently to the center. Authors Barlow and Kaiser were fortunate to have cooperation of many advanced collectors who allowed their Sandwich glass to be photographed. The number of flint patterns shown in color does not truly reflect today's market. Colored flint tableware is difficult to find in comparison to lamps, vases and candlesticks. With patience, a diligent collector does well to acquire one or two pieces a year. However, patience is rewarded because value is based on rarity.

1142 PRESSED BLOCK
(a) Finger bowl 3¼" H. x 4⅝" Dia.
(b) Wooden pattern 1840–1860

This simple though elegant pattern is made up of slightly concave blocks separated vertically and horizontally by grooves. The blocks in the upper row are arched, extending as muted flutes to a smooth rim. The wooden pattern on the right matches the bowl in detail. When used as finger bowls, articles such as this were filled with rosewater and placed on doilies for the convenience of dinner guests who wished to rinse hands and lips between courses. Fingers were then wiped on napkins or on the doilies beneath the bowls. As slop bowls, they held waste from after-dinner tea. If manufactured in clear glass, as most pressed Boston and Sandwich Glass Company pieces were, this bowl could remain unnoticed in an antique shop. However, in color, it is an asset to a Sandwich glass collection as it was to the Nineteenth Century hostess whose table it helped brighten. A goblet was made to match. *Courtesy, Sandwich Glass Museum, Sandwich Historical Society*

1143 PRESSED FOUR PRINTIE BLOCK BOWL ON FOOT

8¼" H. x 9½" Dia. 1850–1870

The pattern derived its name from the four horizontal bands of nineteen blocks, each block enclosing a "printie". Originally, the printies would have been referred to as *concave* or *punties*. It is most unusual to see Four Printie Block on tableware; it was most often adapted to whale oil lamp fonts, Three Printie Block and Four Printie Block examples of which are in photos 2100–2105, and vases as shown in photos 3035–3038. The mold for this deep bowl was beautifully formed, designed so the upper row of printies formed a rim of well-rounded scallops. The bowl was combined with a lower unit pressed in the form of a circular base with a high standard. Concentric circles are beneath the base. Even though the bowl and foot were pressed separately, they are the same color. To date we have not encountered mid-1800's pressed bowls, nappies or salvers with differing colored feet, nor have we documented this occurrence from Sandwich family collections and dug fragments. *Courtesy, Sandwich Glass Museum, Sandwich Historical Society*

1144 PRESSED MIRROR (PUNTY, CONCAVE) BOWL ON FOOT

9½" H. x 10" Dia. 1850–1870

Factory catalogs show that 10" diameter was the largest size in which bowls were routinely pressed, although larger examples are known. An original 1869 catalog of the New England Glass Company in East Cambridge, Massachusetts, illustrated by line drawings a number of bowls in this pattern of half-dropped circles. Their factory name was *Punty*, which was the term for molded or cut dished-out circles. (A man working in the cutting shop dishing out bottoms of articles to remove pontil rod scars was called a *puntier*.) The catalog showed other lower units also made at Sandwich, a low foot with plain rim and high foot with scalloped rim. A McKee and Brothers catalog dated 1864 shows this bowl and a similar foot. The Pittsburgh house called it *Concave*. Boston and Sandwich Glass Company Superintendent William Stutson listed Concave sugars on foot and off foot in his memo book dated 1859–1865. If you look beneath the lower unit of this canary bowl, you will not find scars and sharpness from an early, hand-held pontil rod. This particular lower unit was supported by the type of device perfected by Hiram Dillaway in 1857.

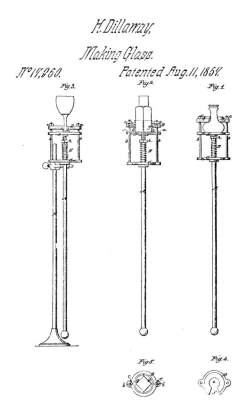

During the first half of the Nineteenth Century, a glass article that required handwork after it was removed from the mold was hand-held by attaching a pontil rod to the center of the bottom or inside the hollow of a pressed standard. Upon completion of the handwork, the rod was snapped off. This left chips in the article or sharp pieces of excess glass that could cut if the article was not handled carefully when it was being washed. By the 1850's, stands were devised to hold the article. The surface remained untouched by the pontil rod, and the device saved the labor cost of an extra glassworker who held the pontil rod while someone else completed the handwork. On August 11, 1857, Sandwich's Hiram Dillaway patented an improved holder that had interchangeable "yokes" to fit many different forms of glass. If you are aware of this change in mass production methods, you will not mistake a good piece of Sandwich glass for a later reproduction.

Continuation follows glossary.

1145 PRESSED DOUBLE LOOP NAPPIE

1⅛" H. x 3¾" Dia. 1840–1860

The center of this nappie is divided into eight sections by spokes that extend to eight small scallops of the rim. They are interrupted by a plain table rest. There are two rows of eight loops, a lower row covering the sidewall and an upper row that forms eight large scallops on the rim. In clear glass, small nappies are found in quantity at almost every antiques show where glass is prominent. The inside diameter of the rim is only 3", so the nappie held only a small serving of berries ladled from a matching larger piece. The larger nappie is usually on a high foot. In the 1880's, the combination of a large nappie and six or more small ones was referred to as a "berry set", but in earlier times each size was marketed individually and combined by the customer to fit household requirements.

1146 PRESSED LOOP (LEAF) NAPPIE AND COVER

(a) Nappie 2⅝" H. x 6⅞" Dia.

(b) Cover 3¾" H. x 5⅜" Dia.

(c) Combined size 5¾" H. x 6⅞" Dia. 1850–1870

When the Boston and Sandwich Glass Company received an order for a butter, the pressing department was instructed to make a 6" or 7" diameter nappie with a cover. The nappie was unfooted as shown here or attached to a low or high foot. (The Cape Cod Glass Company's *List of Glass Ware* noted "All 6-inch Butters on *cast* or *tall* foot if desired.") When adhered to a foot, the covered nappie was sometimes called a *sweetmeat*. This photo shows the way all tableware looked after inspection at the Boston and Sandwich Glass Company. The units match each other in color and the cover fits well. Ten loops on the nappie match ten loops on the cover. Glass flowed smoothly into the finial section of the mold resulting in a well-formed, complete cover. If when removed from the mold a piece was incomplete, badly warped, bubbly or damaged, it was sold as a second if at all possible or was thrown away. Be aware that when a chipped piece is offered to you, it was chipped after it was sold retail. It is not necessary to purchase badly damaged Sandwich glass. Leaf covered butters, sugars, creams and spoon holders appear on Union Glass Company invoices throughout the 1860's. *Courtesy, Sandwich Glass Museum, Sandwich Historical Society*

1147 PRESSED LOOP (LEAF) BOWL ON FOOT

9¾" H. x 5¾" Dia. 1850–1870

Here is a wonderful example of American glass factory ingenuity. Variety in form was obtained by ordering molds in which separate units having common dimensions were pressed, removed from their respective molds and "mixed and matched" at will. The bowl has seven bold loops that extend to a thick, scalloped rim. The cover matches in color and pattern of seven loops that end abruptly below an acorn finial. These two units when combined produced the sugar bowl to the Loop (Leaf) table setting. When marketed as such, the loops at the bottom of the bowl were leveled in the cutting shop to eliminate warp that may have occurred in the mold or annealing leer. By fusing a third unit, the seven-loop circular foot, the article became an elegant footed sugar bowl and saw double-duty as a container for other foodstuffs such as sweetmeats. Variants in finial and foot can be studied in photos 4033 and 4034 where the seven-loop cover and foot are compared with a like diameter Loop candlestick base. Remember the boldness of the Loop pattern made at Sandwich and the manner in which loops terminate in thick rims. Similar flint loop patterns with shallow, undulating rims were not made at the Boston and Sandwich Glass Company. The two most common loop patterns produced in Sandwich were the Leaf in this photo and Gaines. *The Bennington Museum, Bennington, Vermont*

1148 PRESSED LOOP (LEAF) DISH ON FOOT

4¾" H. x 8" Dia. 1850–1870

This Loop dish, suitable for a small amount of fruit, was made by pressing the previously shown seven-loop sugar bowl, taking it from the mold and stretching the upper portion into seven broad loops. The very thick rim had no inner ledge on which a cover rested, so it lent itself nicely to the handwork that converted it to another form to add to inventory. The expanded upper unit was adhered to a Loop (Leaf) foot, one of three styles shown in this series. This foot is rather low with loops that end abruptly near the wafer that joins the units. Following photos show this foot with a knop extension as was used on candlesticks and a tall foot with elongated loops. The fragment in the foreground is one of many dug at the Sandwich factory site of the Boston and Sandwich Glass Company. We do not believe Loop to be a product of the Cape Cod Glass Works.

1149 PRESSED LOOP (LEAF) DISH WITH GAUFFERED RIM ON ELONGATED LOOP FOOT
5½" H. x 7" Dia. 1850–1870

This Loop (Leaf) dish was also made by expanding the sugar bowl. The upper extremity of each broad loop was pulled up and the alternating inner curve was stretched to pull the loops apart. The hand-manipulation resulted in a rim gauffered into seven large flutes. This type of construction is better recognized on tightly-gauffered rims of vases as shown in Chapter 2 of Volume 3. It is most unusual on ordinary pressed tableware; however, we have seen Loop pieces as large as 12" diameter and even wider loops on fragments in the diggings. The tall foot was pressed in a mold with a pattern of Elongated Loop that resulted in a high standard. The foot was not stretched by hand as was the dish. This footed dish was perfect for bunches of grapes overhanging between the broad loops. The pattern is documented as *Leaf* by catalogs of McKee and Brothers of Pittsburgh, Pennsylvania.

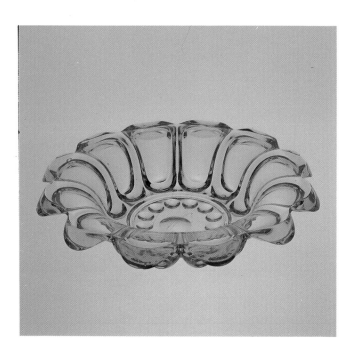

1150 PRESSED LOOP (LEAF) NAPPIE WITH TURNOVER RIM
2¼" H. x 9¾" Dia. 1850–1870

This dish was intended for use as it is pictured. The smoothly dished-out pontil mark in the center is a clue that this piece is complete. If it had been attached to a pressed foot as some were, the center would be rough, showing the breaking away of the wafer by which it was fused to the foot. A ring of large beads surrounds the pontil mark. The twelve loops or leaves on the sidewall flare out to a thick edge that makes them appear to bend downward. On Loop nappies such as this that were intended to set directly on the table, look beneath at the lower extremity of each loop. Some may have been machined to eliminate a wobble caused by warping during the process of annealing. A manufacturing procedure does not deter from value, so a dealer should not discount an early piece because of this characteristic. Heavy patterns designed in the 1850's saw continuous use until the outbreak of the Civil War in 1861. Little tableware was made between 1861 and 1865 because glassworking teams were broken up and factories had all they could do to meet the demand for lighting devices. The same patterns, some newly pressed and some leftover stock, were marketed after the war, but molds fell into disuse as lighter weight styles became popular. *Courtesy, Sandwich Glass Museum, Sandwich Historical Society*

1151 PRESSED LOOP (LEAF) DISH ON FOOT
7⅛" H. x 10⅜" Dia. 1845–1860

As shown on the locator map in Chapter 2 dated 1832–1847, a small furnace was built in 1844 specifically for the manufacture of colored glass. It was called the *canary furnace* in records of meetings of the Boston and Sandwich Glass Company Board of Directors. While some of the pots undoubtedly held glass of other colors (Blue and amethyst were made in the 1820's.), the designation *canary* would indicate a high percentage of colored glass was yellow. Today on the antiques market, when colored flint pressed tableware can be found at all, it is more likely to be canary than not. This nine-loop dish on circular foot was made in several sizes; we are aware of a similarly-formed larger one with eleven loops that is 8¾" high by 12¼" diameter. The circular foot with hexagonal standard was molded in an assortment of sizes from a candlestick size as shown in photo 4019 to a 6" diameter one combined with the 12½" diameter dish. There can be great variation in rim diameter on dishes that came from the same mold, depending on how much labor was expended on hand finishing. *Courtesy, Sandwich Glass Museum, Sandwich Historical Society*

1152 PRESSED LOOP (LEAF) NAPPIE AND COVER

(a) Nappie 2⅛" H. x 6⅝" Dia.
    Cover 3¼" H. x 5⅝" Dia.
    Combined size 5" H. x 6⅝" Dia.
(b) Wooden patterns for both units 1850–1870

Not often can you see a multi-unit piece of Sandwich glass and wooden patterns that were used in the making of molds in which both units were pressed. The patterns are an exact match. The cover pattern appears to be taller because construction did not allow it to be seated inside the scalloped rim of the nappie pattern. On the finished product A, the rim of the cover rests on an inner ledge of the nappie. Covers were deliberately molded with enough play to set firmly inside a lower unit that may be slightly warped. Some may be quite loose, others may have to be rotated until they seat properly. This nappie, which could have been used for butter, has a single row of loops around the sidewall. The stepped cover has two rows. Its finial was pressed as one unit with the cover. *Courtesy, Sandwich Glass Museum, Sandwich Historical Society*

1153 PRESSED LOOP (LEAF) NAPPIE ON FOOT

6" H. x 8½" Dia. 1850–1870

If you feel as author Kaiser does that occasional use justifies ownership, here is the perfect piece to place on the table as a center bowl flanked by a pair of matching canary Petal and Loop candlesticks. A common seven-loop circular base extends to a hexagonal knop. The upper unit has nineteen loops again terminating in a thick, boldly scalloped rim. The bottom of the nappie slopes toward the center and has a circle of nineteen smaller loops placed side to side. Two wafers joined the units together, one wafer applied to the nappie and one to the foot. The upper unit was made one size smaller and several sizes larger and all have nineteen loops.

1154 BLOWN MOLDED ARCH MUSTARD CASTERS

(a) 5¾" H. to finial of metal cap, 2⅛" Dia.
(b) 4⅞" H. x 2⅛" Dia. 1865–1887

Although blown molded, as casters often were, this pattern of strongly defined, simple arches dates after the Civil War. Until the 1860's, rims of peppers and mustards had no threads. Metal caps were pushed on mustard rims and were permanently cemented. If not for the threaded rims, these casters could be mistaken for the early blown molded pattern of arches designated by George and Helen McKearin in *American Glass* as GIV-5. Fragments of Arch casters were dug from the Boston and Sandwich Glass Company site by Sandwich historian Francis (Bill) Wynn, whose extensive fragment collection was incorporated into the Barlow collection. Mr. Wynn placed them in a box labeled "Gothic". The authors mention this as an example of the difficulty of attributing a pattern to a particular factory based on a previous description. A pattern known as *Gothic*, also a Sandwich product, has a similar arch enclosing a small arch, both arches connected by radiating double lines.

1155 PRESSED ELONGATED LOOP DISH ON FOOT

6" H. x 8⅜" Dia. 1850–1870

Here is another of the loop patterns made at the Boston and Sandwich Glass Company. Eighteen elongated loops surround the body and extend into the scallops of the rim. The form of the dish is always the same at the lower ends of the loops, but the final shape of the sidewall and rim depended on the glassworker. After removal from the mold, the upper portion was sometimes reworked. This piece was stretched out to widen the rim, others were pulled up to heighten it. Some were curved out and down to form an attractive turnover rim. This dish was attached to a pressed hexagonal foot common to candlesticks. It was also marketed without a foot. When purchasing the dish "off foot", examine carefully for evidence that a foot did not separate from it. If so, it is a broken dish and has little value. *Courtesy, Sandwich Glass Museum, Sandwich Historical Society*

1156 PRESSED SANDWICH LOOP (GAINES) SUGAR

7¾" H. x 3¾" Dia. 1850–1870

This pattern of elongated loops has incorrectly become known as *Sandwich Loop*, though it is documented as *Gaines* by illustrations in catalogs of McKee and Brothers, flint glass manufacturers in Pittsburgh, Pennsylvania. Out of eleven articles pictured on one page of a McKee 1864 catalog, four are Gaines: quart decanter, quart pitcher, ⅓ quart tumbler and carbon oil lamp. Each loop is convex, a distinguishing feature of Gaines. It is often encountered in translucent white, which in glass industry terminology was called *opal*. When made from a formula that included lead or litharge, it had brilliant overtones described by collectors as "fiery opalescent". Known Sandwich pieces vary in degree of opalescence and it may be that pieces such as this sugar were produced by the Boston and Sandwich Glass Company and the Cape Cod Glass Works (1859–1864) while those less brilliant were a product of the Cape Cod Glass Company (1864–1869). According to a document preserved at The Rakow Library of The Corning Museum of Glass in Corning, New York, a partner of a competing glass house visited the Cape Cod Glass Company on May 18, 1864. He was Thomas Gaffield of Tuttle, Gaffield and Company, owners of the Boston Crystal Glass Works. Gaffield noted, "Mr. Waterman showed us about the works, which are not kept in very neat order. They make and use oyster shell lime.....No lead is used here....." As reprinted on pages 108–109 in Volume 3, the Cape Cod Glass Company's order list itemized "No. 200, Gaines Pattern" in thirty-five forms readily available in opal and flint (meaning colorless glass, whether lead or lime-soda). This sugar has a circular foot, rayed beneath, molded in one piece with the bowl. Twelve vertical loops extend to a scalloped rim. On the matching cover, loops extend downward from a step below an acorn finial. *Courtesy of The Toledo Museum of Art (Acc. No. 65.140)*

1157 PRESSED SANDWICH LOOP (GAINES) BOWL ON FOOT

8¾" H. x 8¾" Dia. 1850–1870

As are all Gaines pieces, this footed bowl is extremely attractive. Its matching foot with high standard was molded as a separate unit which was fused to the beautifully-formed bowl with a wafer that is visible in the photo. The rim of the foot is plain, but the rim of the bowl follows the contour of the elongated loops. Gaines bowls and nappies were made in several sizes that were attached to patterned and unpatterned feet. The Cape Cod Glass Company's *List of Glass Ware* itemized 7" and 8" nappies on cast foot and 8", 9" and 10" bowls on tall foot. Unfooted nappies ranged from 3" to 6" in diameter. The numerous articles made by both Sandwich factories and several Pittsburgh houses showed that Gaines was well-received. Because of its popularity, a collection of Gaines pieces in excellent condition can still be attained today. Even bar and table decanters were listed in opal as well as flint.

1158 PRESSED PLUME AND ACORN NAPPIE

1¼" H. x 5⅛" Dia. 1840–1860

The center of this nappie has two five-lobed plumes separated by two acorns, one on each end of a single stem. The plain table rest is ³⁄₁₆" high, unusually high on a nappie only 5⅛" diameter. The boldly-molded Plume pattern surrounds the table rest to completely cover the border. Smooth rim scallops follow the contour of the plume. At Sandwich, the Plume border was limited to footed and unfooted nappies, some of which have differing central patterns and rims. This Plume and Acorn nappie was manufactured in several colors, most notably amethyst, amber and fiery opalescent. A Plume pattern without the acorn was made in a wide assortment of tableware items by Adams and Company of Pittsburgh, Pennsylvania, in the 1870's and 1880's. The later Plume glass has no lead in it. Sandwich glass companies used lead and litharge (oxide of lead) formulas for tableware during the years this Plume and Acorn nappie was made.

1159 PRESSED DIAMOND POINT WITH PANELS (HINOTO) FOOTED TUMBLERS

(a) Green canary 4" H. x 3⅜" Dia.

(b) Yellow canary 4⅛" H. x 3⅜" Dia. 1850–1870

Diamond Point with Panels footed tumblers take the form of goblets and spoon holders with no stem. Some pieces of the pattern have the common circular foot and others have a six-lobed foot as shown here. An overall pattern of diamonds surrounds the lower portion of the body with nine panels above. The pattern name was given as *Hinoto* by S. T. Millard in his book *Goblets I*. Although tumbler A borders on apple green, a yellow tinge would have caused it to be called *green canary* at the time of production. The term "vaseline" was coined to describe the color, but it was not used at glass factories. The tumblers match in most aspects, but differ slightly in the flare of the rim. Finding this pattern in color is extremely rare. In addition to the two shades of canary, a blue one exists. Whether clear or colored, major differences occurred in the making that add character to mid-1800's flint glass. On a day when the batch was mixed properly, the mold evenly heated and the furnace drafted well, a brilliant finished product resulted. At other times, glass was bubbly, had chill marks and sagged in the annealing leer.

1160 PRESSED DIAMOND POINT WITH CUT PANELS (HINOTO) TABLE DECANTERS

(a) Decanter 8½" H. x 3¾" Dia.

(b) Stopper 4½" H. x 1⅞" Dia.

(c) Combined size 11½" H. x 3¾" Dia. 1850–1870

This pair of decanters with glass stoppers was made to match pressed Diamond Point with Panels stemware and footed tumblers as evidenced by the raised bottom and lobed foot. They were pressed upright in a mold that carried the lobed foot and diamond-patterned sidewall. A large amount of glass left above the pattern was drawn in and hand-tooled into the neck and lip. The decanters were carried to the annealing leer, where they were evenly cooled. Then they were sent to the cutting shop, where the neck was cut and polished into flutes to match the pressed flutes of stemware and tumblers. The Diamond Point stoppers are original and were individually fitted to one of the decanters. A matching number was engraved into the paneled shank of one stopper and the lip of its matching decanter. Another number was placed on the other stopper and decanter. If you are considering the purchase of only one of a pair, make sure the antiques dealer did not switch stoppers. They are not interchangeable and value is affected. There is a subtle difference between these and the similar Diamond Point (Sharp Diamond) decanters. The Diamond Point decanter is flat-sided around the bottom with short flutes beneath the diamonds.

1161 PRESSED DIAMOND POINT (SHARP DIAMOND) BOWL ON FOOT

8" H. x 8¼" Dia. 1850–1870

Diamond Point was listed as *Sharp Diamond* in a late 1860's illustrated catalog of the New England Glass Company of East Cambridge, Massachusetts. A full range of items were made there as well as at the Boston and Sandwich Glass Company. The molds for patterned tableware were manufactured by commercial mold makers who sold them to numerous flint glass houses. The pressed high foot was also common to Sandwich and other glass works. Each factory had a mold for the foot in graduated sizes from 4" diameter, which was joined by a wafer to a 6" diameter bowl or nappie, to 5¾" diameter for a 10" diameter upper unit. Regardless of diameter, each foot has a rim of sixteen scallops. The standard is octagonal. All sizes of this particular scalloped foot, attached to Diamond Point and other bowls, were in the catalog. The bowl is covered with faceted diamonds. Horizontal ribs below the diamonds descend to the bottom. Some goblets also have ribs, but those shown in the New England catalog do not. Footed bowls can be difficult to store, but they are useful when grouped together in varying heights to hold food for festive occasions. A similar pattern was produced in Somerville, Massachusetts, by the Union Glass Company. Invoices in the collection of the authors list Diamond caster bottles.

1162 PRESSED DIAMOND POINT NAPPIE ON DIAMOND FOOT

8¾" H. x 11" Dia. 1850–1870

Fragments dug at the site of the Boston and Sandwich Glass Company reveal that production of diamond patterns was substantial. The number of faceted diamonds per square inch varied enormously from very small ones called "Fine Diamond Point" to the extremely large variant known as "Giant Sawtooth". With little factory documentation to rely on, it is almost impossible to match the size of the diamond to the names of diamond patterns as listed in inventories. Beside varying the size of the diamonds, changes were made in rim design. As you can see, the intricately-patterned cap rings of earlier Lacy molds were discontinued, never to return. Rims still varied, but only as bold scallops, large points and plain. This nappie has a rim of scallops that stand upright. It was fused by a wafer to a completely different foot that has large outlined diamonds with no point in the center. When we see two patterns combined in such a way, the question arises whether each unit was pressed to be deliberately combined or whether it was a way to use up extra units left over from production of those particular forms and patterns in quantity.

1163 PRESSED INVERTED DIAMOND SPOON HOLDERS

(a) No thumbprint 4⅞" H. x 3⅜" Dia.

(b) Thumbprint 4⅝" H. x 3⅜" Dia. 1850–1870

Both spoon holders are covered with diamonds that have facets sunk into the sidewall instead of protruding from it. Above and below is a band of inverted scallops resembling cogs. The circular foot is unpatterned. Spoon holder B has the addition of a large flat diamond repeated three times on the sidewall, once in each of three mold sections. A large punty, or "thumbprint" is centered in each diamond. The molds in which both A and B were pressed were the same height, but the Inverted Diamond and Thumbprint spoon holder sagged in the area between the foot and the lower inverted scallop band. Both patterns were used on lamp fonts, one of which is shown in photos 2130–2131. Two lamps and a matching spoon holder made a set that was used on the kitchen table. *Courtesy, Sandwich Glass Museum, Sandwich Historical Society*

1164 PRESSED INVERTED DIAMOND AND THUMBPRINT SPOON HOLDERS

4½" H. x 3½" Dia. 1850–1870

The large diamond extends from the bottom to the top band of inverted scallops. We show it in color so that it is easily seen. Spoon holders in clear and color are more readily available in the antiques market than other tableware articles for several reasons. A larger quantity was produced because they served a two-fold purpose. One spoon holder and two matching whale oil or fluid lamps held permanent residency on the kitchen table. (Every kitchen had a holder for extra spoons.) And though glassware was not sold in table sets, a spoon holder was often combined with a matching sugar, cream and covered nappie for butter. This style of spoon holder was fairly thick. The amount of material in the stubby stem below the body kept the holder from cracking under the constant bombardment of dropping spoons. Because some were known to contain spills for the lighting of kitchen lamps, they were thought to be "spill holders". Glass factory catalogs listed them as spoon holders regardless of subsequent use. Amethyst and canary are the most common colors. The Kaiser collection includes translucent light green. A variant with flat, divided diamonds replacing the inverted diamonds is called *Checkered Diamond and Thumbprint*.

1165 PRESSED DIAMOND POINT (MITRE DIAMOND)

(a) Celery 9⅜" H. x 4½" Dia.
(b) Spoon holder 5⅜" H. x 3¾" Dia. 1845–1870

Illustrations in the New England Glass Company catalog show this Diamond Point variant as *Mitre Diamond* because of the diamonds that extend to the rim. (*Mitre* is the British spelling of *miter*.) On covered articles, the cover rim was also mitered, the points of both rims fitting together when the cover was in place causing no break in the pattern. These pieces, however, are from the family of Sandwich decorator Annie Mathilda Nye. They were brought home by family members who were Boston and Sandwich Glass Company employees. Celery A has a knopped stem and the usual circular foot. Spoon holder B has a short stem that came into style mid-Century and a circular foot. The unpatterned feet were curved downward in the mold. They were reheated and flattened later. A Boston and Sandwich Glass Company invoice to John Sise dated July 19, 1848, listed Mitre creams. Pittsburgh houses also had a market for Diamond Point articles. Covered nappies and bowls with mitered rims produced by Bryce, Richards and Company were illustrated in their catalog dated 1854. A McKee and Brothers catalog dated 1864 illustrated a sugar and open salt in this diamond pattern. It was called *Diamond*.

1166 PRESSED SAWTOOTH (MITRE DIAMOND) HORSERADISH OR SALT

(a) Lower unit 3⅜" H. x 2⅞" Dia.
(b) Cover 2¼" H. x 2⅞" Dia.
(c) Combined size 5¼" H. x 2⅞" Dia. 1845–1870

This is the larger faceted diamond known as *Sawtooth*. Note how the upper row of diamonds on the footed piece mesh into the lower row of diamonds on the cover. The circular, stepped foot has rays beneath and a thick hexagonal stem. The cover has a faceted finial with a flat top. The wooden pattern for this cover is pictured in photo 3277. The lower unit is often sold as an open salt, but open salts generally have a smooth rather than sawtooth rim. A similar piece with a small acorn finial was produced by Bryce Brothers of Pittsburgh, Pennsylvania, as the sugar of a toy tableware set. Sawtooth was also the product of the Union Glass Company in Somerville, Massachusetts.

1167 PRESSED PANELED WAFFLE CELERY

9⅝" H. x 5¼" Dia. 1850–1870

An overall pattern of waffles is arranged in three panels, one in each side section of the mold. There are twelve short panels below the waffles that extend downward to a stub to which a wafer was adhered. The circular foot with faceted knop standard was pressed as a separate unit. Wrinkly chill marks on the upper surface of the foot resulted when the foot was flattened after removal from the mold. As on several Paneled Waffle and Sandwich Star pieces, a ridge inside the nine heavy rim scallops indicates the piece was designed to be sold with and without a cover and therefore may have had dual use. A Huber covered celery was called a jar in Pittsburgh manufacturer James B. Lyon and Company's 1861 catalog. Numerous Paneled Waffle pieces were made in clear glass and only an occasional piece in color. Lamps are shown in photo 2132.

1168 PRESSED PANELED WAFFLE SWEETMEAT

(a) 6⅛" H. x 5¼" Dia.
(b) 3½" H. x 4" Dia.
(c) Combined size 9¼" H. x 5¼" Dia. 1850–1870

Here is a sweetmeat that matches the previously shown celery. The rim of the very tall cover fits inside the scallops of the lower unit. The block, or waffle, pattern on the cover stops short of the paneled steeple that ends in a large knob finial. The cover is hollow to the finial to allow a spoon to be left in the bowl when the cover was in place between servings. We cannot begin to imagine the problem of flies, ants and other pests that beset the Nineteenth Century homemaker. They quickly congregated on dirty dishes and utensils. If a shorter cover was used, the serving spoon had to be placed in a sauce dish on the table, which in turn was covered with a domed screen. As its name implies, wet sweetmeat was a combination of fruits and nuts sweetened with sugar or honey. *Courtesy, Sandwich Glass Museum, Sandwich Historical Society*

1169 PRESSED PANELED INVERTED WAFFLE NAPPIE ON LOOP (LEAF) FOOT

5" H. x 5" Dia. 1850–1870

The nappie has three panels of the Waffle pattern and a scalloped rim. A seven-loop candlestick base with its knop standard was attached with a wafer. The wafer never has a mold mark on it because it is only a simple disk that was hand formed. The upper and lower units were fused before they were annealed. This footed nappie has an inside ridge to take a dome-shaped, loosely-fitting cover. It is made up of matching Waffle panels like the nappie and has a hexagonal finial that was molded as part of the cover.

1170 BLOWN MOLDED WAFFLE AND THUMBPRINT (PALACE) TABLE DECANTER

(a) Decanter 9" H. x 4" Dia.
(b) Stopper 4¾" H. x 1¾" Dia.
(c) Combined size 12½" H. x 4" Dia. 1850–1870

Most articles of the type collectors call "pattern glass" were pressed by dropping a gather of glass into a metal mold which was placed in a lever or screw pressing machine. A metal plunger was directed downward into the mold to press the glass against all surfaces. Some articles did not lend themselves to this procedure and so a gather of glass was blown into a mold with a like pattern. This decanter was one such item. Canary glass was blown into a mold until the glass completely filled the mold. The gaffer continued to blow while he stretched the glass upward from the opening in the top of the mold. The portion of glass not confined by the mold became thinner, creating the neck. After removal from the mold, the lip was formed. A stopper was blown to match, which was fitted to the decanter by an employee called a *stopper fitter* or *stopperer*. Most patterns can be found in table decanters that had glass stoppers and bar decanters. Bar decanters had a heavy lip applied to the neck. They were sold with metal slide stoppers that had cork plugs as pictured in photos 3222–3224. See also Waffle and Thumbprint lamps in photo 2134, where both pressed and blown molded examples are represented. Three panels of waffles alternate with vertical rows of printies, punties or bull's eyes. The number of printies varies depending on height.

1171 PRESSED FLAT DIAMOND BOWL ON FOOT

7¾" H. x 8" Dia. 1840–1860

Although this Flat Diamond circular foot with tall, lobed standard was usually combined with bowls that differ in pattern, here it is combined with a matching Flat Diamond bowl. Flat diamonds were molded beneath the foot, which has a plain rim. The bowl carries the diamonds on the outer surface. They extend to a heavy, scalloped rim. The shapes of both pressed units were basic to other Sandwich patterns such as Sandwich Star and Diamond and Thumbprint. Nevertheless, it would be difficult to assemble a collection of Flat Diamond alone.

1172 PRESSED DIAMOND THUMBPRINT (DIAMOND AND CONCAVE) SALVER

6½" H. x 13" Dia. 1850–1870

By enclosing a punty in each of the large, flat diamonds, the designer originated a pattern that gained great popularity in the East and Midwest. As is true of the Flat Diamond foot, this foot was removed from its mold having a flat upper surface and a downturned rim. It was wafer-attached to the salver that was pressed in a flat mold. Clear definition of the Diamond Thumbprint to the upturned, scalloped rim points out that a salver was not manufactured by expanding a previously pressed bowl. When used for cake, a pressed cover was available. A proper fit was a cover 1" diameter less than the diameter of the salver. The Cape Cod Glass Company made pressed cake covers from 7" to 18" in diameter. An 18" diameter cover was 10" high. A McKee and Brother catalog in 1859 referred to "D. & C.", an abbreviation for Diamond and Concave. A piece with a scallop and point rim was shown that cannot be attributed to Sandwich. Undoubtedly it was made in a number of factories in Pennsylvania. In the East, manufacture took place at the Boston and Sandwich Glass Company in Sandwich and the Union Glass Works and Union Glass Company in Somerville, Massachusetts.

1173 PRESSED DIAMOND THUMBPRINT (DIAMOND AND CONCAVE) SPOON HOLDER

5½" H. x 3⅞" Dia. 1850–1870

Medium size articles such as this spoon holder were pressed in one piece and therefore have no wafer. The lobes at the bottom of the stem extend upward to form lobes under the body. Three vertical mold seams begin at the rim in the center of three scallops and zigzag to the right of three diamonds before continuing down the stem to the rim of the foot. The lower portion of the mold that formed the foot resembled a mold for a shallow nappie. It was designed to allow gravity to aid the flow of hot glass to the outer extremity of the foot. When the spoon holder was turned out of the mold, the foot was flattened and expanded well beyond the diameter of the upper rim. The pattern and mold seams on the foot are muted due to this expansion. The expanded foot gave stability to the holder, which tended to be top-heavy when filled with spoons, especially when used in railroad dining cars and aboard ships. The scallops on the rim flare outward. We find this to be true on all Diamond Thumbprint holloware we have seen to date except the celery, which has scallops extending upward.

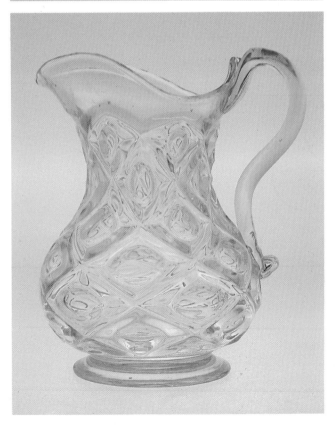

1174 PRESSED DIAMOND THUMBPRINT (DIAMOND AND CONCAVE) JUG

10" H. x 7" Dia. 1850–1870

In addition to a cream that in size matched a sugar, two or three larger sizes of pitchers were standard production items. Called *jugs*, they were wholesaled by capacity, i.e., three pint, quart and pint. At the retail level, the largest was earmarked for water and the next largest for milk. The plain foot was pressed as part of the jug and was not applied. Note the elongated thumbprints on the upper half of the body. This was caused by reheating the top to shear the rim and shape a spout and a point at the opposite end to receive an applied handle. The extended point allowed a greater length of handle to be fused to the body without covering the pattern. This jug weighs over seven pounds empty and when filled is difficult to use. Handles were easily broken if the jug was not supported at the foot by the other hand. When examining items with applied handles, do not pick them up by their handles. Study the handle and the jug or cream at the points where both ends of the handle were attached. A crack in any place is unacceptable and value should be reduced by at least 75 percent. There is no question that the jug shown here is old, but reproductions in clear and color were made for the Sandwich Glass Museum. Produced by the Viking Glass Company, each piece carries the museum logo "SM", which can be removed.

1175 PRESSED SANDWICH STAR (QUARTER DIAMOND) BOWL ON FOOT

11" H. x 12" Dia. 1840–1870

In the beginning of the pressed glass era, much thought seemed to have been given to the design of each article and its pattern, an acceptable procedure for a new, experimental branch of the glass industry. The Panic of 1837 caused mold makers and glassmakers to rethink production methods. Standard shapes, to which a variety of patterns could be adapted, cut down on mold making costs. And the new, sturdy pieces had a market in the middle of our country as the United States expanded West. The flat diamond was divided into fourths from corner to corner into a pattern known in Sandwich as *Quarter Diamond*. The broken pieces are some of many fragments found in large concentration at the Boston and Sandwich Glass Company. Unearthed at the site were colors now seldom or never seen in a finished product such as opaque lavender, opaque white, canary, blue, green and amethyst. The circular fragment on the right is a foot. The two in the foreground are the sidewall and flared, scalloped rim of the bowl. Note how the pattern resembles the German iron or Maltese cross, which is discussed in photo 1177. Most rims are flared. An occasional piece has upright scallops as taken from the mold.

1176 PRESSED SANDWICH STAR (QUARTER DIAMOND) BOWL ON THREE-DOLPHIN STANDARD WITH CIRCULAR BASE

9⅝" H. x 11¾" Dia. 1850–1870

One of the most difficult units to mold that was made in quantity is a Three-Dolphin standard. It and the circular base were pressed as one piece. The three heads rest on a base that has concentric circles beneath it. The S-curved bodies extend upward to a knop. The tails curve downward and are joined together. The top of the knop was flattened to accept a disk-shaped wafer. To the wafer was mounted the Sandwich Star bowl. This combination is very rare. Several have been recorded, but to date we have not encountered a Three-Dolphin tableware article with a differing pattern used as an upper unit. Three-Dolphin standards with circular and hexagonal bases were made in numerous wonderful transparent, translucent and opaque colors. They served as lower units for lamp glasses as shown in photos 2144–2146, 4049 and 4050. They are highly valued by lamp collectors when fastened by brass connectors to kerosene fonts as pictured in photos 2284, 2301, 2371 and 2372. *Courtesy, Sandwich Glass Museum, Sandwich Historical Society*

1177 PRESSED SANDWICH STAR (QUARTER DIAMOND) DISH

2" H. x 8⅜" L. x 5⅛" W. 1840–1870

In *Early American Pressed Glass*, author Ruth Webb Lee wrote, "For lack of a better title and as a means of identification, it seems proper to call it 'Sandwich Star'". When viewing this rectangular dish from above, one can see how she arrived at the title. William Germain Dooley, who wrote articles on glass for the magazine *Hobbies* and a booklet entitled *Old Sandwich Glass*, interviewed a glassmaker who began working at the Boston and Sandwich Glass Company in 1873. Quoting the glassmaker, "The name given to Sandwich Star by the older men was Quarter Diamond". According to legend as repeated by one-time Sandwich Glass Museum Director Doris Kershaw, the design was fabricated by a German worker at Sandwich who intended to glorify the German iron or Maltese cross. To his surprise and disappointment, the star became more prominent than did the cross. We prefer to believe the glassworker.

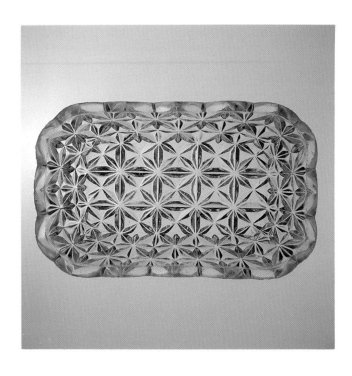

1178 PRESSED SANDWICH STAR (QUARTER DIAMOND) BAR DECANTER

10⅜" H. x 4¼" Dia. 1840–1870

This is a very refined bar decanter. Most bar decanters have a very thick donut of glass applied to the neck. The donut gave added strength to withstand the corking and uncorking of a metal slide stopper (see photos 3222–3224 for details). This nicely flanged thick lip also took a metal stopper. Note the thickness of glass which happened to have been made during a period when families moved to the West in covered wagons. Their journey was interrupted often to rest and change horses. The many taverns that sprang up along the trails created a market for heavy bar ware. The Sandwich Star decanter was also finished with a thinner lip and smaller diameter neck to which was usually fitted a blown molded Block pattern stopper.

1179 PRESSED SANDWICH STAR (QUARTER DIAMOND) SPOON HOLDERS

5¼" H. x 3⅝" Dia. 1840–1870

This form of spoon holder is erroneously called "spill holder", but glass company catalogs list it as a spoon holder. One order indicated they sometimes held cigars. *Spill* is first defined in Webster's 1859 Appendix to *An American Dictionary of the English Language* as "A small roll of paper or slip of wood for lighting lamps, &c." A study of early sloar books and catalogs failed to disclose an item that was blown or pressed specifically to hold spills. *Spill* defined as such does not appear in Webster's 1847 dictionary. We believe the practice of lighting lamps with spills that were stored in special glass containers began in the kerosene era. The making of glass spill holders at the Boston and Sandwich Glass Company is documented in a sloar book in 1887. Nicholas Black's shop made ninety-four 6½" by 2½" spills beginning the week of October 3. During the week of December 5, Thomas Dean's group made 496 4½" opal spills. When spill holders became necessary in the American home, spoon holders found a secondary use.

1180 PRESSED PRISM NAPPIE ON FOOT

6⅛" H. x 7⅛" Dia. 1840–1860

This nappie was made in four sizes, this one being next to the smallest. Regardless of diameter, all have twenty-two sharp ribs placed side to side around the body. Each ends in a diamond that extends into the mitered rim. The nappie was manufactured with and without a foot, called "on foot" and "off foot" by the industry. A matching cover was made with a mitered rim that fit into the mitered rim of the nappie. There is no way to tell if a particular nappie at one time had a cover because there is no inner ridge on which the cover rested. Because of its simple lines, unfooted clear ones are unrecognized in antiques shops. In an antiques shop we visited regularly, a fairly priced covered one remained for two years and was still there at the time the shop discontinued business. The hexagonal foot is usually referred to as a "candlestick base" because it is the 4¼" diameter size that was adhered to a blown candle socket as shown in photo 4010 and a pressed socket as pictured in photo 4022. Candlesticks were sometimes made in two colors, but two colors on a footed nappie may mean the units were glued together. Look for glue around the wafer. It did not come from the factory in combination colors. *Courtesy, Sandwich Glass Museum, Sandwich Historical Society*

1181 PRESSED SMOCKING

(a) Plate 2" H. x 8½" Dia.
(b) Open sugar 4" H. x 6" Dia. 1850–1870

The large inverted diamond pattern resembles shirred, decorative stitching used in gathering cloth—hence the name *Smocking*. Both articles in this photo have a six-lobed foot that was pressed as part of the piece. Plate A was made by stretching the rim of a shallow footed nappie; three seam marks that would ordinarily have remained vertical during the procedure were twisted in the area between the foot and the plate. The blue Smocking piece appears to be a true open sugar in which loaf sugar was placed to be removed with small tongs. Its secondary use could have been as a slop bowl. Smocking pattern was said by Ruth Webb Lee in *Victorian Glass* not to have been found in color. As recently as 1990, Bill Jenks and Jerry Luna listed it only in clear in their massive study *Early American Pattern Glass 1850–1910*. An amethyst plate sold at auction in 1978 and the two pieces shown here are the only ones in color we have been able to attribute to the Boston and Sandwich Glass Company. Two styles of spoon holders were made, one with a lobed and one with a circular foot. Smocking variants were made also abroad. In England, it was registered by Joseph Webb of Coalborn Hill Glassworks in Stourbridge on August 3, 1854. According to Colin R. Lattimore in *English 19th Century Press-Moulded Glass*, the article shown in Webb's presentation was a covered dish. Lattimore pictured a celery with a register mark molded into the stem.

1182 PRESSED FLAT DIAMOND AND PANEL

(a) Table decanter 9" H. x 4" Dia.
   Stopper 4½" H. x 2" Dia.
   Combined size 12¼" H. x 4" Dia.
(b) Jelly 5¾" H. x 2¾" Dia. 1850–1870

Decanter A was pressed in a mold that had three side sections. Three large pointed ovals alternate with flat diamonds that resemble a lattice. A fourteen-point star is molded into the bottom, which has a wide table rest that was machined to level the decanter. After the pattern was pressed, the upper portion was shaped by hand tools. The matching stopper was blown molded and is therefore hollow. Article B is a rather large jelly, a dessert dish often unrecognized as such. It is usually thought to be a drinking vessel because it is stemmed, but it was not intended for such use. Beneath its foot is a twelve-pointed star. Flat Diamond and Panel was sometimes engraved in unpatterned areas such as the shoulder of the decanter and the smooth surface enclosed by the pointed oval. *Courtesy, Sandwich Glass Museum, Sandwich Historical Society*

1183 PRESSED TULIP SALT

3½" H. x 2¾" Dia. 1850–1870

Tulip was produced at several flint glass manufactories including the Boston and Sandwich Glass Company. It was illustrated by the Pittsburgh, Pennsylvania, firm of Bryce, Richards and Company in a catalog believed to date 1854. The main element of the pattern is a large three-petaled tulip blossom that covers the surface from top to bottom. The ground between the tulip is covered with diamond point. Tulips are molded three times around this salt, but the number varies according to the shape of the article. The manner in which petals from two adjoining blossoms meet to form a large scallop is an interesting design device. The heavy circular foot is rayed beneath. A matching pomade was made by reworking glass above the tulips into a wide mouth as shown on a Sawtooth pomade in photo 3275. Fitted to it was a wide cover roughed to grip the inside of the jar. Collectors sometimes call this pattern "Tulip and Sawtooth" to differentiate it from a tulip-like pattern used on fluid lamp fonts as shown in photos 2147–2148. *Courtesy, Sandwich Glass Museum, Sandwich Historical Society*

1184 PRESSED NEW ENGLAND PINEAPPLE (PINEAPPLE, LOOP AND JEWEL) BOWL ON FOOT

9½" H. x 10¾" Dia. 1850–1870

New England Pineapple in clear glass is highly appealing. The Boston and Sandwich Glass Company manufactured a large assortment of tableware pieces that can still be readily purchased in the antiques market. Its beauty in clear glass was lost in opaque white. The pattern does not show through the bowl, and unless you are at eye level, it is lost on the outside as well. Because it is difficult to focus on the pattern, at a quick glance it could be mistaken for Tulip, which has faceted diamonds low on the body between large stylized tulip blossoms. In their day, New England Pineapple and Tulip may have been variants first produced in the same mold shop. The bowl in this photo has diamonds enclosed by a motif thought to resemble a pineapple. However, in Frederick T. Irwin's *The Story of Sandwich Glass* published in 1926 it was called *Loop and Jewel*. (Irwin's father was a Boston and Sandwich Glass Company employee beginning in 1851.) The large pineapple alternates with bold tulips around the bowl, which was mounted on a high foot with panels on the base and standard. New England Pineapple stemware was reproduced in the 1960's, but the copies should not fool a knowledgeable dealer or collector.
Courtesy, Sandwich Glass Museum, Sandwich Historical Society

1185 PRESSED LYRE (HARP) SPOON HOLDER

4⅝" H. x 3½" Dia. 1840–1870

This spoon holder varies in color from delicate fiery opalescent to almost clear. This soft opal is described as "moonstone", a term not found in Sandwich documents. The mold in which it was pressed had a well-defined pattern showing no wear from extended use, although the pattern itself was popular for a very long time. It had been in a collection of glass maintained by a Sandwich glassmaker before eventual inclusion in the Kaiser collection. Harp was also a product of Jarves' Mount Washington Glass Works and some Pittsburgh houses. A covered nappie was illustrated in Bryce, Richards and Company's 1854 catalog and McKee and Brother listed uncolored Harp spoon holders at $2.30 per dozen in their 1859/1860 price list. The harps on fragments found at the Boston and Sandwich Glass Company site vary in size, indicating use on many articles. Several styles of lamps are pictured in photos 2142–2143 and a cologne is shown in photo 3103.

1186 PRESSED WASHINGTON

(a) Egg cup 3⅞" H. x 2½" Dia.

(b) Low foot on Fine Rib (Reeded) bowl 3¾" H. x 6¼" Dia. 1850–1870

Egg cups were for poached or coddled eggs eaten without their shells. They have the capacity of champagnes but stems are shorter. Six panels of pattern surround this egg cup. Two vertical, concave thumbprints (The term is interchangeable with *printie* or *puntie*.) alternate with a concave oval three times around the body, separated by a vertical groove. An arch above each panel is made up of three pointed ovals end to end. The number of thumbprints varies with the height of the article; jugs and decanters have three. A shallow nappie has thumbprints in each panel because it lacks height for the oval. While the pattern is concave on the egg cup, it is convex on the Washington foot attached by a wafer to a Fine Rib bowl. The New England Glass Company devoted two pages to the Washington pattern showing many large pieces that are rare today. The Cape Cod Glass Company's *List of Glass Ware* itemized "Mt. Washington" articles, obviously named for Deming Jarves' Mount Washington Glass Works in South Boston where assuredly it was also produced. It may or may not be the Washington shown here.

1187 PRESSED PUNTY AND ELLIPSE (MONROE)

(a) Spoon holder 5" H. x 3⅞" Dia.

(b) Cream 5⅜" H. 1840–1865

Minnie Watson Kamm, author of *A Sixth Pitcher Book*, stated in 1949 that she had never seen a pitcher to match the pattern she named *Monroe*. Because she illustrated only pitchers but had not seen one in this pattern, she drew an imaginary cream. However, she did not realize that cream B was manufactured by pressing spoon holder A and reshaping its rim to form a crude spout. Better known as *Punty and Ellipse*, the hexagonal spoon holder has a large oval molded into three sides and two smaller punties molded into three alternating sides. The spout was made by drawing up and flaring one of the six sides made up of two punties. This maneuver caused the misshaping of the two large ovals on either side. The horizontal band around the rim was flattened in the area of the spout but the rim remained thick. After pouring, liquid continues to trickle down the outside of the cream. A thick, solid handle was applied opposite the spout, its upper end conforming to the curve of the large oval beneath it. While not one-of-a-kind, a cream produced by altering a spoon holder is unique. A matching molasses jug has a metal hinged cover bearing the patent date May 10, 1864.

1188 PRESSED STAR AND PUNTY SPOON HOLDER

4" H. x 3½" Dia. 1840–1870

While most hexagonal spoon holders have a foot, this example from the Barlow collection does not. However, the Star and Punty spoon holder was made both ways as shown in photo 2119. The fragments on either side match in form and pattern. They were retrieved from the Boston and Sandwich Glass Company factory yard. The large oval alternating with two punties follow those of the previously pictured Punty and Ellipse. A five-pointed star with its longest point centered at the bottom is enclosed by the three ellipses. A star with five equal points is centered in the lower three punties. A matching flat-bottomed cream is known but seldom seen. The simple, heavy, hexagonal patterns created during the height of glass pressing in Sandwich were easily adapted to various articles. Star and Punty lamp fonts permanently attached to glass bases can be seen in photos 2118–2121. Fonts with pegs beneath them were used in girandoles as pictured in photos 2123–2124. Star and Punty colognes can be studied in photos 3101–3102.

1189 PRESSED STAR AND PUNTY SUGAR

(a) Sugar 5⅜" H. x 5¼" Dia.

(b) Cover 3½" H. x 4⅛" Dia.

(c) Combined size 8¾" H. x 5¼" Dia. 1840–1870

Note that the footed bowl and its matching cover is octagonal. Each of eight sides of the bowl carries the motif of an oval or ellipse enclosing a five-pointed star with its longest point centered downward. The eight sides of the cover present a mirror image; the long point of each star extends onto the dome. The finial with its nipple center was used on a number of different covers manufactured during the mid-1800's. If you find this footed bowl alone, you are purchasing only one unit of a two-unit article. The scarcity of covers makes their value exceed that of the bowls. You are far better off to purchase a cover alone. A lower unit would eventually surface and would probably match in clarity. Bowls and covers were not necessarily pressed the same day at the factory. Unless there is a marked difference in the glass, the units would not be considered "married".

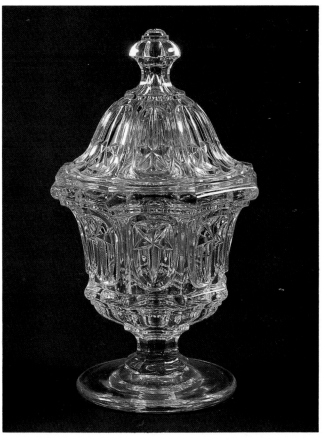

1190 PRESSED COLONIAL GOBLET
(a) Wooden pattern
(b) Goblet 3¾" H. 1840–1860

A pattern closely resembling this Sandwich one was illustrated in a catalog believed to have been issued in 1842 by the Paris, France, glass distributor Launay Hautin & Compagnie. This form was listed as a goblet rather than a tumbler since it does have a short, thick stem. Numerous odd pieces of tableware were produced in the 1840's that are difficult for today's collector to categorize or find useful. If we were able to observe business transactions in a glass showroom, we may discover that customers bought items for uses not described in the catalog. For example, this weighted piece could have held toothbrushes or loose tooth powder into which family members dipped a moistened toothbrush. The familiar stemmed goblet came into being in the mid-1840's. The reason why the matching wooden pattern is dark brown is that patterns were soaked in oil prior to use. The oil penetrated the grain of the wood and kept plaster-of-Paris from adhering to the pattern when it was removed from the plaster casting. After the mold was made, the commercial mold making establishment sent the mold with its matching wooden pattern to the glass factory. The price of the pattern was included in the mold cost. When the first glass articles were pressed in the new mold, they were compared to the wooden pattern and checked for mold defects. The wooden pattern remained at the factory. It was sent back to the mold maker when another mold was needed.

1191 EARLY MOON AND STAR (STAR AND PUNTY, STAR AND CONCAVE)
(a) Sugar 3¾" H. x 4⅝" Dia.
    Cover 3¼" H. x 4¾" Dia.
    Combined size 6⅞" H. x 4¾" Dia.
(b) Cream 5¾" H. x 3" Dia. body 1850–1870

Designs for patterns were sometimes taken from things that surrounded people. Stars appeared as sunbursts on blown molded pieces and as rays beneath bottoms. This pattern of alternating six-pointed stars and circles completely covering the surface was named *Early Moon and Star* by collectors to distinguish it from a late Pittsburgh pattern called *Moon and Star*. Pittsburgh houses knew it as *Star and Concave*. It appeared in the Cape Cod Glass Company's *List of Glass Ware* as *Star and Punty* where five forms were listed and "goblet" was handwritten. Colored fragments were retrieved from both Sandwich factory yards. A stand lamp and hand lamp can be seen in photo 2167. The stand lamp was sometimes sold in pairs with a matching spoon holder as a kitchen set. An inner rim on the sugar cover keeps the cover in place. As there is no inner ledge on the sugar bowl, it may be mistaken for an open sugar. Note the contour of the rim of the cream. The rim and wonderfully formed spout balanced by an equally well-executed handle combined to produce a piece that should please any pattern glass collector. *Courtesy, Sandwich Glass Museum, Sandwich Historical Society*

1192 PRESSED PRISM AND CRESCENT TUMBLER
2¾" H. x 2¾" Dia. 1845–1860

Prism and Crescent was pressed in a limited number of pieces over a relatively short period. It is made up of vertical prisms that separate columns of horizontal prisms and printies. A matching whale oil lamp shown in photo 2165 helped establish the date. The tumbler in this photo was also made with a handle that was applied after the tumbler was pressed. A handled tumbler was for lemonade. Lemonades are illustrated in the New England Glass Company catalog. (A study of toy lemonades made by the Boston and Sandwich Glass Company and the Cape Cod Glass Company is included in Chapter 10 of Volume 3.) Prism and Crescent is likely to be found in tumblers and stemware. Therefore, be on the lookout for decanters. Glass companies received large orders for bar tumblers and bar decanters from public eating establishments such as those in large city hotels and on passenger ships. When designed for such use, patterns were sturdy. Glass sugars, creams and serving pieces were not required because tableware was made of china.

1193 BLOWN MOLDED PILLAR TABLE DECANTER

10" H. x 4½" Dia. 1845–1875

Wooden patterns of Pillar stemware were found at Sandwich, as well as wooden patterns of two lamp fonts as shown in photo 2163. Although a sauce dish (nappie) was reported by Ruth Webb Lee, one most often finds ales, bar decanters and table decanters. This table decanter minus its glass stopper was in the family collection of glassmaker John Murray. As you can see, the inside of the neck was ground for a stopper. When you purchase a table decanter without its correct stopper, you are acquiring only one unit of a two-unit item. Its name was derived from the vertical convex pillars in which are concave "printies". The number of "printies" varies with the height of the article. Bakewell, Pears and Company also produced Pillar in their Pittsburgh, Pennsylvania, factory.

1194 PRESSED SNOWFLAKE SPOON HOLDER

5" H. x 3¼" Dia. 1850–1870

This spoon holder is circular, but carries the heavy horizontal bands below and above the pattern that one finds on hexagonal spoon holders. The main element of design is a six-pointed rosette thought to resemble a snowflake. The outer extremity of each point is faceted. There are twelve snowflakes in each of four horizontal rows. A twenty-four point star is molded in deep relief beneath the foot, which cannot be seen through the translucent, fiery opalescent glass. When patterns were designed, the mold maker had clear glass in mind through which all of the pattern reflected. All of the spoon holders were regularly made in clear flint glass. Snowflake resembles another Sandwich pattern called *Rosette*, which has six rounded petals and a bead center.

1195 BLOWN MOLDED OVAL HOBNAIL SPILL HOLDER

4⅛" H. x 3⅛" Dia. 1845–1870

One of the most interesting patterns documented as Sandwich is that of hobnails that are wider than they are high. It lent itself to blown molded finials, vases and colognes. This is the only Oval Hobnail article that resembles tableware and may be a spill holder. If so, it was made during the latter part of the time period because the glass spill holder was not a marketable item until the United States was well into the use of kerosene as a fuel for lighting devices. Because the glass was blown into a mold, the reverse of the pattern can be felt on the inside surface, ruling the piece out as a footed tumbler. Sandwich glass made to hold food or drink is smooth on the surface that came into contact with its contents. As shown in the foreground, the number of fragments unearthed at the Boston and Sandwich Glass Company in various stages of completion attest to Sandwich manufacture. However, Oval Hobnail objects were also made in France.

1196 PRESSED BUCKLE

(a) Sugar 5⅜" H. x 4⅛" Dia.
     Cover 3" H. x 4⅛" Dia.
     Combined size 8¼" H. x 4⅛" Dia.
(b) Cream 6¼" H. x 3⅛" Dia. body 1860–1880

Buckle was made in a range of tableware items by the Boston and Sandwich Glass Company in Sandwich; the Union Glass Works and Union Glass Company in Somerville, Massachusetts; Gillinder and Sons of Philadelphia, Pennsylvania; and the Burlington Glass Works in Hamilton, Ontario, Canada. At Gillinder it was known as No. 15 with no other designation. Because it was manufactured at the time flint glass factories began to press tableware with glass made from less expensive litharge and lime formulas, Buckle pieces vary in quality. Shown here are a sugar A and matching cream B, both having the hexagonal stem and plain, circular foot of a goblet. Narrow, vertical ribs, called *reed*, surround the bottom of the body. Fine diamond point covers the surface of open ovals thought to resemble buckles. The matching sugar cover has an inner rim that fits inside the rim of the bowl. The acorn finial with a diamond point cap was part of the cover mold. The diameter of the cream is given for the widest part of the pressed body. Dimensions vary at the top depending on the habits of the glassworker who shaped the rim and spout. The handle was applied by adhering it along its length at the top and applying pressure with a crimper at the bottom. Old glass is brittle and should not be held by the handle. Buckle fonts for kerosene lamps were produced. *Courtesy, Sandwich Glass Museum, Sandwich Historical Society*

1197 PRESSED BUCKLE BOWL WITH TURN OVER RIM INSERT FOR METAL BASKET

1860–1880

This large bowl was dug at the Boston and Sandwich Glass Company site. It had been discarded because the rim fractured as the glass cooled. Rims such as this were called *turn over* rims by the industry. When this bowl is found at an antiques show or shop, it is thought to be incomplete because it is top-heavy and looks as though a foot should have been adhered to it. But the foot was part of the metalwork into which the bowl was inserted. Most commonly the Buckle bowl was manufactured in clear and blue. It was marketed in a wire basket as well as a quadruple plate frame with a handle manufactured by Reed and Barton in Taunton, Massachusetts. Reed and Barton began business in 1824. Their invoices, showing sales to the Boston and Sandwich Glass Company and Deming Jarves, date as early as April 17, 1832. No dimensions are available for this particular bowl. It was lost in a fire that destroyed the Barlow-Kaiser Publishing Company, Inc. warehouse in 1983. Some Buckle nappies have a central pattern of a nine-pointed star covered with fine diamond point. A variant known as *Banded Buckle* was also a Sandwich product. It has a horizontal band of fine diamond point surrounding the body above the buckles.

1198 PRESSED BUCKLE

(a) Goblet 6" H. x 3¼" Dia.

(b) Plaster-of-Paris cast of mold 1860–1880

The Buckle pattern goblet on the left was pressed in a cast iron three-section mold that was manufactured by using the plaster-of-Paris cast as an intermediate step. Sandwich historian Francis (Bill) Wynn, while digging at the Boston and Sandwich Glass Company site in 1947, unearthed the two side sections shown here. Some damage had occurred when the sections were discarded, but the Buckle pattern and the cylindrical extensions by which the sections were fastened together remained intact. When the Buckle goblet is placed in the plaster cast, the fit is perfect with the pattern on the goblet matching the location of the pattern on the inside surface of the cast.

1199 THIRD SECTION OF PLASTER-OF-PARIS CAST OF BUCKLE MOLD

When William Casey of Carver, Massachusetts, was digging at the Boston and Sandwich Glass Company site in 1959, he uncovered this third section of the plaster-of-Paris cast. Mr. Wynn, realizing its importance to the completion of his 1947 find, offered to purchase the Casey section. When Casey refused, Wynn gave Casey the first two sections because according to Wynn, "History would never forgive us if we do not put the three pieces together." All three sections were incorporated into the Barlow collection after the death of William Casey.

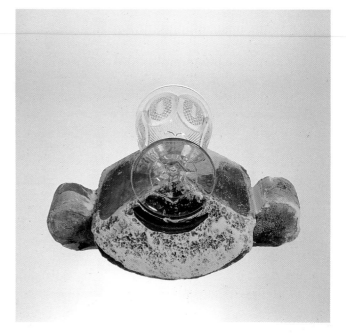

1200 PRESSED HUBER ENGRAVED WITH GRAPES

(a) Bowl on foot 5¼" H. x 7½" Dia.

(b) Nappies 1⅛" H. x 3½" Dia. 1855–1875

The footed bowl A, nappies B and the goblets that follow are the items remaining from a larger selection. They were part of the collection of Ella (Mrs. Ralph) Freeman, daughter-in-law of the former Annie Mathilda Nye, a Sandwich decorator. Mrs. Freeman remembered other pieces now broken such as a sugar and butter. All of their Huber pieces were engraved with leaves and unpolished grapes as shown here. The panels of Huber bowls extend to a rim of shallow scallops. This bowl has a low, unpatterned foot that was a standard unit applied to numerous patterned bowls and nappies. This footed bowl was illustrated in five sizes by the New England Glass Company of East Cambridge, Massachusetts, in their 1869 catalog. It was also combined with a high, scalloped foot as shown on the Diamond Point bowl in photo 1161. The matching nappies have a rosette as a central pattern and panels that end in shallow arches near a smooth rim. The 3½" diameter size shown was the smallest in the New England catalog. A 7" diameter nappie was listed as a "Preserve Nappie on foot, covered". The combination of a large bowl or nappie with small nappies to match was sold in later years as a "berry set". A Huber individual salt with engraving is known.

1201 PRESSED HUBER GOBLETS ENGRAVED WITH GRAPES

6½" H. x 3½" Dia. 1855–1875

The two Huber goblets were part of the Nye/Freeman collection brought home from the Boston and Sandwich Glass Company by members of Annie Mathilda Nye's family. Like the nappies, vertical panels end in a shallow scallop below a smooth rim. There were two types of Huber goblets, those in this photo with a break between the panels on the body and the hexagonal stem and a hotel goblet with panels that extend from a rounded body to the bottom of the stem. Beer mugs were produced in four sizes, smaller in diameter at the rim than the bottom and with pressed handles. In addition to the Boston and Sandwich Glass Company, New England Glass Company, Mount Washington Glass Works and Portland Glass Company, a limited number of Huber articles were listed in the Cape Cod Glass Company's *List of Glass Ware* as reprinted on pages 108–110 in Volume 3. Pieces from Annie Nye's family collection can be seen throughout *The Glass Industry in Sandwich*, many of which were decorated by her hand.

1202 PRESSED HUBER

(a) Bottle with applied string ring 6¼" H. x 2⅝" Dia.
(b) Wooden pattern for bitter bottle 1855–1875

This nine-paneled Huber bottle A is the size of a Huber bitter bottle as illustrated in the 1869 New England Glass Company catalog. It was pressed in a Huber pattern mold and after removal was held on the bottom to a pontil rod while the neck was drawn up and a string ring applied ¼" below the rim. The bottom was dished out into a large punty mark that was polished to remove a scar from the pontil rod. The still-visible, handwritten label that reads "Cherry Wine 1875" documents its use. The bottle was filled with cherry wine most likely made in the home and was stopped with the cork that was still with the bottle at the time of purchase by author Kaiser, as was the string and leather remnants. A leather strap was run up one side, across the cork and down the other side. The string was tied tightly around the ends of the leather below the string ring. With the cork driven into place and pressure against it from the leather, the wine could be stored for an extended period. After the bottle was purchased for the Kaiser collection, we realized the wooden pattern B for the matching bitter bottle was in the possession of author Barlow.

1203 PRESSED FINE RIB (REEDED)

(a) Goblet 6⅜" H. x 3½" Dia.
(b) Champagne 5½" H. x 2⅞" Dia.
(c) Wine 4⅛" H. x 2¼" Dia.
(d) Cordial 3¼" H. x 1¾" Dia. 1850–1875

Goblet is defined as "A kind of cup or drinking vessel without a handle". Yet only the largest was termed a goblet while smaller ones were named for their contents. In order of rarity, a set of goblets and wines can still be assembled, champagnes are found on occasion and cordials are scarce. In twenty years of collecting this pattern for the Kaiser home, we have only three cordials. The pattern of fine vertical ribs was originally called *Reeded*. Two pages of the New England Glass Company catalog were devoted to it and the number of fragments dug from the Boston and Sandwich Glass Company site indicate prolific production there as well. Other makers were the Union Flint Glass Works and Union Flint Glass Company in Somerville, Massachusetts; McKee and Brothers in Pittsburgh, Pennsylvania; Bakewell, Pears and Company also of Pittsburgh and assuredly many more. Most pieces are good quality flint, but production extended into the non-flint era. Mass production of colored pieces was limited to toy tumblers and lemonades as shown in photos 3328–3329 and an occasional lamp font. A colored flint adult-size tableware item would be considered very rare.

1204 PRESSED FINE RIB (REEDED)

(a) Custard 4" H. x 2½" Dia.

(b) Pomade, with shield 3½" H. x 2⅝" Dia.

(c) Egg cup 4" H. x 2⅝" Dia. 1850–1875

To the novice antiques dealer and collector, all three forms are called egg cups. Only C is a true egg cup. The same mold was used to press egg cup C and custard A. After taking the custard from the mold in which it was pressed, a handle with a long crimped tail was applied. Forms A and C are shown in the 1869 New England Glass Company catalog, an original of which is preserved at The Rakow Library of The Corning Museum of Glass in Corning, New York. Under the name of *Reeded*, the catalog accurately illustrated seventy pieces and their use. This priceless document is one of the most detailed relating to American pressed glass that we have had the pleasure to study. Centered in this photo is the lower unit of a pomade, a commercial covered jar in which pomade was sold. The distributor's firm name was sometimes molded in the shield. Its matching cover has an acorn finial. Fine Rib tableware was pressed in molds with three side sections. The pomade came from a less expensive two-section mold. Pomade jars made in various tableware patterns were called "covered egg cups" by scholar and writer Ruth Webb Lee, and the name persists. For a study of pomades that resemble egg cups, see photos 3265–3273.

1205 PRESSED FINE RIB (REEDED) WITH CUT OVALS EGG CUP

3⅞" H. x 2⅝" Dia. 1850–1875

Occasionally, pressed articles were used as blanks that after annealing were engraved or cut. The glass company "dressed" the piece at little extra cost but reaped a larger profit. Although Fine Rib was pressed in a large and varied assortment of pieces, cut blanks are rare. We have seen the egg cup, wine, goblet, decanter, celery and nappie with horizontal rows of cut ovals, which are nothing more than dished-out punties. The value of cut pieces is much higher than the same form not cut. Very rarely a Bellflower design was cut into the Fine Rib blank that followed the pattern of pressed Bellflower pieces. Cut Bellflower pieces are usually in less-than-perfect condition because it was difficult to maintain the curve of the horizontal vine without damaging the pressed vertical ribs.

1206 BLOWN MOLDED FINE RIB (REEDED) CASTERS

(a) Pepper 6⅝" H. x 2¼" Dia. 1865–1875

(b) Vinegar 6⅞" H. x 2¼" Dia.

(c) Mustard 5½" H. x 2¼" Dia. 1860–1875

Glass factory catalogs listed casters for metal stands in three forms—pepper, vinegar and mustard—regardless of the condiment they would later contain. Most stands manufactured during the 1860's had a revolving plate with four or five holes in which the casters were suspended. Pepper A was used for pepper as well as other dry condiments that were sprinkled, *but not salt*. The perforated metal caps that screwed onto the threaded necks of two matching peppers may have different size holes for finely- and coarsely-ground pepper. Arthur G. Peterson's preliminary research in preparation for his book *Glass Salt Shakers: 1,000 Patterns* led to his conclusion that the perfection of a screw thread on the neck of a bottle took place in the early 1860's. Our study of the McKee and Brothers' catalogs bears out his statement, which is why the Fine Rib pepper is dated 1865. The 1859/1860 and 1864 McKee catalogs show casters, including Bellflower (R. L.), only with push-on caps. Screw caps are illustrated in the 1868 catalog. Vinegar B was used for liquids such as soy, vinegar and oil. Its neck was flanged into a lip with two spouts and was machined for a narrow, pressed, hexagonal or matching blown molded Reeded stopper. Mustard C held mustard, horseradish, relish or jam. Its cap was affixed with cement to a wide rim. The hinged cover has a slot for the handle of a metal, bone or olive wood mustard spoon that was left in the caster when the cover was in place.

1211 PRESSED PRISM PANEL (PRISM) TOYS

(a) Tumbler 1¾" H. x 1¾" Dia.
(b) Lemonade 1¾" H. x 1¾" Dia.
(c) Chamber pot 1¼" H. x 2¼" Dia. 1859–1869

This pattern of vertical grooves arranged in panels was designated *Prism* in a catalog of the King Glass Company, a Pittsburgh firm. It is known to collectors as *Prism Panel* to differentiate it from a prism pattern that is not paneled. At Sandwich, it is documented as a product of the Cape Cod Glass Works (1859–1864) and the Cape Cod Glass Company (1864–1869). Tumbler A was made in a large size for adults and with an applied handled was sold as a lemonade. The toy size was made with a pressed handle as pictured in B. An amethyst one can be seen in photo 3325. Chamber pot C matches in pattern, pressed handle and base diameter. It, too, was made in color. Toys are often mistakenly sold as Twentieth Century "whiskey tasters", open salts and nut dishes. For more information about toys made in Sandwich, see Chapter 10 in Volume 3.

1212 PRESSED RIBBED ACORN (ACORN)

(a) Nappie 1½" H. x 6⅛" Dia.
  Cover 2¾" H. x 5⅝" Dia.
  Combined size 4¼" H. x 6⅛" Dia.
(b) Nappie on foot 4" H. x 6⅛" Dia.
  Cover 2¾" H. x 5⅝" Dia.
  Combined size 6½" H. x 6⅛" Dia. 1855–1875

Covered nappie A was most often used for butter and covered nappie B on foot was sometimes called a *sweetmeat*. Several similar patterns were designed by adding different forms of vegetation to the stems of a vine that undulated around the body of a piece. These nappies have acorns on a ground of vertical ribs. The ribs served to reflect the light, making tableware items produced from less expensive litharge, lime and soda formulas appear more brilliant. Most Ribbed Acorn pieces were made from flint glass. The Ribbed Acorn pattern was molded into the outside surface of the nappies but into the inside surface of the covers and high foot. Each piece was attractive when pressed in transparent glass, but much of the pattern was lost when molds were filled with translucent and opaque glass. In the 1870's at the Boston and Sandwich Glass Company, estimates by the authors are that no more than four of the forty working pots held glass with no lead content. Production of pressed tableware decreased during the 1870's as the glass industry in New England saw a surge in the manufacture of blown glass to be cut, engraved and etched. Acorn plates were listed on Union Glass Company invoices as early as April 6, 1858. *Courtesy, Sandwich Glass Museum, Sandwich Historical Society*

1213 PRESSED BELLFLOWER (R. L.) GOBLET

6¼" H. x 3¼" Dia. 1855–1875

A bell-shaped, tulip-like blossom on a continuous undulating vine is called *Bellflower* by collectors. McKee and Brothers listed the pattern as "R. L.", thought to be an abbreviation for Ribbed Leaf, but the terminology of that time suggests that "R. L." stood for *Reeded and Leaf*. Three elements appear on the vine: the bellflower, a single leaf and a group of three berries resembling a three-leaf clover. There are many variations in pattern, form and mold design. Vertical ribs can be spaced closely together, in which case the article is called "fine rib". A heavier, wider rib is known as "coarse rib". On some variants, two undulating vines intertwine, but this "double vine" cannot be documented as a Sandwich product. All fragments dug at the Boston and Sandwich Glass Company site have only a single vine. Because Bellflower was manufactured during the time that glass factories were converting from flint to litharge and non-flint formulas, quality varies tremendously. Reproductions abound, many produced in clear and color by the Imperial Glass Company for The Metropolitan Museum of Art.

1214 BLOWN MOLDED BELLFLOWER (R. L.) MOLASSES JUG

6⅛" H. x 3" Dia. 1855–1875

This single vine, fine rib Bellflower molasses jug, or can, is typical of molasses cans blown molded during this time period. They were made in many patterns with a rim diameter to take a cemented metal cap with a spout and hinged cover. The metal cover of this cap has an eight-lobed tab that opens the cover by thumb pressure. If this thumb piece is broken, the value of the jug, or can, is greatly reduced. The handle had to be applied to form a high loop so that, when grasped by the hand, the thumb reached the metal tab. It was indiscriminately attached with no thought as to which portion of the pattern is obliterated. The "R. L. Mo. Can, Brit." top was shown in McKee and Brothers' 1871 catalog. The Cape Cod Glass Company used the term *molasses jug*. *Courtesy, Sandwich Glass Museum, Sandwich Historical Society*

1215 PRESSED RIBBED GRAPE (MOUNT VERNON) SPOON HOLDER

5¾" H. x 3½" Dia. 1855–1875

In her book *Early American Pressed Glass*, Ruth Webb Lee commented that Ribbed Grape "is usually found in clear glass. Fragments in blue were recovered from Sandwich, but perfect pieces in color are extremely rare." Her statement holds true for other patterns as well—the value of a colored piece is many times that of the same piece in clear. The same undulating vine previously shown is here combined with grape leaves and bunches of grapes in which the grapes were stylized into rigid, horizontal rows. Vertical ribs that repeat the rays beneath the foot stop short of the rim of blunted miters. A variant of the spoon holder has ribs extending into the miters. The authors believe Ribbed Grape is the pattern listed as "Mount Vernon Pattern. Grape Vine." by the Cape Cod Glass Company. If so, it was also made by the Union Glass Company of Somerville, Massachusetts. A Union invoice dated June 14, 1865, listed 4" Mount Vernon nappies. *Courtesy of The Toledo Museum of Art (Acc. No. 65.157)*

1216 PRESSED RIBBED GRAPE (MOUNT VERNON)

(a) Goblet 6¼" H. x 3½" Dia. 1855–1875

(b) Nappie on foot 4⅝" H. x 6⅛" Dia.

Cover 3½" H. x 5⅝" Dia.

Combined size 7¾" H. x 6⅛" Dia. 1855–1873

The Cape Cod Glass Company's *List of Glass Ware* is reprinted in full on pages 108–110 of Volume 3. It itemizes under "Mount Vernon Pattern. Grape Vine." all articles on which the Ribbed Grape pattern has been found including a 6" cheese plate. On goblet A, the pattern of grapes and leaves on an undulating vine shows clearly. However, the pattern is lost when pressed in opaque and translucent colors. Many collectors and dealers overlook the footed nappie and cover thinking the units were married at a later time. The pressed cover appears to have no pattern because the grapes and ribs are inside. The high foot has vertical ribs inside the standard and concentric circles around the base as shown on the low foot of the Prism nappie in photo 1207. Cover finials shaped like acorns are common to this era. *Courtesy, Sandwich Glass Museum, Sandwich Historical Society*

1217 UNITS OF ABOVE NAPPIE ON FOOT

The grapes and leaves are concave on the outer surface of the nappie unit. The pattern is reversed on the inner surface of the cover; the grapes and leaves are convex. Yet, the pieces are original to each other. Be aware of these differences when you are considering a purchase. Note also that there is an inner ledge inside the scallops of the rim on which the cover rests. Look for the ledge when contemplating the purchase of what is believed to be an "open compote", a term not in use at the time this Ribbed Grape (Mount Vernon) article was made. If there is a ledge but a cover is not included in the sale, you are buying only the lower unit of a two-unit item.

1218 PRESSED RIBBED IVY CORDIAL DECANTER

(a) Decanter 6" H. x 2½" Dia.
(b) Stopper 2½" H. x 1¼" Dia.
(c) Combined size 7½" H. x 2½" Dia. 1855–1875

Throughout the Nineteenth Century, production costs were cut by mass producing molds as well as glass. All of these ribbed or reeded patterns are similar in form with rayed stars beneath the feet, short stems on spoon holders and almost identical dimensions. This small decanter could have been pressed in any of the ribbed patterns, but here it is pictured with a three-pointed ivy leaf on the single vine that surrounds the body. The rim was flared into a lip to which a pressed Tulip stopper was fitted. A pontil mark on such a piece does not indicate early manufacture. Even in 1870, pontil rods held holloware while upper portions were hand formed. The stopper is a smaller version of the Tulip stopper of a large capacity Magnet and Grape with Frosted Leaf syrup dispenser used at soda fountains. Reshaping after removal from the mold resulted in a different configuration. The original factory pattern name is not known. *Courtesy, Sandwich Glass Museum, Sandwich Historical Society*

1219 PRESSED REEDED PATTY-PAN

8⅜" H. x 2⅛" Dia. 1850–1860

This is a pressed, finely-ribbed, flat-sided pan with a center circle that would have camouflaged the outline of a wafer if the pan were combined with a foot. The circle is the center of a ribbed star that has twenty-two points. At first glance, the ribs on the sidewall resemble those on the outermost band of Hamilton (Cape Cod) and Hamilton With Leaf (Rose Leaf). But this pattern is reversed; the ribs extend from the rim downward rather than upward from the table rest. Matching fragments were found at the Boston and Sandwich Glass Company factory site, but we have not encountered other forms in this ribbed pattern.

1220 PRESSED HAMILTON (CAPE COD) NAPPIE ON FOOT

5" H. x 7" Dia. 1855–1875

The Boston and Sandwich Glass Company and the Cape Cod Glass Company both made the pattern called *Hamilton* and its several variants. Fragments in clear and deep blue were unearthed at the Boston and Sandwich site, and a sugar is illustrated on page 1 of the *List of Glass Ware Manufactured by Cape Cod Glass Company* as reprinted on page 108 in Volume 3. Originally known as *Cape Cod*, it is the first pattern detailed in the list and was produced in twenty-five tableware forms. Small quantities appear to have been made by Deming Jarves at his Mount Washington Glass Works. In September 1866, Jarves sent James Lloyd to the South Boston factory to assess operating costs prior to leasing the works to William Langdon Libbey. In a letter to Lloyd on Cape Cod Glass Company stationery dated September 28, Jarves wrote, "Our mould cleaner must be careful not to rub off the fine work on our Cape Cod moulds." The pattern is composed of three distinct bands encircling the body. Straight-sided pieces have a band of vertical ribs around the lower portion that appear as rays in the bottoms of bowls and nappies. A band of divided diamonds, definitely "fine work", surrounds the center, above which is a band of vertical ribs that extend upward ending in a zigzag. In the early 1970's, author Kaiser passed up an opaque light blue cream with an applied handle because she thought the price tag read $200, only to find out after it was sold that it had been marked $20. "I don't write as well as you do," said the dealer. "I wondered why you didn't take it."

1221 HAMILTON WITH LEAF (ROSE LEAF) COVERED BOWL ON FOOT

(a) Bowl 8⅛" H. x 8" Dia.
(b) Cover 4⅝" H. x 7½" Dia.
(c) Combined size 11⅞" H. x 8" Dia. 1855–1875

This pattern has all of the ribbed features found on Hamilton (Cape Cod), but the "fine work" in the center band was replaced by large, stylized, nine-pointed leaves on an undulating vine. A study of the Cape Cod Glass Company's *List of Glass Ware* shows it to be their *Rose Leaf*. Twenty-one articles were available with "Plain" and "Rough" corresponding to Hamilton with Leaf shown here and Hamilton with Frosted Leaf which follows. This is the largest bowl the authors have seen and is the largest listed by the Cape Cod works. The lower unit is made up of an octagonal standard and a circular foot with the rose leaf band and band of ribs ending in a zigzag near a plain rim. A wafer attached to the top of the standard is tilted, but securely holds the bowl with a deeply scalloped rim. The matching cover rests on a ledge inside the rim. Its finial resembles a gourd and is difficult to grasp, owing to the weight of the cover. Fragments of Hamilton with Leaf were found at the Boston and Sandwich site. We can find no patterns in the Cape Cod list that were exclusive to that factory.

1222 (A) PRESSED HAMILTON WITH FROSTED LEAF (ROSE LEAF) SPOON HOLDER

5½" H. x 3⅜" Dia. 1855–1875

(B) BLOWN MOLDED BANDED LEAF (ROSE LEAF) PEG LAMP, WHALE OIL BURNER

3⅞" H. x 3" Dia. 1830–1855

One of the most difficult problems facing a historian is to read the written word and relate it to a glass article with some degree of certainty. In the case of the Hamilton variants, the illustration at the top of the Cape Cod Glass Company list (see pages 108–110 in Volume 3) served as a stepping stone to guide us on our paper trail. Note the eight-pointed leaves that surround spoon holder A. They were deliberately molded in deep relief to be frosted by machining their surface in the cutting shop. The description of a frosted leaf can be found in the Cape Cod list under the Rose Leaf pattern, where it is noted it could be ordered "roughed". Note this pattern's similarity to that of the earlier blown molded peg lamp B. Vertical ribs, though rounded, are at the bottom and top. Detailed, naturalistic, veined leaves in the center band more closely resemble rose leaves than the later, stylized Hamilton with Leaf version. The authors conclude that pressed Hamilton with Leaf was a simplified continuation of the earlier blown molded pattern that may also have been called *Rose Leaf*. See photos 2077–2079 for more information about the Banded Leaf peg lamp and a matching whale oil lamp with attached glass base.

1223 PRESSED RIBBED PALM (SPRIG)

(a) Sugar 7½" H. x 4¼" Dia.

(b) Cream 5" H. x 3¼" Dia. body 1863–1875

On April 21, 1863, Frederick McKee was issued design patent No. 1748 for "A 'sprig pattern' composed of a series of leaves branching out on both sides of a stem. The intermediate space between the sprigs may be furrowed." The pattern appeared under the name of *Sprig* in McKee and Brothers' 1864 catalog. It was to become a complete assortment of tableware pieces. Collectors dubbed the pattern *Ribbed Palm* because McKee's sprigs resemble single broad palm leaves rather than multi-leaved stems. How Ribbed Palm came to be produced by a number of other glass companies is uncertain. Possibly the pattern was released when McKee's patent ran out. The sugar and cream shown here are two of many pieces that were taken home from the Boston and Sandwich Glass Company factory by a Sandwich glassworker. The feet were designed with a downward slant that allowed the hot glass to completely fill the molds; yet the feet were large enough in diameter to support the bodies without needing to be flattened after removal from their molds. Deming Jarves first patented a method of pressing a handle in one piece with the body on May 28, 1830. Thirty-five years later, it was still less expensive to make a handleless cream mold and apply the handle in a separate operation.

1224 PRESSED RIBBED PALM (SPRIG)

(a) Cover 6" Dia.

(b) Covered nappie 6¼" H. x 6" Dia. 1863–1875

The earliest annealing leers with uneven heat caused glass to warp as it cooled. Covers were designed to rest loosely on wide inner ledges of lower units so that, if either or both units warped, they still combined to result in a saleable covered article. By the 1850's, annealing leers were better designed to take stress out of the glass with less distortion. The inner ledge could be eliminated from the lower unit and the cover could rest directly on the edge of the lower unit to present to the customer a clean-lined contour from the bottom of the bowl to the top of the cover. A narrow ridge inside the cover, as shown in A, prevented the cover from slipping from side to side. By eliminating the inner ledge from nappie B, it could be sold with and without a cover. Covers are difficult to find, therefore, because less covers than nappies were manufactured and in use were more easily broken. If you find a cover alone, purchase it. The value of a cover is greater than the value of its lower unit. You will eventually find the lower unit.

1225 PRESSED GREEK KEY (GREEK BORDER)

(a) Sugar 5¾" H. x 4⅜" Dia.

   Cover 3¼" H. x 4½" Dia.

   Combined size 7¼" H. x 4½" Dia.

(b) Cream 6½" H. x 3¼" Dia. body 1860–1880

Greek Key was a popular design when engraved into the thin blown glass known to the industry as "bubble glass". Forty pieces of blown tableware were photographed for the Boston and Sandwich Glass Company's 1874 catalog (see also photo 4210). It adapted easily to pressed glass and with very little extra labor could be "dressed" by roughing the surface of the border in the cutting shop. By doing so, two patterns were added to inventory: Greek Key with clear border as taken from the mold and the roughed variant today called Frosted Greek Key. It is a documented product of the Union Glass Company in Somerville, Massachusetts, and the Portland Glass Company in Portland, Maine. Frosted Greek Key may be the pattern referred to as "Altered Grecian" in notes written by a visitor to the Portland works in the 1860's. Coarse, rounded ribs surround the lower part of the bodies. The feet are not rayed—what you see in the photo are reflections of the ribs. When considering a purchase, do not accept a sugar bowl without a cover and examine the applied handle carefully for damage. *Courtesy, Sandwich Glass Museum, Sandwich Historical Society*

1226 PRESSED LINCOLN DRAPE OPEN SUGAR
5½" H. x 4⅞" Dia. 1865–1875

Tradition states that Lincoln Drape was designed to commemorate the assassination of United States President Abraham Lincoln. With the surrender on April 9, 1865, of the Confederate army to General Ulysses Grant, commander in chief of Union forces, the Civil War was virtually over. On the night of April 14, 1865, Lincoln and his wife relaxed by attending a play at Ford's Theatre in Washington, where he was allegedly shot by secession zealot John Wilkes Booth. He fell unconscious into his wife's arms and died the following morning. The drape pattern on glass depicted the drapery in Lincoln's booth on the balcony of the theatre. The number of drapes held by large ovals varies with the diameter of the article. As was common in the 1860's, vertical ribs cover the remaining surface and match rays beneath the feet of stemware and footed nappies. This piece appears to be a true open sugar that did not have a cover. Open sugars were used for loaf sugar. The variant Lincoln Drape with Tassel cannot be documented as a Sandwich product. The large ovals are replaced by circular rings from which a cord and large tassel depends.

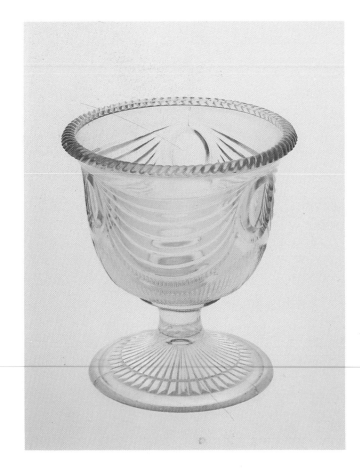

1227 BULL'S EYE (LAWRENCE) CELERY
9⅛" H. x 4⅝" Dia. 1855–1875

According to the New England Glass Company catalog that dates from the late 1860's, this Bull's Eye pattern was marketed as *Lawrence*. Perhaps it was on its way out when the catalog was produced because only a few forms were illustrated under "various patterns of pressed glass". Since most patterns were manufactured in several glass houses, there is no way to determine the origin of a particular Bull's Eye (Lawrence) item purchased on the open market. Its value in colorless glass should be based on supply and demand regardless of origin. When a piece is found in color, value increases substantially. Fragments of colored Bull's Eye (Lawrence) pomades were dug from the Cape Cod Glass Company site, as discussed under photo 3268. The Boston and Sandwich Glass Company also made numerous pieces of tableware as well as lamp fonts as shown in photo 2285. *Courtesy, Sandwich Glass Museum, Sandwich Historical Society*

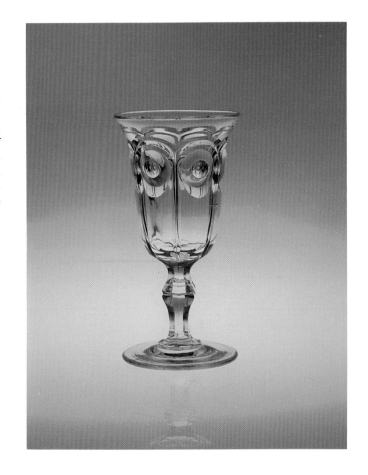

1233 PRESSED HONEYCOMB (NEW YORK, UTICA) TABLE DECANTERS WITH BLOWN MOLDED STOPPER

(a) Decanter 9½" H. x 5" Dia.
(b) Stopper 4⅞" H. x 2" Dia.
(c) Combined size 13¼" H. x 5" Dia. 1860–1880

Several forms of decanters were available in the Honeycomb pattern. When a bar lip was applied at the rim, the decanter was sold with a metal *slide stop* as pictured in photos 3222–3224. A decanter for the table had a rim flared out to a thin lip, as shown here, to which was fitted one of several styles of "glass stops". Rarest of glass stoppers is the Honeycomb blown in the form of an acorn with the pattern covering the surface of the acorn cap as shown here. Occasionally the smooth shoulder of the decanter and nut of the acorn stopper were engraved. The unpatterned upper portion of the stopper was easily broken. If either acorn stopper is broken, the value of these decanters as a pair is greatly diminished. Less rare is a flat-topped stopper with the Honeycomb pattern on its lower portion. Although several Honeycomb variants were produced in Sandwich, none had the pattern completely covering the surface into scallops of the rim.

1234 PRESSED FLOWERED OVAL (FLOWER MEDALLION)

(a) Sugar 4¼" H. x 4" Dia.
   Cover 3¼" H. x 4⅛" Dia.
   Combined size 7¼" H. x 4⅛" Dia.
(b) Cream 6⅝" H. x 2⅞" Dia. body 1865–1880

Patterns mass produced in Sandwich after the Civil War, when the changeover from lead to lime-soda formulas took place, are noted for their similarities rather than differences. Forms and sizes were standardized and several "rules of thumb" apply. The bodies of sugars, spoon holders and creams followed the forms of stemmed drinking vessels. They have stems and circular feet and were easily manufactured. Handles were applied to creams after completion of the body. This pattern is made up of a single horizontal row of large ovals or medallions, each enclosing an eight-lobed rosette. Each rosette is the Honeycomb pattern in miniature; one finds the motif centered in Honeycomb nappies. Although pleasing, it apparently had limited appeal. Few forms have been found. *Courtesy, Sandwich Glass Museum, Sandwich Historical Society*

1235 PRESSED MAGNET AND GRAPE WITH FROSTED LEAF GOBLET

6½" H. x 3½" Dia. 1855–1875

The Boston and Sandwich Glass Company produced two variants of Magnet and Grape, one with a stippled leaf and one with a frosted leaf as shown here. The frosted effect was accomplished by machine-roughing the surface of the leaf and sometimes the grapes after the piece was annealed. This goblet was pressed in a four-section mold that resulted in an octagonal rather than hexagonal stem. The foot, which has a rayed star beneath it, was not reheated and flared after removal from the mold. Advances in mold-heating techniques eliminated this necessity. Two opposite mold sections have a horseshoe-shaped magnet covered with fine diamond point. They alternate with a frosted grape leaf over a bunch of frosted or clear grapes. The shape of a magnet is repeated around the grape bunch. Numerous reproductions were created by the Imperial Glass Company in Bellaire, Ohio, for The Metropolitan Museum of Art. Although marked "MMA", they can fool the uninitiated. *Courtesy, Sandwich Glass Museum, Sandwich Historical Society*

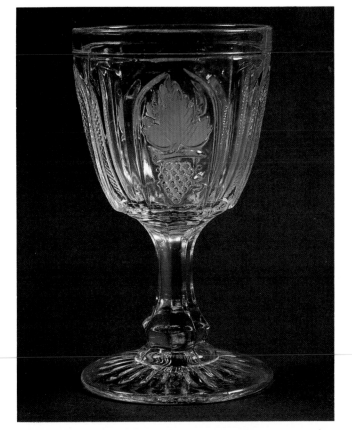

1236 PRESSED GRAPE VINE SPOON HOLDER

4¾" H. x 3¼" Dia. 1850–1865

This translucent green spoon holder has a pattern of a grape vine ascending diagonally and repeated three times on a smooth background. The circular body is unpaneled with a plain, horizontal band at bottom and rim. It was pressed in a three-section mold that included the stubby stem and rather flat foot. Opal colors are attributed to the expertise of Sandwich chemist James Danforth Lloyd. Formulas for opal tints were written by Lloyd in a notebook dated August 7, 1868, when he was employed by Deming Jarves at the Cape Cod Glass Company (see page 105 in Volume 3). A clear Grape Vine spoon holder with decorated vines from the Lloyd family collection can be seen in photo 2241.

1237 PRESSED MORNING GLORY

(a) Sugar 5⅛" H. x 4⅛" Dia.
   Cover 3" H. x 4½" Dia.
   Combined size 8" H. x 4½" Dia.
(b) Cream 6⅜" H. x 3⅛" Dia. body 1865–1880

The Morning Glory pattern was not exclusive to glass. A similar pattern was molded and decorated on European porcelain. In glass, the molds were so finely detailed and thought out that they may have been difficult to keep clean. It may be the reason why cream B has little depth, little detail and is dull. Or it could have been pressed in a worn-out mold that was too expensive to replace. Note the sharp detail of sugar A. From the rim of the circular foot to the uppermost leaves, mold seams were hidden by the pattern. A vine follows each seam downward from the body and across the foot to a leaf that extends onto the thickness of the rim. (The leaves on reproductions usually stop short of the rim.) On nappies, four blossoms about to burst are in deep relief to provide feet for a table rest. Vines, leaves, buds and blossoms are very finely stippled to provide contrast against a smooth background. Although thought was given to designing the finished product, little thought was expended by the glassworker who formed the spout and applied the handle of cream B. They do not line up in any way with the leaves on the foot. Morning Glory pieces command highest prices. Because of cost and rarity, assembling enough tableware for use is out of the question for most pattern glass collectors. *Courtesy, Sandwich Glass Museum, Sandwich Historical Society*

1244 BLOWN MOLDED BEADED GRAPE MEDALLION CASTERS IN FIVE-HOLE STAND

(a) Cruets 6⅝" H. x 2⅛" Dia.

   Pressed Beaded Mirror (Beaded Medallion) stopper 2¾" H. x ⅞" Dia.

   Combined size 8" H. x 2⅛" Dia.

(b) Mustard 5" H. x 2⅛" Dia.

(c) Peppers 6⅜" H. x 2⅛" Dia. 1865–1880

Glass casters can be found in all kinds of pewter and britannia stands and wire frames. The metal holders did not last long under heavy daily use and were replaced from time to time. Mustard covers broke at the hinge, pepper caps split when screwed too tightly onto the thread molded in the rim, the two spouts on the lip of the cruet broke, and matching stoppers mysteriously disappeared under cupboards and food safes. Unless a family had the forethought to purchase twenty or so matching casters and three or four stands, sets were eventually mixed and matched. Finding them that way today is common. This set is one of the best we have had the privilege of photographing. All five Beaded Grape Medallion casters in this revolving stand match in pattern and all were made from a lime-soda formula. All three forms—cruet, mustard and pepper—were blown in molds with three hinged sections. The stopper is a good example of mass production ingenuity; it was pressed in the Beaded Medallion pattern that could be combined with cruets in the three medallion patterns. The pretty wooden mustard spoon has inscribed double rings around the handle. The patina on the handle stops at the point where the spoon is suspended in the cover slot, showing it was with the mustard for a very long time and may be the original one used.

1245 PRESSED TREE OF LIFE FOOTED TUMBLER

5⅝" H. x 3⅛" Dia. 1865–1887

This pattern of branches and twigs is sometimes confused with Overshot (Frosted Ware), a blown product of the Boston and Sandwich Glass Company. As detailed in Chapter 6 of Volume 4, Overshot glass was manufactured by applying tiny particles of glass to the surface. When the particles were adhered before the piece was blown to its full size as shown in photo 4102, smooth areas developed between the rough particles that resemble the branches of pressed Tree of Life. There are three types of pressed Tree of Life, one of which was made at Sandwich. As shown in this photo, Sandwich pieces have a distinct vertical branch or slender trunk that follows the mold seams and therefore hides them. Side branches are also well delineated. If you look for these distinctions, you will not confuse Sandwich Tree of Life with the two types that are similar to each other but not to Sandwich. One version was designed by William Otis Davis for the Portland Glass Company in Portland, Maine. Some Portland pieces carry his name molded as an intricate part of the pattern, which resembles bark of a tree indiscriminately sectioned. A similar pattern was marketed by Hobbs, Brockunier and Company of Wheeling, West Virginia. Their version was sometimes pressed in molds that had wide, rounded ribs like those of a melon.

1246 BLEEDING HEART (FLORAL) SPOON HOLDER

5⅜" H. x 3⅜" Dia. 1870–1887

Bleeding Heart was produced during the waning years of the Boston and Sandwich Glass Company and by glass works on both sides of the Monongahela River into the 1900's. Some was made in Canada. Thirty pieces accurately illustrated were named *Floral Ware* in Pittsburgh's King, Son and Company catalog believed to date from the mid-1870's. Articles from the 1870's made from a lime-soda formula are relatively bright with each delicate Bleeding Heart (dielytra spectabilis) precise in detail as shown by this spoon holder. Later pieces pressed in worn, outdated molds have blossoms with hearts reduced to indistinct ovals. When the Boston and Sandwich Glass Company became defunct on January 1, 1888, their inventory *and molds* were sold to Boston glass and china distributor Jones, McDuffee and Stratton, who advertised their occupation of the Boston and Sandwich Glass Company warehouse on Federal Street "for the exhibition and sale of it" (see page 19 in Volume 4). These molds added to the inventory of later western Pennsylvania and Ohio factories would have been responsible for the gray, dull goblets that, when covered, were sold containing condiments after the turn of the century.

1247 PRESSED BRADFORD BLACKBERRY (BRADFORD GRAPE) GOBLET

6" H. x 3¼" Dia. 1875–1887

According to Ruth Webb Lee in *Victorian Glass* published in 1944, this pattern was named *Bradford Blackberry* by the late Emma Fitts Bradford, who first called it to Lee's attention. Minnie Watson Kamm in *A Fifth Pitcher Book* argued for *Bradford Grape*, so designated by earlier writer S. T. Millard in *Goblets I* published in 1938. The goblet in this photo has ten panels that begin above a swelling at the top of a hexagonal stem. Its form is that of Huber but its quality is not. An undulating vine surrounds the body, from which drops in every other panel a poorly-executed grape bunch or pointed blackberry with stylized drupelets. Five of them alternate with five six-pointed leaves. The two-part mold, off-color lime-soda formula, static design and the stocky form of its matching cream proves manufacture when the pressing of colorless glass was in its declining years.

1248 PRESSED SCALLOPED LINES (SCALLOPED BAND) SPOON HOLDER

5⅜" H. x 3⅜" Dia. 1880–1887

As the Boston and Sandwich Glass Company struggled to stay afloat, what molds were needed were purchased from mold makers such as Anthony Kribs in New York and William J. Wilkinson and Son in Philadelphia. Patterns and forms lost their regional flavor. Unless supplied with strong documentation, a collector cannot remotely attribute a pattern such as Scalloped Lines to a particular area of the United States, let alone a specific factory. According to Albert Christian Revi in his book *American Pressed Glass and Figure Bottles*, John Ernest Miller designing for Sweeney, McCluney and Company of Wheeling, West Virginia, obtained a patent for this pattern on September 12, 1871. Manufacture at the Boston and Sandwich Glass Company and possibly at that site by later companies would have taken place upon expiration of Miller's patent. A wide band around the center has a ribbon of seven scalloped lines facing upward and seven draping downward in shallow relief. The mold was made with very little play between the three side sections and the plunger, so the glass is only ³⁄₃₂" thick at the scallops of the rim. Its matching goblet has the thinnest of stems, just heavy enough to prevent it from snapping. By employing molds that held a minimum of glass, many more items were made from each pot of hot metal, now reduced to the lowest acceptable quality.

1249 PRESSED RIPPLE BOWL ON FOOT

5" H. x 6¼" Dia. 1880–1887

Here is another indistinct pattern documented as a Sandwich product at a time when Pennsylvania, Ohio, West Virginia and Indiana factories were introducing non-flint tableware in vivid color. A ribbon of wavy lines surrounds an otherwise smooth bowl and matching foot. A rope pattern follows a thickened rim that provides the illusion of heaviness. In the 1870's and 1880's, some footed bowls were supplied with a metal cover, each half of which was hinged to open independently. They were marketed as bar bowls for sugar and crackers. A blown molded Punty bar bowl with britannia cover can be seen on page 15 of the Boston and Sandwich Glass Company Catalog from 1874, reprints of which are available.

1250 PRESSED CHRYSANTHEMUM LEAF NAPPIES

(a) Small 1¼" H. x 4" Dia.
(b) Large 3½" H. x 8" Dia. 1875–1887

The origin of this flamboyant pattern is uncertain. The scrolled foliage resembles elements on earlier Lacy patterns. A similar pattern also with chains of beads was produced on Moriage, a type of Japanese pottery and porcelain. The squatty, paneled forms identify them as typical of articles designed toward the end of the Nineteenth Century. Each panel extends to a shallow scallop of the rim. Numerous Chrysanthemum Leaf articles were pressed in clear glass at the Boston and Sandwich Glass Company, and some were gilded to brighten an otherwise heavy, unexciting pattern. It is believed that the molds found their way to Midwest factories after the Boston and Sandwich Glass Company closed. They were filled with an opaque brown glass called *Chocolate glass* from a formula perfected by Jacob Rosenthal shortly after he was employed by the Indiana Tumbler and Goblet Company in Greentown, Indiana, in 1900. This was one year after the Greentown works and eighteen others merged to form the National Glass Company. According to Greentown glass authority James Measell, with whom we corresponded, no fragments of Chocolate Chrysanthemum Leaf were found at the Greentown site. Dr. Measell and his predecessor, Dr. Ruth Herrick, believe it was manufactured at another National Glass Company facility, possibly McKee and Brothers, after Rosenthal's formula was purchased by National in 1902.

1251 PRESSED CHRYSANTHEMUM LEAF BUTTER

5½" H. x 7½" Dia. 1875–1887

Wholesalers and manufacturers may have continued to market tableware pieces individually, but retailers and catalog companies advertised sets. The previously shown Chrysanthemum Leaf large nappie and six small ones became a berry set. The butter was part of a four piece set that included a sugar, cream and spoon holder. Note the change in form of the butter from a nappie with shallow cover to a flat plate with dome cover. The pattern on the cover was still a mirror image, upside down unless it depicted a person, animal or stemmed flower that had direction. There is no pattern on the bottom of the plate. It is beneath the scalloped border. The large ball finial was an improvement over earlier hexagonal and acorn finials that were difficult to grasp. Two Chrysanthemum Leaf vases are shown in photos 3078–3079. A cracker jar can be seen in photo 4187.

1252 PRESSED SHELL DISHES

(a) Large 4¼" H. x 10" L. x 5¾" W.
(b) Small 3⅛" H. x 5" L. x 3" W. 1895–1908

Several attempts to reopen the Boston and Sandwich Glass Company resulted in limited production of inexpensive items made from non-flint formulas that found their way to the retail market. Dishes such as these were called *shell dishes* in glass company catalogs because of form as much as pattern. The opaque white glass with a shiny surface is known as "milk glass", a term we do not find in Nineteenth Century documentation. These dishes were used for grapes, a fruit widely cultivated at homes in eastern Massachusetts. The oval form was made in four sizes from 4" to 10" long. A second form documented as a Sandwich product was 10" square. The shell foot at each end was copied from an earlier reeded claw foot that was applied to blown pieces. It is splayed and terminates in a pronounced ball. The triangular-shaped foot in the center of each side is reinforced by a bracket. The underside of all four rounded feet has a grainy surface, part of which was machined at the factory to level the piece. This factory procedure does not affect value. Matching fragments were dug near the surface, indicating it was made very late in Sandwich glassmaking history.

INVENTORY OF SANDWICH GLASS

No.	Description	Condition	Date Purchased	Amount	Date Sold	Amount

GLOSSARY

ACID CUTBACK Cameo glass, made by treating the surface of cased glass with acid. An acid-resistant design was transferred onto the surface. Acid was applied, which "cut back", or ate through, the unprotected portions of the casing to reveal the glass beneath.

ADVENTURINE See *goldstone*.

AGENCY The office of an agent, or factor.

AGENT One entrusted with the power to negotiate the business of another, usually in a different location.

ANNEAL The gradual reheating and slow cooling of an article in a leer—an oven built for the purpose. This procedure removes any stress that may have built up in the glass during its manufacture.

APPLIED The fastening of a separate piece of glass, such as a base, handle, prunt, or stem, to an article already formed.

APPRENTICE One who was bound by indenture for a specified period to an experienced glassworker or mold maker for the purpose of instruction in the art and skill of creating glassware.

ASHERY A place where potash was made for mixing in a batch of glass.

BARYTES Sulphate of baryta, generally called heavy-spar.

BATCH Mixture of sand, cullet, and various raw materials that are placed in the pot to be heated into metal, or molten glass.

BLANK A finished piece of glass requiring additional work, such as decorating or engraving.

BLOWN GLASS Glass made by the use of a blowpipe and air pressure sufficient to give it form.

BLOWN MOLDED GLASS Glass made by blowing hot glass into a plain or patterned mold, and forcing it with air pressure to conform to the shape of the mold.

BOX A container of any shape and any size (e.g., it could be square, rectangular, circular or oval).

BUTTON STEM A connector between the base and the body of any article, with a button-shaped extrusion in its center.

CANE In *paperweight making*, a bundle of various colored glass rods that are arranged into a design, fused by reheating, pulled until it is long and thin, cooled and then cut into segments.

CASING A different colored layer of glass, either on the inside or outside of the main body of a blown piece, which adhered to the piece at the time it was blown.

CASTOR PLACE The location in the furnace room where large goods were blown, such as apothecary show globes, lamp shades and decanters. The size of such items necessitated that the glassworkers used as a glory hole an empty furnace pot with a widened mouth.

CAVE Ash pit under the furnace.

CAVE METAL Hot glass that flowed into the cave from a broken pot.

CHAIR A term used interchangeably with *shop*. Quoting Deming Jarves in a July 2, 1827, letter to William Stutson, "Do you think it advisable to form another chair for making small articles?"

CLAW FOOT An applied reeded foot resembling a scallop shell.

CLUSTER On *cut glass*, a grouping of similar designs in close proximity.

COMPOTE An assortment of fruit stewed in syrup. In the late 1800's, a long-stemmed, shallow dish, also known as a *comport*, in which to serve compote or fresh fruit, nuts and candies. Both terms superseded *nappie on foot*.

CRAQUELLE Glass that has been deliberately fractured after it has been formed, and reheated to seal the fractures, leaving the scars as a permanent design.

CROSSCUT DIAMOND On *cut glass*, a diamond that is divided into quarters.

CULLET Glass made in the factory and saved from a pot to be used in making future batches. Waste glass trimmed from rims and spouts was dropped into a cullet box. Also, glass items already annealed, either produced in the factory or purchased, and broken to be included in future batches.

CUTTING The grinding away of a portion of the surface of a blank, using wheels and wet sand to produce a design.

DARTER The boy who throws, or darts, dried sticks of wood into the furnace or annealing leer. The sticks were split into 1″ diameter width from 3½′ lengths of pine and oak cordwood.

DECORATING The ornamenting of a blank by painting or

staining it with a non-glass substance.

DESIGN The ornamentation of glass after it has been annealed, by cutting, engraving, etching or decorating.

DIAMOND SQUARES A pattern of perfect squares with equal sides and 90 degree corners set at a 45 degree angle.

DIP MOLD A shallow mold into which a blown gather of glass was dipped to form items such as nappies and dishes.

DONUT On *Trevaise*, the wafer-size glob of glass applied to the base. In most cases, the center of the wafer is dished out, leaving the shape of a donut.

ELECTRIC INCANDESCENT LAMP Original term for the item now called a *light bulb*. The first electric lamps were globe-shaped.

ENAMEL Colored glass made with lead. Most often, the term referred to opaque white glass. However, Deming Jarves noted in an 1867 memo, "Enamelled Glass deep color", meaning that the items listed should be made in color from glass containing lead.

ENGRAVING The process of cutting shallow designs and letters into a blank using a lathe with copper wheels and an abrasive.

ETCHING An inexpensive method of producing a design by using hydrofluoric acid to eat into the surface of a blank.

EXTINGUISHER A cone which, when placed on a burning lamp or candlestick, extinguishes the flame.

FACTOR An agent.

FILIGREE ROD A rod that has spiral or straight threads running through it. Also called *latticinio*.

FINIAL The decorative, terminal part of a newel post, writing pen, etc. The part of a cover used as a handle.

FIRE POLISHING Reheating a finished piece to remove marks left by tools or molds, leaving the article with a smooth surface.

FITTER The lower rim of a globe, shade or chimney that fits onto a metal ring or burner.

FLASHED A method developed during the 1880's of coating pressed and blown molded glass with a layer of colored glass after it was removed from the mold. The *flashed* layer was made from a formula that melted at a much lower temperature than the originally molded piece, so the original piece did not warp. On *cut glass*, a fan-like design located between the points of a fan, hobstar, or star.

FLINT A variety of quartz composed of silica with traces of iron. It is very hard, and strikes fire with steel.

FLINT GLASS Originally made from pulverized flints, it later became glass made from a batch containing lead. The term *flint* continued to be used, however. In the 1800's, it became the factory term for clear glass.

FLOATED In *decorated opal glass*, the method used to apply a solid color background.

FLUTE The hand-crimping of a rim. On *pressed* or *cut glass*, a panel rounded at the top.

FLY The shattering of an article due to uneven cooling in the annealing leer, particularly a problem with cased or flashed glass with layers that expand and contract at different temperatures.

FOLDED RIM A rim on either the body or base of a piece, the edge of which is doubled back onto itself, resulting in greater strength.

FRAGMENTS Broken pieces of finished glass, discarded at the time of production.

FREE-BLOWN GLASS Glass made by blowing hot glass and shaping it into its final form by the use of hand tools.

GAFFER In a group of glassworkers, called a *shop*, the most skilled artisan; the master glass blower.

GASOMETER The place where gas was generated for lighting.

GATHER The mass of hot metal that has been gathered on the end of a blowpipe.

GATHERER The assistant to the master glass blower, who gathers the hot metal on the end of the blowpipe.

GAUFFER To crimp or flute.

GILDING The application of gold for decorative purposes.

GLASS GALL Impurities skimmed from the surface of melted glass. Also called *sandever*, *sandiver*.

GLORY HOLE A small furnace into which a partly-finished article was inserted for reheating or fire polishing.

GOLDSTONE Glass combined with copper filings.

GREEN GLASS Glass in its natural color, generally used for bottles.

HOBSTAR On *cut glass*, a many-pointed geometrically cut star.

INDENTURE A contract binding an apprentice to his master.

KNOP A round knob, either hollow or solid, in the center of a stem.

LAMP CAPPER The worker who fits a lamp cap, or burner and its accompanying cork or metal collar, to a particular lamp font.

LAMPWORK The making and assembly of leaves, petals, stems, fruit and other small parts from rods of glass that have been softened by heating them over a gas burner. Originally, oil lamps produced the open flame.

LAPIDARY STOPPER A cut, faceted stopper.

LATTICINIO A rod of glass or a paperweight background composed of threads arranged in lattice, spiral or swirl configurations. The threads are usually white. Also, an article of glass made by arranging differently colored rods in a circular configuration and fusing them to a blown gather. The gather is then manipulated into the desired form, such as a creamer or lamp font.

LEER A tunnel-shaped oven through which glass articles are drawn after formation for the purpose of annealing. Also spelled *lear*, *lehr*.

LIGHTING DEVICE Any wooden, metal or glass primitive or sophisticated contrivance that emits light.

LIME Oxide of calcium; the white, caustic substance obtained from limestone and shells by heat. The heat expells carbonic acid, leaving behind the lime. Documentation shows the Cape Cod Glass Company and other glass factories obtained their lime from oyster shells.

LIME-SODA GLASS Glass made from non-lead formulas that include lime and bicarbonate of soda.

MAKE-DO A damaged item that has been repaired to "make it do" what was originally intended.

MANTLE A chemically treated tube of fabric that produces an incandescent glow when suspended over the flame of a gas burner.

MARBRIE In *blown glass*, a loop design made by looping and trailing threads of glass through another color, such as in paperweights and witch balls.

MARVER Iron plate on which hot glass is first shaped by rolling, in preparation for blowing into its final form.

MERESE A wafer-shaped piece of hot glass, used to connect individual units to make a complete piece, such as the base and socket of a candlestick or the bowl and standard of a footed nappie.

METAL Glass either in a molten condition in the pot, or in a cold, hardened state.

MOLD A form into which glass is blown or pressed to give it shape and pattern. Also spelled *mould*.

MOLD MARKS On glass that has been blown or pressed into a mold, the marks or seam lines left by the edges of the units of the mold.

MOVE A period of time during which a shop makes glass continuously. A glass blower is expected to make ten *moves* each week.

NAPPIE A shallow bowl of any size, whether round bottomed or flat bottomed, which can be on a standard. Also spelled *nappy*.

NEEDLE ETCHING Done by coating a blank with an acid-resisting substance, then inscribing a design into the resist with a sharp needle. The blank is then dipped into hydro-fluoric acid, which etches the glass where the design was inscribed.

NIB The writing point of a pen.

OVERFILL On pieces that have been blown or pressed into a mold, the excess hot glass that seeps into the seams of the mold, sometimes creating fins.

PANEL A section with raised margins and square corners.

PATTERN (ON GLASS) The specific ornamentation into which *hot glass* is formed.

PATTERN (WOODEN) Wooden model carved in detail that is sent to the foundry, used as a guide to shape a mold.

PEG On a *lamp*, the unit that holds the oil and is attached to the base with a metal connector.

PICKWICK A pointed instrument used for raising, or "picking", the wick of a whale oil lamp.

PILLAR-MOLDED GLASS Glass made by first blowing a hot gather of glass into a mold with vertical ridges (pillars). A second cooler gather is blown into the first. The hot outer layer conforms to the shape of the mold, while the cooler inner layer remains smooth.

PINWHEEL On *cut glass*, a design resembling a hobstar in motion, its points angled in a clockwise or counter-clockwise position.

PLINTH A square block forming the base for a standard. Also, a base and standard molded in one piece, used as the lower unit of a lamp.

PONTIL MARK Rough spot caused by breaking away the pontil rod or spider pontil.

PONTIL ROD A rod of iron used by glassworkers to take glass from a pot or hold an article while it is being formed. Also called *punt*.

POT A one-piece container in which glass is melted, usually made of clay and able to withstand extreme heat.

POT STONE A gray-white stone deposited in the molten glass at the time of production, according to a Professor Barff, who analyzed pot stones and reported his findings in April 1876. Alumina, an oxide of aluminum present in the clay from which the pot was made, separated from the inner wall of the pot and combined with elements in the glass and solidified.

PRESSED GLASS Glass made by placing hot glass into a mold and forcing it with a plunger to conform to the shape of the mold.

PRISM A pattern or design of deep parallel V-grooves that reflect the light.

PROCELLO An iron spring tool resembling tongs used to expand and contract glass into its final form. Also called *pucella*.

PRUNT A blob of glass applied to the surface of a vessel, for the purpose of decorating or hiding a defect.

PUNT See *pontil rod*.

PUNTIER A glass cutter who dishes out concave circles, sometimes as part of a design and usually to remove the rough mark left by the pontil rod.

PUNTING The process of dishing out a circle with a cutting wheel, usually to remove the mark left by the pontil rod.

PUNTY A concave circle made by dishing out the glass with a cutting wheel.

QUILTING In *art glass*, an all-over diamond design, permanently molded into the piece as it was being blown.

RIBBON ROD A rod that has twisted flat ribbons of glass running through it.

RIGAREE A heavy thread of glass applied to the surface of a piece, giving a decorative rippled or fluted effect.

ROD A straight shaft of glass that will be reheated to form other things. Thin rods are fused together to make canes, and are also softened to supply glass for lampwork. Thick rods are formed into arms for epergne units. Reeded rods are used to form handles and claw feet on Late Blown Ware, as well as nibs for glass writing pens.

SAFE According to Webster's 1847 *An American Dictionary of the English Language*, "a chest or closet for securing provisions from noxious animals". Erroneously called a "pie safe", it was the forerunner of the ice box.

SERVITOR The first assistant to the gaffer in a group of glassworkers called a *shop*.

SHEDDING The flaking of the surface of finished glass, sometimes caused by minute particles of fire clay in the sand. Too much alkali in the glass and moisture in the air drawing out the soda are also contributing factors.

SHELL FOOT See *claw foot*.

SHOP A group of workmen producing glass at the furnace, consisting of a master glass blower and his help.

SICK GLASS Discoloration of the surface of an article.

SILVER NITRATE A stain prepared by dissolving silver in nitric acid. It turns amber in color when brushed onto annealed glass and fired in a decorating kiln.

SLOAR BOOK The book in which an accounting was kept of the output of glass produced by each shop at the furnace.

SLOAR MAN The employee who entered the output of each shop in the sloar book.

SNUFF The part of a wick that has been charred by the flame.

SNUFFER A scissors-like instrument for trimming and catching the charred part of a wick.

SOCKET EXTENSION On a *candlestick*, the section between the socket and the wafer, molded in one piece with the socket.

SPIDER PONTIL An iron unit placed on the end of the pontil rod, consisting of several finger-like rods. The fingers gave support to items that could not be held by a single rod in the center.

STAINED GLASS A finished piece of clear glass that is colored wholly or in part by the application of a chemical dye—most commonly ruby. The article is refired, making the dye a permanent finish.

STICKER-UP BOY The boy who carries hot glass on a V-shaped stick in a group of glassworkers called a *shop*.

STOPPERER The glass cutter who sizes, roughs and polishes the plug of a stopper to fit the neck of a particular object. Also called *stopper fitter*.

STRAWBERRY DIAMOND On *pressed* and *cut glass*, a diamond which is crosshatched. Also the name of a pressed pattern and a cut glass design that utilize crosscut diamonds.

TAKER-IN BOY The boy who carries the hot finished product to the leer in a group of glassworkers called a *shop*. During slow periods, he assists in the removal of glass from the cold end of the leer.

TALE Articles sold by count rather than by weight. In the words of Deming Jarves, "Tale was derived from the mode of selling, the best glass being sold only by weight, while light articles were sold tale."

UNDERFILL An insufficient amount of glass blown or pressed into a mold, resulting in an incomplete product. This is a characteristic, not a defect.

VESICA On *cut glass*, a pointed oval.

WAFER A flattened piece of hot glass, sometimes called a merese, used to join separately made units into a complete piece, such as the base and socket of a candlestick or the bowl and standard of a footed nappie.

WELTED RIM See *folded rim*.

WHIMSEY Unusual, one-of-a-kind item made of glass by a worker in his spare time.

WHITE GLASS Transparent, colorless flint glass.

CONTINUATIONS

DILLAWAY PATENT 17,960

UNITED STATES PATENT OFFICE.

HIRAM DILLAWAY, OF SANDWICH, MASSACHUSETTS.

GLASSWARE-HOLDER.

Specification of Letters Patent No. 17,960, dated August 11, 1857.

To all whom it may concern:

Be it known that I, HIRAM DILLAWAY, of Sandwich, in the county of Barnstable and State of Massachusetts, have invented a new and Improved Holder for Holding Glassware While Being Manufactured; and I do hereby declare that the following is a full, clear, and exact description of the same, reference being had to the accompanying drawings, forming part of this specification, in which —

Figure 1 is a side view of one of my improved holders, adapted for the holding of a decanter or such like article. Fig. 2 is a side view of the same, partly in section, with a different yoke adapted to the holding of a square parallel-sided bottle. Fig. 3 is a side view of the same, with another yoke adapted to the holding of a goblet. This view illustrates the manner of admitting and liberating the article. Fig. 4 is a front view of the yoke shown in Fig. 1. Fig. 5 is a front view of the yoke shown in Fig. 2.

Similar letters of reference indicate corresponding parts in the several figures.

This invention consists in a holder for holding bottles, all shank ware, lamps, bowls, and other glass articles during the manipulations that are necessary in their manufacture, which may be termed the "yoke-holder," and is more simple in its construction, more capable of universal application, lighter and consequently more easily handled, more easily kept in repair, and less liable to break ware than the tools heretofore used.

To enable other skilled in the art to make and use my invention, I will proceed to describe its construction and operation.

A, is a handle consisting of a straight rod of iron, having riveted or otherwise firmly secured to one end a flat or concave plate of iron B standing perpendicular to it, said plate being preferably of circular form and having on opposite sides two lugs in which there are holes *a, a,* (Fig. 2) through which pass freely two rods *b, b,* which constitute portions of a yoke C, D, *b, b.* The lower or back piece C of the yoke, which is fitted to slide as a guide on the rod A, is simply of the form of a cross-head, and has the rods *b, b,* permanently attached to it. The upper or front portion D of the yoke piece, whose duty is to clamp the article to be operated upon against the plate B, which may be termed the supporting plate, is secured by nuts *c, c,* against shoulders on the side rods *b, b,* so as to be capable of being readily removed, and replaced by another, two or more of these yoke-pieces being generally provided for each holder. The external form of the several yoke-pieces D may be like that of the supporting plate B. Those which are intended for holding round articles, such as the decanter shown in Fig. 1, or the shank of the goblet shown in Fig. 3, in red outline, are made with a round hole *e,* in the center, as shown in Fig. 4, and a slot *f,* on one side the neck or shank or other small part of the article, and with the inner margin of the hole chamfered to such a form as will enable it to fit without indenting itself into an article of rounded form; but those yoke-pieces which are made for parallel-sided articles, such as the square bottle shown in red outline in Fig. 2, are made with a round taper hole to receive a lining die *g, g,* (see Figs. 2 and 5) which is divided centrally into two or more parts which are formed internally to fit the article to be held, and externally to fit the taper hole in the yoke piece, the largest side of which hole is next the plate B, as shown in Fig. 2. A strong spiral spring E, is coiled around the rod or handle A, between the yoke and the plate B, to draw the yoke-piece D, toward the plate B, to clamp the article; and a nut *h,* fitted to a screw thread on that part of the exterior of the rod A, near the plate B, to serve as a bearing for the spring, serves also to adjust the yoke to clamp the articles of different height, depth, or thickness.

To enable any article to be inserted in the holder, the handle is taken in the hand, and the part C, of the yoke pulled against a stand H, I, such as is represented in Fig. 3, or against what is known among glassworkers as the "chair-arm," which moves the yoke-piece D, away from the supporting plate B, and thus allows the article—if of a swelling shape with a neck or shank—to be inserted laterally through the slot *f,* or if of a parallel-sided form to be inserted directly into the die *g, g;* and on the pull being slackened, the yoke piece D is brought by the spring either upon the article itself or upon the tapering exterior of the holding die *g, g;* in either case, clamping the article firmly so that it may be submitted to pulling or pressing endwise in the manufacture. One yoke-piece like those shown

---

2   17,960

in Figs. 1, 3, and 4, will serve for many articles of different form; but generally when a clamping die *g, g,* is used, a separate die will be required for every article of different form, though the yoke-piece need not be changed with the die, as several dies may be fitted to the same yoke-piece. The dies *g, g,* are caused to clamp the article laterally with great firmness, by the pulling of the yoke-piece over their conical exterior; and the harder the article held by the said dies is pulled, the harder they will grip it. The article is liberated again by pulling the part C, of the yoke against the stand I, or chair arm. This holder never fails to hold the articles exactly in the center, which is of great advantage, and it will adapt itself readily to variations in the size of the articles, and in short, it has nothing of the positive unaccommodating character of tools heretofore used.

What I claim as my invention and desire to secure by Letters Patent is:

An instrument composed of a handle, a supporting plate, a yoke, and a spring, combined to operate substantially as herein described, for the purpose set forth, whether the yoke be provided or not with an internal holding die *g, g,* as herein specified.

HIRAM DILLAWAY.

Witnesses:
CHARLES SOUTHACK,
GEO. L. FESSENDEN.

DILLAWAY PATENT 79,737

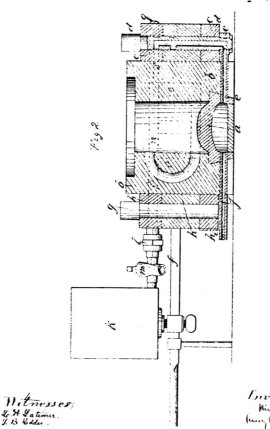

2 Sheets. Sheet 2.

H. Dillaway,
Glass Mold.

Nº 79,737.   Patented July 7, 1868.

Fig. 2

Witnesses:
L. H. Latimer.
J. B. Elder.

Inventor:
Hiram Dillaway
Allys

DILLAWAY PATENT 79,737

United States Patent Office.

HIRAM DILLAWAY, OF SANDWICH, MASSACHUSETTS.

Letters Patent No. 79,737, dated July 7, 1868.

IMPROVED GLASSWARE-MOULDS.

The Schedule referred to in these Letters Patent and making part of the same.

TO ALL WHOM IT MAY CONCERN:

Be it known that I, HIRAM DILLAWAY, of Sandwich, in the county of Barnstable, and State of Massachusetts, have invented an Improvement in Glassware-Moulds; and I do hereby declare that the following, taken in connection with the drawings which accompany and form part of this specification, is a description of my invention sufficient to enable those skilled in the art to practise it.

This invention has special reference to means of supplying water to the bodies of such glassware-moulds as open in sections or parts to deliver the ware moulded therein.

Figure 1 of the drawing shows, in plan, a sectional mould-body, supplied with means for cooling each section of the body, in accordance with my invention, and

Figure 2 is a sectional elevation of the same.

In an application for United States Letters Patent made by me, of even date herewith, I have set forth, as my invention, the combination, with the body of a glassware-mould, of a water-reservoir, so arranged as to be moved with the mould-body, so as to keep up a supply of water from the reservoir to the body, without making and breaking the connection at each impression received in the mould.

Said invention is the foundation on which my improvements herein described are based, they consisting in such an arrangement and combination of parts as enables me, through a connection formed by the hinges on which the sections move, to supply them all, or more than one of them, from one reservoir, if desired.

And my invention also consists in the combination, with separate sections of a sectional glassware-mould, of separate water-reservoirs.

The sectional mould-body shown in the drawings is one for making plain-handled mugs, the body being made in three parts or sections, a bottom section, a, and two side sections, b c. The side sections are hinged upon a hinge-pin, d, and embrace the bottom section, as shown, the bottom section being made hollow, in any convenient way, and connected by a pipe, e, to the hinge-pin d, which the end of said pipe encompasses, as shown in fig. 2. Each side section is provided with a handle-tang, f, by which the mould is opened and closed, there being the locking-pin g and locking-ears h, usual in moulds for holding the parts together.

On each section of the mould is a hook-piece, i, which acts on the pipe j, to keep the bottom a of the mould in a central position relative to the side sections b c, when they are fully opened; the pipe j also serving to allow such steam to escape as may be formed in the water-space made in the bottom, a.

On each or either tag f is fixed a water-reservoir, k, preferably so as to be removable, if desired, there being a coupling-joint, l, in the water-conveying pipe, which pipe is provided with a stop-cock, m, designed to regulate the flow of water from the reservoir k to the side sections of the mould.

The water-passages in the side sections are formed by drilling upper and lower horizontal holes in the direction most clearly shown in fig. 1, said holes being marked n, and by vertical holes connecting the horizontal holes, the vertical holes being marked o, all the holes being stopped with plugs at the places where the drill entered.

The water-pipe from either reservoir connects with a hole, marked p, communicating with the water-passages formed in the sections c b, there being an escape-pipe, q, for egress of steam or hot water from each side section.

To supply water to the bottom, a, from either reservoir f, or to supply both the bottom, a, and both side sections from one reservoir, the hinge-pin is made to perform the functions of a water-conveyer, and is bored vertically in its axial line, as seen in fig. 2, the bore being stopped or plugged at each end.

In the side sections are drilled passages, (see fig. 1,) marked s, which communicate with grooves or scores turned around the hinge-pin, at the places where the passages s emerge into the hinge-pin hole, and in the hinge-pin, at the scores, lateral holes are drilled, which communicate with the vertical bore of said pin.

It will be seen that, with but one reservoir, water can be supplied to both sections b c, in which case it will be advisable to stop the vent q of the section bearing the reservoir, thus causing a flow through the entire circuit from the reservoir to the open vent.

2

79.737

At the lower part of the hinge-pin, and opposite the pipe e, a score is turned in the hinge-pin, so that communication is always had from the vertical bore of said pin with the pipe e, by means of a short lateral bore from said groove into the vertical bore of the hinge-pin; and it will be seen that the bottom, a, can be supplied with water from either or both reservoirs, and that, if both of the vents q are stopped, vent will be found through pipe j, thus keeping a circulation of water throughout all the sections of the body of the mould, from a reservoir or reservoirs which are mounted on the body, and always move with it, so that the water-connection is not made and broken at each impression taken.

I claim a sectional glassware-mould body, when constructed with a hollow hinge-pin, so that water can flow from one section to another through said pin, substantially as described.

Also, in combination with the bottom and side sections of a mould-body, the hooks i, arranged to operate substantially as described.

HIRAM DILLAWAY.

Witnesses:
LUTHER DRAKE,
JAMES D. LLOYD.

TURPIE PATENT 75,604

United States Patent Office.

DAVID TURPIE, OF SANDWICH, MASSACHUSETTS, ASSIGNOR TO "BOSTON AND SANDWICH GLASS COMPANY."

Letters Patent No. 75,604, dated March 17, 1868.

IMPROVEMENT IN GLASS-MOULDS.

The Schedule referred to in these Letters Patent and making part of the same.

TO ALL WHOM IT MAY CONCERN:

Be it known that I, DAVID TURPIE, of Sandwich, in the county of Barnstable, and State of Massachusetts, have invented an Improvement in Moulds for Forming Glassware with Handles; and I do hereby declare that the following, taken in connection with the drawings which accompany and form part of this specification, is a description of my invention sufficient to enable those skilled in the art to practise it.

Moulded articles of glassware having handles have heretofore shown on the outer surface from rim to base at least two vertical seams, occasioned by vertical joints in the moulds, at the parts where the casing separates to discharge or free the moulded handle, and the object of my invention is to mould articles of glassware with handles, (like beer-mugs for example,) without seams continuing them from the top or rim to the base of the glass.

In moulding or pressing handled mugs, &c., the mould has heretofore been composed of the following principal parts—a base, an outer vertical shell, in two or more parts, having in one joint thereof the part of the mould in which the handle is formed, a plunger, and a top-piece, which forms the rim of the glass, and guides the plunger.

Now, my invention consists in adding to said parts a hollow slotted cylinder, and certain pieces which are attached to the outer shell, and extend into the slot in the hollow cylinder, and nearly through it.

In the old arrangement, the outer vertical shell formed the outer surface of the glassware, as well as the whole of the handle. In my arrangement, a part only of the handle is formed in the outer vertical shell, and all of the outer upright surface of the body of the glass being formed by the inner surface of the slotted cylinder. Of the drawings which represent a glass-mould, embodying my invention—

Figure 1 is a vertical central section, taken in the plane of line s s, seen in

Figure 2, which is a plan of the mould with the top-piece and plunger removed.

Figure 3 is a horizontal section of a part of the mould, taken on the line y y seen in fig. 1.

a denotes the plunger, which forms the cavity or interior of the moulded article b. c is the top-piece, which guides the plunger and forms the top edge of b. d is the outer vertical shell, which is made in halves, and is hinged and held together by a pin and ears in the usual manner. e is the base, which is locked in the outer case in the usual manner. f is the slotted cylinder, which forms the outer part of the body of b, and a portion of the handle, the bore of f being somewhat taper, so that said cylinder can be lifted off from the glass with ease, by means of the handles g, which are let into slots formed in d, and by which the relative position of the slot in f is determined with regard to so much of the handle-mould as is formed in d. On each side of the joint in d, on the side of the pin h, are secured pieces i and j, said pieces entering and filling a portion of the slot in f, and the vertical joint of the outer case continuing through the vertical central plane of said pieces. The piece i forms the part of the surface of the mould which makes the inside of the handle, and the piece j forms a part which makes a portion of the lower outer surface of the handle, and the inner surfaces of the pieces i and j are made so as to form flat surfaces or faces, or a kind of panel on the surface of the body of b, within and beneath the handle.

Now, when the outer part, d, of the mould is closed upon the base-piece e, and is secured by the pin h, the slotted cylinder f is pushed into its place, the slot therein sliding down over the pieces i and j, and the handles g entering the slots in the casing d; then the top, c, is applied, and the plunger a is forced, by the action of a press, down upon the molten glass, which has been previously deposited in the mould. The action of the plunger displaces the molten glass, causing it to fill all the vacant space in the mould, pressing into the channel which forms the handle. The plunger being then withdrawn, the top-piece is removed, and the slotted cylinder f is lifted out of the mould off from the glass, and the pin h being withdrawn, the two parts of the outer casing d are swung open, and the moulded glass is left standing on the base, e, from which it is then lifted off.

It will be seen that by the described construction of the mould, but one seam or joint line is shown on the article, said seam extending along the centre of the handle to the base of the mug, but not from the top of the handle to the top of the mug. Of course the inner surface of the slotted cylinder f may be formed so as to mould fluted as well as plain ware.

I claim a glass-mould, constructed and arranged to operate substantially as and for the purpose described.

DAVID TURPIE.

Witnesses:
GEO. P. DREW,
O. H. BURGESS.

BIBLIOGRAPHY

UNPUBLISHED SOURCES

Account book of various activities of the Boston and Sandwich Glass Company, such as the company store, sea-going vessels, wages, and wood for construction and fuel. April 17, 1826, to July 1830. Ms. collection in the Tannahill Research Library, Henry Ford Museum, Edison Institute, Dearborn, Michigan.

Barbour, Harriot Buxton. *Sandwich The Town That Glass Built*. Ms. and related correspondence in the Boston University Library, Boston, Massachusetts.

Burbank, George E. *History of the Sandwich Glass Works*. Ms. in the Barlow collection.

Corporate records. Office of the Secretary of State, The Commonwealth of Massachusetts, Boston, Massachusetts.

Correspondence pertaining to the management of the Boston and Sandwich Glass Company and the Cape Cod Glass Company, such as glass formulas, letters, special notices and transfers. Ms. collection in the Tannahill Research Library, Henry Ford Museum, Edison Institute, Dearborn, Michigan.

Correspondence pertaining to the management of the Boston and Sandwich Glass Company, the Boston and Sandwich Glass Company II and the Cape Cod Glass Company, such as glass formulas, letters, statements, etc. Ms. collection in the Rakow Library, The Corning Museum of Glass, Corning, New York.

Correspondence pertaining to the management of the New England Glass Company, such as invoices and bills of lading to William E. Mayhew and Company. Ms. collection in the Maryland Historical Society, Baltimore, Maryland.

Correspondence to and from glass authorities and writers on the subject of glass, pertaining to the excavation of the Boston and Sandwich Glass Company site and the discussion of fragments. Ms. consisting of the Francis (Bill) Wynn papers, now in the Barlow collection.

Dillaway family documents, such as genealogy. Ms. in the private collections of Dillaway family descendants.

Documentation in the form of fragments dug from factory and cutting shop sites. Private collections and the extensive Barlow collection, which includes the former Francis (Bill) Wynn collection.

Documentation of Sandwich glass items and Sandwich glass-workers, such as hand-written notebooks, letters, billheads, contracts, pictures, and oral history of Sandwich families recorded on tape by descendants. Ms. in the Barlow collection, Kaiser collection and private collections.

Documents pertaining to the genealogy of the family of Deming Jarves, including church records. Ms. in the care of City Registrar, City of Boston Vital Records, Boston, Massachusetts. Ms. in the Massachusetts State Archives, Boston, Massachusetts. Ms. in Sandwich Vital Records, Sandwich, Massachusetts. Ms. in the Genealogy Room, Sturgis Library, Barnstable, Massachusetts. Ms. at Mount Auburn Cemetery, Cambridge, Massachusetts.

Documents pertaining to the genealogy of the family of William Stutson, including church records. Ms. in the care of City Registrar, City of Boston Vital Records, Boston, Massachusetts. Ms. in the Massachusetts State Archives, Boston, Massachusetts. Ms. in Sandwich Vital Records, Sandwich, Massachusetts. Ms. in the Genealogy Room, Flower Memorial Library, Watertown, New York.

Documents pertaining to the Sandwich glass industry, such as letters, invoices, statements, photographs, family papers and original factory catalogs. Ms. collection in the care of the Sandwich Glass Museum, Sandwich Historical Society, Sandwich, Massachusetts.

Documents pertaining to the Sandwich glass industry and other related industries, such as statistics from Sandwich Vital Records, information from property tax records, maps, photographs, family papers and genealogy. Ms. in the care of the Town of Sandwich Massachusetts Archives and Historical Center, Sandwich, Massachusetts.

Documents pertaining to the Cheshire, Massachusetts, glass sand industry, such as statistics from vital records, information from property tax records, maps and genealogy. Ms. in the care of the Town of Cheshire, Massachusetts, and the Town of Lanesborough, Massachusetts.

Documents relating to the Cheshire, Massachusetts, glass sand industry, such as original manuscripts and newspaper articles. Ms. in the care of the Cheshire Public Library, Cheshire, Massachusetts, and the Berkshire Athenaeum, Pittsfield,

Massachusetts.

Documents relating to the North Sandwich industrial area, such as photographs, account books and handwritten scrapbooks. Ms. in the private collection of Mrs. Edward "Ned" Nickerson and the Bourne Historical Society, Bourne, Massachusetts.

Documents relating to the Sandwich Co-operative Glass Company, such as account books, correspondence and glass formulas. Ms. in the private collection of Murray family descendants.

Glass formula book. "Sandwich Aug. 7, 1868, James D. Lloyd." Ms. collection in the Tannahill Research Library, Henry Ford Museum, Edison Institute, Dearborn, Michigan.

Hubbard, Howard G. *A Complete Check List of Household Lights Patented in the United States 1792–1862.* South Hadley, Massachusetts: 1935.

Irwin, Frederick T. *The Story of Sandwich Glass.* Ms. and related documents in the Barlow collection.

Kern family documents, such as pictures and genealogy. Ms. in the private collections of Kern family descendants.

Lapham family documents, such as pictures and genealogy. Ms. in the private collections of Lapham family descendants.

Lloyd family documents, such as genealogy. Ms. in the private collections of Lloyd family descendants.

Lutz family documents, such as pictures, handwritten biographies and genealogy. Ms. in the private collections of Lutz family descendants.

Mary Gregory documents, such as diaries, letters and pictures. Ms. in the Barlow collection, Kaiser collection, other private collections, and included in the private papers of her family.

Minutes of annual meetings, Board of Directors meetings, special meetings and stockholders meetings of the Boston and Sandwich Glass Company. Ms. collection in the Tannahill Research Library, Henry Ford Museum, Edison Institute, Dearborn, Michigan.

Minutes of meetings of the American Flint Glass Workers Union, Local No. 16. Ms. in the Sandwich Glass Museum, Sandwich Historical Society, Sandwich, Massachusetts.

Nye family documents relating to the North Sandwich industrial area and the Electrical Glass Corporation. Ms. in the Barlow-Kaiser collection.

Oral history recorded on tape. Tales of Cape Cod, Inc. collection in the Cape Cod Community College Library, Hyannis, Massachusetts.

Patents relating to the invention of new techniques in glassmaking, improved equipment for glassmaking, new designs and styles of glass, and the invention of other items relating to the glass industry. United States Department of Commerce, Patent and Trademark Office, Washington, District of Columbia.

Population Schedule of the Census of the United States. Ms. from National Archives Microfilm Publications, National Archives and Records Service, Washington, District of Columbia.

Property deeds and other proofs of ownership, such as surveys, mortgage deeds, and last will and testaments. Ms. in the Barnstable County Registry of Deeds and Barnstable County Registry of Probate, Barnstable, Massachusetts.

Property deeds and other proofs of ownership relating to the Cheshire, Massachusetts, glass sand industry, such as maps. Ms. in the Berkshire County Registry of Deeds, North District, North Adams, Massachusetts.

Property deeds and other proofs of ownership, such as contracts, mortgage deeds and last will and testaments relating to the Jarves family. Ms. in the Barnstable County Registry of Deeds and Barnstable County Registry of Probate, Barnstable, Massachusetts. Ms. in the Suffolk County Registry of Deeds and Suffolk County Registry of Probate, Boston, Massachusetts. Ms. in the Middlesex County Registry of Deeds, Cambridge, Massachusetts. Ms. in the Essex County Registry of Deeds, South District, Salem, Massachusetts. Ms. in the Plymouth County Registry of Deeds, Plymouth, Massachusetts. Ms. in the Berkshire County Registry of Deeds, North District, North Adams, Massachusetts.

Property deeds and other proofs of ownership, such as mortgage deeds and last will and testaments relating to the Stutson family. Ms. in the Barnstable County Registry of Deeds and Barnstable County Registry of Probate, Barnstable, Massachusetts. Ms. in the Suffolk County Registry of Deeds and Suffolk County Registry of Probate, Boston, Massachusetts. Ms. in the care of City Clerk, Jefferson County Clerk's Office, Watertown, New York. Ms. in the care of Hounsfield Town Clerk, Sackets Harbor, New York. Ms. in the care of Sackets Harbor Village Clerk, Sackets Harbor, New York.

Sloar books, a weekly accounting of glass produced at the Sandwich Glass Manufactory and the Boston and Sandwich Glass Company, and the workers who produced it. July 9, 1825, to March 29, 1828. Ms. collection in the Tannahill Research Library, Henry Ford Museum, Edison Institute, Dearborn, Michigan. May 31, 1887, to December 26, 1887. Ms. in the care of the Town of Sandwich Massachusetts Archives and Historical Center, Sandwich, Massachusetts.

Spurr family documents, such as pictures, handwritten autobiographies, glass formulas and genealogy. Ms. in the private collections of Spurr family descendants.

Vessel documentation records. Ms. in the National Archives and Records Service, Washington, District of Columbia.

Vodon family documents, such as pictures and genealogy. Ms. in the private collection of Vodon family descendants.

Waterman, Charles Cotesworth Pinckney. Notes on the Boston and Sandwich Glass Company, dated November 1876, and deposited in the Sandwich Centennial Box. Ms. in the care of the Town of Sandwich Massachusetts Archives and Historical Center, Sandwich, Massachusetts.

Wright, David F. *The Stetson Family in the Boston and Sandwich Glass Company.* Ms. in the care of the Town of Sandwich Massachusetts Archives and Historical Center, Sandwich, Massachusetts, 1974.

PRINTED SOURCES

Amic, Yolande. *L'Opaline Francaise au XIXᵉ Siecle.* Paris, France: Library Gründ, 1952.

Anthony, T. Robert. *19th Century Fairy Lamps.* Manchester, Vermont: Forward's Color Productions, Inc., 1969.

Avila, George C. *The Pairpoint Glass Story.* New Bedford, Massachusetts: Reynolds-DeWalt Printing, Inc., 1968.

Barber, John Warner. *Historical Collections, being a general collection of interesting facts, traditions, biographical sketches, Anecdotes, &c., relating to the History and Antiquities of Every Town in Massachusetts.* Worcester, Massachusetts: Dorr, Howland & Co., 1839.

Barbour, Harriot Buxton. *Sandwich The Town That Glass Built.*

Boston, Massachusetts: Houghton Mifflin Company, 1948.

Barret, Richard Carter. *A Collectors Handbook of American Art Glass*. Manchester, Vermont: Forward's Color Productions, Inc., 1971.

————. *A Collectors Handbook of Blown and Pressed American Glass*. Manchester, Vermont: Forward's Color Productions, Inc., 1971.

————. *Popular American Ruby-Stained Pattern Glass*. Manchester, Vermont: Forward's Color Productions, Inc., 1968.

Belden, Louise Conway. *The Festive Tradition; Table Decoration and Desserts in America, 1650–1900*. New York, New York, and London, England: W. W. Norton & Company, 1983.

Belknap, E. McCamly. *Milk Glass*. New York, New York: Crown Publishers, Inc., 1949.

Bilane, John E. *Cup Plate Discoveries Since 1948; The Cup Plate Notes of James H. Rose*. Union, New Jersey: John E. Bilane, 1971.

Bishop, Barbara. "Deming Jarves and His Glass Factories," *The Glass Club Bulletin*, Spring 1983, pp. 3–5.

Bishop, Barbara and Martha Hassell. *Your Obd^t. Servt., Deming Jarves*. Sandwich, Massachusetts: The Sandwich Historical Society, 1984.

Bredehoft, Neila M. and George A. Fogg, and Francis C. Maloney. *Early Duncan Glassware; Geo. Duncan & Sons, Pittsburgh 1874–1892*. Boston, Massachusetts, and Saint Louisville, Ohio: Published privately, 1987.

Brown, Clark W. *Salt Dishes*. Leon, Iowa: Mid-America Book Company, reprinted in 1968.

————. *A Supplement to Salt Dishes*. Leon, Iowa: Prairie Winds Press, reprinted in 1970.

Brown, William B. *Over the Pathways of the Past*. Cheshire, Massachusetts: Cheshire Public Library, 1938.

Burbank, George E. *A Bit of Sandwich History*. Sandwich, Massachusetts: 1939.

Burgess, Bangs. *History of Sandwich Glass*. Yarmouth, Massachusetts: The Register Press, 1925.

Burns, Charles. *Glass Cup Plates*. Philadelphia, Pennsylvania: Burns Antique Shop, 1921.

Butterfield, Oliver. "Bewitching Witchballs," *Yankee*, July 1978, pp. 97, 172–175.

Cataldo, Louis and Dorothy Worrell. *Pictorial Tales of Cape Cod*. (Vol. I) Hyannis, Massachusetts: Tales of Cape Cod, Inc., 1956.

————. *Pictorial Tales of Cape Cod*. (Vol. II) Hyannis, Massachusetts: Tales of Cape Cod, Inc., 1961.

Childs, David B. "If It's Threaded...," *Yankee*, June 1960, pp. 86–89.

Chipman, Frank W. *The Romance of Old Sandwich Glass*. Sandwich, Massachusetts: Sandwich Publishing Company, Inc., 1932.

Cloak, Evelyn Campbell. *Glass Paperweights of the Bergstrom Art Center*. New York, New York: Crown Publishers, Inc., 1969.

Conat, Robert. *A Streak of Luck; The Life and Legend of Thomas Alva Edison*. New York, New York: Seaview Books, 1979.

Covill, William E., Jr. *Ink Bottles and Inkwells*. Taunton, Massachusetts: William S. Sullwold Publishing, 1971.

Cronin, J. R. *Fakes & Forged Trade Marks on Old & New Glass*. Marshalltown, Iowa: Antique Publications Service, 1976.

Cullity, Rosana and John Nye Cullity. *A Sandwich Album*. East Sandwich, Massachusetts: The Nye Family of America Association, Inc., 1987.

Culver, Willard R. "From Sand to Seer and Servant of Man,"

The National Geographic Magazine, January 1943, pp. 17–24, 41–48.

Deyo, Simeon L. *History of Barnstable County, Massachusetts*. New York, New York: H. W. Blake & Co., 1890.

DiBartolomeo, Robert E. *American Glass from the Pages of Antiques; Pressed and Cut*. (Vol. II) Princeton, New Jersey: The Pyne Press, 1974.

Dickinson, Rudolphus. *A Geographical and Statistical View of Massachusetts Proper*. 1813.

Dickinson, Samuel N. *The Boston Almanac for the Year 1847*. Boston, Massachusetts: B. B. Mussey and Thomas Groom, 1846.

Dooley, William Germain. *Old Sandwich Glass*. Pasadena, California: Esto Publishing Company, n.d.

————. "Recollections of Sandwich Glass by a Veteran Who Worked on It," *Hobbies*, June 1951, p. 96.

Drepperd, Carl W. *The ABC's of Old Glass*. Garden City, New York: Doubleday & Company, Inc., 1949.

Dyer, Walter A. "The Pressed Glass of Old Sandwich". *Antiques*, February 1922, pp. 57–60.

Eckardt, Allison M. "Living with Antiques; A Collection of American Neoclassical Furnishings on the East Coast". *The Magazine ANTIQUES*, April 1987, pp. 858–863.

Edison Lamp Works. *Pictorial History of the Edison Lamp*. Harrison, New Jersey: Edison Lamp Works, c. 1920.

Farson, Robert H. *The Cape Cod Canal*. Middletown, Connecticut: Wesleyan University Press, 1977.

Fauster, Carl U. *Libbey Glass Since 1818*. Toledo, Ohio: Len Beach Press, 1979.

Fawsett, Marise. *Cape Cod Annals*. Bowie, Maryland: Heritage Books, Inc., 1990.

Ferson, Regis F. and Mary F. Ferson. *Yesterday's Milk Glass Today*. Pittsburgh, Pennsylvania: Published privately, 1981.

Freeman, Frederick. *History of Cape Cod: Annals of the Thirteen Towns of Barnstable County*. Boston, Massachusetts: George C. Rand & Avery, 1862.

Freeman, Dr. Larry. *New Light on Old Lamps*. Watkins Glen, New York: American Life Foundation, reprinted in 1984.

Fritz, Florence. *Bamboo and Sailing Ships; The Story of Thomas Alva Edison and Fort Myers, Florida*. 1949.

Gaines, Edith. "Woman's Day Dictionary of American Glass," *Woman's Day*, August 1961, pp. 19–34.

————. "Woman's Day Dictionary of Sandwich Glass," *Woman's Day*, August 1963, pp. 21–32.

————. "Woman's Day Dictionary of Victorian Glass," *Woman's Day*, August 1964, pp. 23–34.

Gores, Stan. *1876 Centennial Collectibles and Price Guide*. Fond du Lac, Wisconsin: The Haber Printing Co., 1974.

Grover, Ray and Lee Grover. *Art Glass Nouveau*. Rutland, Vermont: Charles E. Tuttle Company, Inc., 1967.

————. *Carved & Decorated European Art Glass*. Rutland, Vermont: Charles E. Tuttle Company, Inc., 1970.

Grow, Lawrence. *The Warner Collector's Guide to Pressed Glass*. New York, New York: Warner Books, Inc., 1982.

Hammond, Dorothy. *Confusing Collectibles*. Des Moines, Iowa: Wallace-Homestead Book Company, 1969.

————. *More Confusing Collectibles*. Wichita, Kansas: C. B. P. Publishing Company, 1972.

Harris, Amanda B. "Down in Sandwich Town," *Wide Awake* 1, 1887, pp. 19–27.

Harris, John. *The Great Boston Fire, 1872*. Boston, Massachusetts: Boston Globe, 1972.

Hartung, Marion T. and Ione E. Hinshaw. *Patterns and Pinafores*. Des Moines, Iowa: Wallace-Homestead Book Company, 1971.

Hayes-Cavanaugh, Doris. "Early Glassmaking in East Cambridge, Mass.," *Old Time New England*, January 1929, pp. 113–122.

Haynes, E. Barrington. *Glass Through the Ages*. Baltimore, Maryland: Penguin Books, 1969.

Hayward, Arthur H. *Colonial and Early American Lighting*. New York, New York: Dover Publications, Inc., reprinted in 1962.

Hayward, John. *Gazetteer of Massachusetts*. Boston, Massachusetts: John Hayward, 1847.

Heacock, William. *Encyclopedia of Victorian Colored Pattern Glass; Book 1 Toothpick Holders from A to Z*. Jonesville, Michigan: Antique Publications, 1974.

————. *Encyclopedia of Victorian Colored Pattern Glass; Book 2 Opalescent Glass from A to Z*. Jonesville, Michigan: Antique Publications, 1975.

————. *Encyclopedia of Victorian Colored Pattern Glass; Book 3 Syrups, Sugar Shakers & Cruets from A to Z*. Jonesville, Michigan: Antique Publications, 1976.

————. *Encyclopedia of Victorian Colored Pattern Glass; Book 4 Custard Glass from A to Z*. Marietta, Ohio: Antique Publications, 1976.

————. *Encyclopedia of Victorian Colored Pattern Glass; Book 5 U. S. Glass from A to Z*. Marietta, Ohio: Antique Publications, 1978.

————. *Encyclopedia of Victorian Colored Pattern Glass; Book 6 Oil Cruets from A to Z*. Marietta, Ohio: Antique Publications, 1981.

————. *1000 Toothpick Holders; A Collector's Guide*. Marietta, Ohio: Antique Publications, 1977.

Heacock, William and Patricia Johnson. *5000 Open Salts; A Collector's Guide*. Marietta, Ohio: Richardson Printing Corporation, 1982.

Hebard, Helen Brigham. *Early Lighting in New England*. Rutland, Vermont: Charles E. Tuttle Company, 1964.

Heckler, Norman. *American Bottles in the Charles B. Gardner Collection*. Bolton, Massachusetts: Robert W. Skinner, Inc., 1975.

Hildebrand, J. R. "Glass Goes To Town," *The National Geographic Magazine*, January 1943, pp. 1–16, 25–40.

Hollister, Paul, Jr. *The Encyclopedia of Glass Paperweights*. New York, New York: Clarkson N. Potter, Inc., 1969.

Hough, Walter. *Collection of Heating and Lighting Utensils in the United States National Museum*. Washington, District of Columbia: United States Government Printing Office, 1928.

Hunter, Frederick William. *Stiegel Glass*. New York, New York: Dover Publications, Inc., 1950.

Ingold, Gérard. *The Art of the Paperweight; Saint Louis*. Santa Cruz, California: Paperweight Press, 1981.

Innes, Lowell. *Pittsburgh Glass 1797–1891*. Boston, Massachusetts: Houghton Mifflin Company, 1976.

Irwin, Frederick T. *The Story of Sandwich Glass*. Manchester, New Hampshire: Granite State Press, 1926.

Jarves, Deming. "The Manufactures of Glass" (numbers 1–8), *Journal of Mining and Manufactures*, September 1852–April 1853.

————. *Reminiscences of Glass-making*. Great Neck, New York: Beatrice C. Weinstock, reprinted in 1968.

Jarves, James Jackson. *In Memoriam James Jackson Jarves*. (Jr.) Published privately, 1890.

————. *Why and What Am I?*. Boston, Massachusetts: Phillips, Sampson and Company, 1857.

Jenks, Bill and Jerry Luna. *Early American Pattern Glass 1850–1910*. Radnor, Pennsylvania: Wallace-Homestead Book Company, 1990.

Jones, Olive R. and E. Ann Smith. *Glass of the British Military 1755–1820*. Hull, Quebec, Canada: Parks Canada, 1985.

Jones, Olive and Catherine Sullivan. *The Parks Canada Glass Glossary*. Hull, Quebec, Canada: Parks Canada, 1985.

Jones, Thomas P. *Journal of the Franklin Institute*. (Vol. 3, rebound as Vol. 7) Philadelphia, Pennsylvania: Franklin Institute, 1829.

Kamm, Minnie W. and Serry Wood. *The Kamm-Wood Encyclopedia of Pattern Glass*. (II vols.) Watkins Glen, New York: Century House, 1961.

Keene, Betsey D. *History of Bourne 1622–1937*. Yarmouthport, Massachusetts: Charles W. Swift, 1937.

Knittle, Rhea Mansfield. *Early American Glass*. New York, New York: The Century Co., 1927.

Lane, Lyman and Sally Lane, and Joan Pappas. *A Rare Collection of Keene & Stoddard Glass*. Manchester, Vermont: Forward's Color Productions, Inc., 1970.

Lanmon, Dwight P. "Russian Paperweights and Letter Seals?" *The Magazine ANTIQUES*, October 1984, pp. 900–903.

————. "Unmasking an American Glass Fraud," *The Magazine ANTIQUES*, January 1983, pp. 226–236.

Lanmon, Dwight P., Robert H. Brill and George J. Reilly. "Some Blown 'Three-Mold' Suspicions Confirmed," *Journal of Glass Studies*, vol. 15 (1973), pp. 151–159, 172–173.

Lardner, Rev. Dionysius. *The Cabinet Cyclopedia; Useful Arts*. Philadelphia, Pennsylvania: Carey and Lea, 1832.

Lattimore, Colin R. *English 19th Century Press-Moulded Glass*. London, England: Barrie & Jenkins, Ltd., 1979.

Lechler, Doris Anderson. *Children's Glass Dishes, China, and Furniture*. Paducah, Kentucky: Collector Books, 1983.

Lechler, Doris and Virginia O'Neill. *Children's Glass Dishes*. Nashville, Tennessee, and New York, New York: Thomas Nelson, Inc., Publishers, 1976.

Lee, Ruth Webb. *Antique Fakes & Reproductions*. Wellesley Hills, Massachusetts: Lee Publications, 1966.

————. *Early American Pressed Glass*. Wellesley Hills, Massachusetts: Lee Publications, 1960.

————. *Nineteenth-Century Art Glass*. New York, New York: M. Barrows & Company, Inc., 1952.

————. *Sandwich Glass*. Wellesley Hills, Massachusetts: Lee Publications, 1939.

————. *Victorian Glass*. Wellesley Hills, Massachusetts: Lee Publications, 1944.

Lee, Ruth Webb and James H. Rose. *American Glass Cup Plates*. Wellesley Hills, Massachusetts: Lee Publications, 1948.

Lindsey, Bessie M. *American Historical Glass*. Rutland, Vermont: Charles E. Tuttle Co., 1967.

Lovell, Russell A., Jr. *The Cape Cod Story of Thornton W. Burgess*. Taunton, Massachusetts: Thornton W. Burgess Society, Inc., and William S. Sullwold Publishing, 1974.

————. *Sandwich; A Cape Cod Town*. Sandwich, Massachusetts: Town of Sandwich Massachusetts Archives and Historical Center, 1984.

Mackay, James. *Glass Paperweights*. New York, New York: The Viking Press, Inc., 1973.

Manheim, Frank J. *A Garland of Weights*. New York, New York:

Farrar, Straus and Giroux, 1967.

Manley, C. C. *British Glass*. Des Moines, Iowa: Wallace-Homestead Book Co., 1968.

Manley, Cyril. *Decorative Victorian Glass*. New York, New York: Van Nostrand Reinhold Company, 1981.

Mannoni, Edith. *Opalines*. Paris, France: Editions Ch. Massin, n.d.

Maycock, Susan E. *East Cambridge*. Cambridge, Massachusetts: Cambridge Historical Commission, 1988.

McKearin, George S. and Helen McKearin. *American Glass*. New York, New York: Crown Publishers, Inc., 1941.

McKearin, Helen and George S. McKearin. *Two Hundred Years of American Blown Glass*. New York, New York: Bonanza Books, 1949.

McKearin, Helen and Kenneth M. Wilson. *American Bottles & Flasks and Their Ancestry*. New York, New York: Crown Publishers, Inc., 1978.

Measell, James. *Greentown Glass; The Indiana Tumbler and Goblet Company*. Grand Rapids, Michigan: The Grand Rapids Public Museum with the Grand Rapids Museum Association, 1979.

Metz, Alice Hulett. *Early American Pattern Glass*. Columbus, Ohio: Spencer-Walker Press, 1965.

_____. *Much More Early American Pattern Glass*. Columbus, Ohio: Spencer-Walker Press, 1970.

Millard, S. T. *Goblets II*. Holton, Kansas: Gossip Printers and Publishers, 1940.

Miller, Robert W. *Mary Gregory and Her Glass*. Des Moines, Iowa: Wallace-Homestead Book Co., 1972.

Moore, N. Hudson. *Old Glass*. New York, New York: Tudor Publishing Co., 1924.

Morris, Paul C. and Joseph F. Morin. *The Island Steamers*. Nantucket, Massachusetts: Nantucket Nautical Publishers, 1977.

Mulch, Dwight. "John D. Larkin and Company: From Factory to Family," *The Antique Trader Weekly*, June 24, 1984, pp. 92–94.

Neal, L. W. and D. B. Neal. *Pressed Glass Salt Dishes of the Lacy Period 1825–1850*. Philadelphia, Pennsylvania: L. W. and D. B. Neal, 1962.

Nelson, Kirk J. *A Century of Sandwich Glass*. Sandwich, Massachusetts: Sandwich Glass Museum, 1992.

Padgett, Leonard. *Pairpoint Glass*. Des Moines, Iowa: Wallace-Homestead Book Company, 1979.

Pearson, J. Michael and Dorothy T. Pearson. *American Cut Glass Collections*. Miami, Florida: The Franklin Press, Inc., 1969.

_____. *American Cut Glass for the Discriminating Collector*. Miami, Florida: The Franklin Press, Inc., 1965.

Pellatt, Apsley. *Curiosities of Glass Making*. Newport, England: The Ceramic Book Company, reprinted in 1968.

Pepper, Adeline. *The Glass Gaffers of New Jersey*. New York, New York: Charles Scribner's Sons, 1971.

Perry, Josephine. *The Glass Industry*. New York, New York, and Toronto, Ontario: Longmans, Green and Co., 1945.

Peterson, Arthur G. *Glass Patents and Patterns*. Sanford, Florida: Celery City Printing Co., 1973.

_____. *Glass Salt Shakers: 1,000 Patterns*. Des Moines, Iowa: Wallace-Homestead Book Co., 1960.

Raycraft, Don and Carol Raycraft. *Early American Lighting*. Des Moines, Iowa: Wallace-Homestead Book Co., n.d.

Raynor, Ellen M. and Emma L. Petitclerc. *History of the Town of Cheshire, Berkshire County, Massachusetts*. Holyoke, Massachusetts, and New York, New York: Clark W. Bryan & Company, 1885.

Revi, Albert Christian. *American Art Nouveau Glass*. Exton, Pennsylvania: Schiffer Publishing, Ltd., 1981.

_____. *American Cut and Engraved Glass*. Nashville, Tennessee: Thomas Nelson Inc., 1972.

_____. *American Pressed Glass and Figure Bottles*. Nashville, Tennessee: Thomas Nelson Inc., 1972.

_____. *Nineteenth Century Glass*. Exton, Pennsylvania: Schiffer Publishing, Ltd., revised 1967.

Righter, Miriam. *Iowa City Glass*. Des Moines, Iowa: Wallace-Homestead Book Co., 1966.

Robertson, Frank E. "New Evidence from Sandwich Glass Fragments," *The Magazine ANTIQUES*, October 1982, pp. 818–823.

Robertson, R. A. *Chats on Old Glass*. New York, New York: Dover Publications, Inc., 1969. Revised and enlarged by Kenneth M. Wilson.

Rose, James H. *The Story of American Pressed Glass of the Lacy Period 1825–1850*. Corning, New York: The Corning Museum of Glass, 1954.

Rushlight Club. *Early Lighting; A Pictorial Guide*. Talcottville, Connecticut: 1972.

Sandwich Glass Museum. *The Sandwich Glass Museum Collection*. Sandwich, Massachusetts: Sandwich Glass Museum, 1969.

Sauzay, A. *Wonders of Art and Archaeology; Wonders of Glass Making*. New York, New York: Charles Scribner's Sons, 1885.

Schwartz, Marvin D. *American Glass from the Pages of Antiques; Blown and Moulded*. (Vol. I) Princeton, New Jersey: The Pyne Press, 1974.

Slack, Raymond. *English Pressed Glass 1831–1900*. London, England: Barrie & Jenkins, 1987.

Smith, Allan B. and Helen B. Smith. *One Thousand Individual Open Salts Illustrated*. Litchfield, Maine: The Country House, 1972.

_____. *650 More Individual Open Salts Illustrated*. Litchfield, Maine: The Country House, 1973.

_____. *The Third Book of Individual Open Salts Illustrated*. Litchfield, Maine: The Country House, 1976.

_____. *Individual Open Salts Illustrated*. Litchfield, Maine: The Country House, n.d.

_____. *Individual Open Salts Illustrated; 1977 Annual*. Litchfield, Maine: The Country House, 1977.

Smith, Frank R. and Ruth E. Smith. *Miniature Lamps*. New York, New York: Thomas Nelson Inc., 1968.

Smith, Ruth. *Miniature Lamps II*. Exton, Pennsylvania: Schiffer Publishing Ltd., 1982.

Spillman, Jane Shadel. *American and European Pressed Glass in The Corning Museum of Glass*. Corning, New York: The Corning Museum of Glass, 1981.

_____. *Glass Bottles, Lamps & Other Objects*. New York, New York: Alfred A. Knopf, Inc., 1983.

_____. *Glass Tableware, Bowls & Vases*. New York, New York: Alfred A. Knopf, Inc., 1982.

_____. "Pressed-Glass Designs in the United States and Europe," *The Magazine ANTIQUES*, July 1983, pp. 130–139.

Spillman, Jane Shadel and Estelle Sinclaire Farrar. *The Cut and Engraved Glass of Corning 1868–1940*. Corning, New York: The Corning Museum of Glass, 1977.

Stanley, Mary Louise. *A Century of Glass Toys*. Manchester, Vermont: Forward's Color Productions, Inc., n.d.

Steegmuller, Francis. *The Two Lives of James Jackson Jarves*. New Haven, Connecticut: Yale University Press, 1951.

Stetson Kindred of America. *The Descendants of Cornet Robert Stetson*, Vol. 1, No. 3. Stetson Kindred of America, Inc., 1956.

Stetson, Nelson M. *Booklet No. 3; Stetson Kindred of America*. Campbello, Massachusetts: The Stetson Kindred of America, n.d.

_____. *Booklet No. 6; Stetson Kindred of America*. Campbello, Massachusetts: The Stetson Kindred of America, 1923.

Stow, Charles Messer. *The Deming Jarves Book of Designs*. Yarmouth, Massachusetts: The Register Press, 1925.

Swan, Frank H. *Portland Glass*. Des Moines, Iowa: Wallace-Homestead Book Company, 1949. Revised and enlarged by Marion Dana.

_____. *Portland Glass Company*. Providence, Rhode Island: The Roger Williams Press, 1939.

Taylor, Katrina V. H. "Russian Glass in the Hillwood Museum." *The Magazine ANTIQUES*, July 1983, pp. 140–145.

Teleki, Gloria Roth. *The Baskets of Rural America*. New York, New York: E. P. Dutton & Co., Inc., 1975.

The Toledo Museum of Art. *American Glass*. Toledo, Ohio: The Toledo Museum of Art, n.d.

_____. *Art in Glass*. Toledo, Ohio: The Toledo Museum of Art, 1969.

_____. *The New England Glass Company 1818–1888*. Toledo, Ohio: The Toledo Museum of Art, 1963.

Thuro, Catherine M. V. *Oil Lamps; The Kerosene Era in North America*. Des Moines, Iowa: Wallace-Homestead Book Co., 1976.

_____. *Oil Lamps II; Glass Kerosene Lamps*. Paducah, Kentucky, and Des Moines, Iowa: Collector Books and Wallace-Homestead Book Co., 1983.

Thwing, Leroy. *Flickering Flames*. Rutland, Vermont: Charles E. Tuttle Company, 1974.

_____. "Lamp Oils and Other Illuminants." *Old Time New England*, October 1932, pp. 56–69.

Towne, Sumner. "Mike Grady's Last Pot," *Yankee*, March 1968, pp. 84, 85, 136–139.

United States House Executive Documents. *Documents Relative to The Manufactures in the United States Collected and Transmitted to The House of Representatives by the Secretary of the Treasury*. Washington, 1833.

VanRensselaer, Stephen. *Early American Bottles & Flasks*. Stratford, Connecticut: J. Edmund Edwards, 1971.

Van Tassel, Valentine. *American Glass*. New York, New York: Gramercy Publishing Company, 1950.

Vuilleumier, Marion. *Cape Cod; a Pictorial History*. Norfolk, Virginia: The Donning Company/Publishers, 1982.

Walsh, Lavinia. "The Romance of Sandwich Glass," *The Cape Cod Magazine*, July 1926, pp. 9, 26.

_____. "Old Boston and Sandwich Glassworks....," *Ceramic Age*, December 1950, pp. 16, 17, 34.

Warner, Oliver. *Statistical Information Relating to Certain Branches of Industry in Massachusetts for the Year Ending May 1, 1865*. Boston, Massachusetts: Wright & Potter, 1866.

Watkins, Lura Woodside. *American Glass and Glassmaking*. New York, New York: Chanticleer Press, 1950.

_____. *Cambridge Glass 1818 to 1888*. New York, New York: Bramhall House, 1930.

Webber, Norman W. *Collecting Glass*. New York, New York: Arco Publishing Company, Inc., 1973.

Webster, Noah. *An American Dictionary of the English Language*. Springfield, Massachusetts: George and Charles Merriam, 1847. Revised.

_____. *An American Dictionary of the English Language*. Springfield, Massachusetts: George and Charles Merriam, 1859. Revised and enlarged by Chauncey A. Goodrich.

_____. *An American Dictionary of the English Language*. Springfield, Massachusetts: G. & C. Merriam, 1872. Revised and enlarged by Chauncey A. Goodrich and Noah Porter.

Wetz, Jon and Jacqueline Wetz. *The Co-operative Glass Company Sandwich, Massachusetts: 1888–1891*. Sandwich, Massachusetts: Barn Lantern Publishing, 1976.

Williams, Lenore Wheeler. *Sandwich Glass*. Bridgeport, Connecticut: The Park City Eng. Co., 1922.

Wilson, Kenneth M. *New England Glass & Glassmaking*. New York, New York: Thomas Y. Crowell Company, 1972.

Winsor, Justin. *The Memorial History of Boston; Including Suffolk County, Massachusetts 1630–1880*. (IV vols.) Boston, Massachusetts: James R. Osgood and Company, 1881.

(no author). "Cape Cod, Nantucket, and the Vineyard." *Harper's New Monthly Magazine* LI (c. 1870), pp. 52–66.

CATALOGS

A. L. Blackmer Co. Rich Cut Glass 1906–1907. Shreveport, Louisiana: The American Cut Glass Association, reprinted in 1982.

Amberina; 1884 New England Glass Works; 1917 Libbey Glass Company. Toledo, Ohio: Antique & Historical Glass Foundation, reprinted in 1970.

Averbeck Rich Cut Glass Catalog No. 104, The. Berkeley, California: Cembura & Avery Publishers, reprinted in 1973.

Boston & Sandwich Glass Co., Boston. Wellesley Hills, Massachusetts: Lee Publications, reprinted in 1968.

Boston & Sandwich Glass Co. Price List. Collection of the Sandwich Glass Museum, Sandwich Historical Society, Sandwich, Massachusetts, n.d.

Catalog of 700 Packages Flint Glass Ware Manufactured by the Cape Cod Glass Works, to be Sold at the New England Trade Sale, Wednesday, July 14, 1859 at 9½ O'clock. Collection of the Rakow Library, The Corning Museum of Glass, Corning, New York, 1859.

C. Dorflinger & Sons Cut Glass Catalog. Silver Spring, Maryland: Christian Dorflinger Glass Study Group, reprinted in 1981.

Collector's Paperweights; Price Guide and Catalog. Santa Cruz, California: Paperweight Press, 1983.

Cut Glass Produced by the Laurel Cut Glass Company. Shreveport, Louisiana: The American Cut Glass Association, reprinted, n.d.

Dietz & Company Illustrated Catalog. Watkins Glen, New York: American Life Books, reprinted in 1982.

Egginton's Celebrated Cut Glass. Shreveport, Louisiana: The American Cut Glass Association, reprinted in 1982.

Elsholz Collection of Early American Glass (III vols.) Hyannis, Massachusetts: Richard A. Bourne Co., Inc., 1986–1987.

Empire Cut Glass Company, The. Shreveport, Louisiana: American Cut Glass Association, reprinted in 1980.

F. X. Parsche & Son Co. Shreveport, Louisiana: American Cut Glass Association, reprinted in 1981.

Glassware Catalogue No. 25 Gillinder & Sons, Inc. Spring City,

Tennessee: Hillcrest Books, reprinted in 1974.

Higgins and Seiter Fine China and Cut Glass Catalog No. 13. New York, New York: Higgins and Seiter, n.d.

Illustrated Catalog of American Hardware of the Russell and Erwin Manufacturing Company 1865. Association for Preservation Technology, reprinted in 1980.

J. D. Bergen Co., The; Manufacturers of Rich Cut Glassware 1904–1905. Berkeley, California: Cembura & Avery Publishers, reprinted in 1973.

Lackawanna Cut Glass Co. Shreveport, Louisiana: The American Cut Glass Association, reprinted, n.d.

Launay Hautin & Cie. Collection de dessins representant... Collection of the Rakow Library, The Corning Museum of Glass, Corning, New York, n.d.

Launay Hautin & Cie. Des Fabriques de Baccarat, St. Louis, Choisey et Bercy. Collection of the Rakow Library, The Corning Museum of Glass, Corning, New York, n.d.

Launay Hautin & Cie. Repertoire des Articles compris dans la Collection... Collection of the Rakow Library, The Corning Museum of Glass, Corning, New York, 1844.

Launay Hautin & Cie. Usages principaux pour services de table... Collection of the Rakow Library, The Corning Museum of Glass, Corning, New York, n.d.

Libbey Glass Co., The; Cut Glass June 1st, 1896. Toledo, Ohio: Antique & Historical Glass Foundation, reprinted in 1968.

List of Glass Ware Manufactured by Cape Cod Glass Company. Collection of the Sandwich Glass Museum, Sandwich Historical Society, Sandwich, Massachusetts, n.d.

M'Kee Victorian Glass; Five Complete Glass Catalogs from 1859/60 to 1871. New York, New York: Dover Publications, Inc., reprinted in 1981.

Monroe Cut Glass. Shreveport, Louisiana: American Cut Glass Association, reprinted, n.d.

Morey, Churchill & Morey Pocket Guide to 1880 Table Settings. Watkins Glen, New York: Century House, reprinted, n.d.

Mt. Washington Glass Co. Clinton, Maryland: Leonard E. Padgett, reprinted in 1976.

Mt. Washington Glass Company (cut glassware). Collection of the Rakow Library, The Corning Museum of Glass, Corning, New York, n.d.

Mt. Washington Glass Company; Crystal Gas Fixtures. Collection of the Rakow Library, The Corning Museum of Glass, Corning, New York, n.d.

Mt. Washington Glass Works (glass prisms and beads). Collection of the Rakow Library, The Corning Museum of Glass, Corning, New York, n.d.

Mt. Washington Glass Works Price List. Collection of the Rakow Library, The Corning Museum of Glass, Corning, New York, n.d.

New England Glass Company. Collection of the Rakow Library, The Corning Museum of Glass, Corning, New York, n.d.

New England Glass Company (list of glassware). Collection of the Rakow Library, The Corning Museum of Glass, Corning, New York, n.d.

Picture Book of Authentic Mid-Victorian Gas Lighting Fixtures; A Reprint of the Historic Mitchell, Vance & Co. Catalog, ca. 1876, with Over 1000 Illustrations. Mineola, New York: Dover Publications, Inc., reprinted in 1984.

Plume & Atwood Manufacturing Company, The. Simpson, Illinois: J. W. Courter Enterprises, reprinted in 1975.

Public Auction Richard A. Bourne Company, Inc. Boston, Massachusetts: The Nimrod Press, Inc., 1970–1992.

Quaker City Cut Glass Co. Shreveport, Louisiana: American Cut Glass Association, n.d.

Rich Cut Glass Pitkin & Brooks. Berkeley, California: Cembura & Avery Publishers, reprinted in 1973.

Sandwich Glass Patterns. West Englewood, New Jersey: Bernadine Forgett, c. 1960.

Taylor Bros. & Company, Inc., Manufacturers of Cut Glass. Shreveport, Louisiana: American Cut Glass Association, n.d.

Whitall, Tatum & Co. Price List 1895. Philadelphia, Pennsylvania; New York, New York; Boston, Massachusetts: Whitall, Tatum & Co., 1895.

BUSINESS DIRECTORIES

Boston City Directories. 1789–1891.

Longworth's American Almanac, New York Register, and City Directory. 1824–1833.

Resident and Business Directory of Bourne, Falmouth and Sandwich, Massachusetts. Hopkinton, Massachusetts: A. E. Foss & Co., 1900

NEWSPAPERS AND TRADE PAPERS

Academy Breezes. 1884–1886.

Acorn, The. Sandwich, Massachusetts: The Sandwich Historical Society, 1967–1987, 1990–1992.

American Collector. New York, New York: Educational Publishing Corporation, 1933–1946.

Barnstable County Gazette. 1826.

Barnstable Patriot. 1846–1869.

Barnstable Patriot and Commercial Advertiser. 1830–1846.

Barnstable Patriot, The. 1869–1905, 1912–1916, 1918–1923.

Berkshire Evening Eagle. Pittsfield, Massachusetts: Eagle Publishing Company, 1948.

Berkshire Hills, The. Pittsfield, Massachusetts: 1904.

Boston Commercial Gazette. 1818–1828.

Bourne Pioneer, The. 1906–1907.

Brockton Searchlight, The. 1909.

Cape Cod Advocate, and Nautical Intelligencer. 1851–1864.

Cape Cod Gazette. 1870–1872.

Casino Bulletin. 1884–1885.

Chronicle of the Early American Industries Association, The. Flushing, New York: Leon S. Case, January 1938.

Crockery & Glass Journal. New York, New York: George Whittemore & Company, 1885–1890.

Crockery Journal. New York, New York: George Whittemore & Company, 1874–1884.

Cullet from the Glass Museum. Sandwich, Massachusetts: The Sandwich Historical Society, 1987–1992.

Glass Club Bulletin, The. The National Early American Glass Club, 1938–1992.

Hyannis Patriot, The. 1908–1909, 1916–1918, 1923–1925.

Illuminator, The. Toronto, Ontario, Canada: The Historical Lighting Society of Canada, 1987–1988.

Independent, The. 1895–1908.

Independent Chronicle, The. 1787.

Nautical Intelligencer, and Barnstable County Gazette. 1824.

Nautical Intelligencer and Falmouth and Holmes'-Hole Journal. 1823–1824.

Old Colony Memorial. 1827–1832.

Old Colony Memorial & Plymouth County Advertiser. 1822–1827.

Pittsburg Glass Journal. The Pittsburgh Chapter of the National Early American Glass Club, 1989–1991.

Sandwich Collector, The. East Sandwich, Massachusetts: McCue Publications, 1984–1985.

Sandwich Independent. 1920–1921.

Sandwich Independent, The. 1908–1909.

Sandwich Mechanic and Family Visitor. 1851.

Sandwich Observer. 1846–1851.

Sandwich Observer, The. 1884–1895, 1910–1911.

Sandwich Review, The. 1889–1890.

Seaside Press, The. 1873–1880.

Village Broadsider, The. 1978–1985.

Weekly Review, The. 1881–1882.

Yarmouth Register and Barnstable County Advertiser. 1836–1839.

Yarmouth Register and Barnstable County Weekly Advertiser. 1839–1846.

Yarmouth Register. 1849–1906.

BARLOW-KAISER
SANDWICH GLASS PRICE GUIDE

for pieces in perfect condition

FOURTH EDITION

to be used with Volumes 1, 2, 3 and 4 of

THE GLASS INDUSTRY IN SANDWICH
and
A GUIDE TO SANDWICH GLASS

**BARLOW-KAISER
PUBLISHING COMPANY, INC.**
P.O. BOX 265
WINDHAM, NEW HAMPSHIRE 03087

INTRODUCTION TO PRICE GUIDE

It is most important to determine the condition of a glass item before you purchase it. We are often so fascinated by a good "find" that we miss its obvious condition. The prices in this guide are for items that are in perfect, or *mint*, condition. *Mint condition* is an article of glass that is pristine. It has no defects. If there is roughage only in places where there are mold marks, it is still considered to be mint, because if the item was good enough to pass inspection at the time of production, it is good enough to be called mint today. Shear marks (often called "straw marks"), caused by cutting through a glob of glass while it was hot, do not detract from value. They are a fact of construction procedure. Manufacturing errors, such as annealing marks, bent or twisted pieces, off-center pieces, underfilled or overfilled molds, and overheating, add character to a piece of glass. However, the mint condition status of the glass is not affected. Rapid reductions in pricing are caused by damage after the time of manufacture in the following order, using the 100 percent value of a mint item as a base.

An unusually rare article, even though broken, must be considered for purchase regardless of price, if the serious collector is to have an example of that article.

Glass cannot be repaired without removing additional glass to smooth out or eliminate a chip. The "repair" rarely adds to value because the form of the article is altered. A goblet that has been machined down to eliminate a rim chip will not match its undamaged counterparts.

CONDITION	MAXIMUM VALUE OF MINT
CHIPPED Damage serious enough to penetrate into the body of an article, but small or shallow enough so that it cannot be glued back or replaced.	80%
BRUISED When an article has been struck with enough force to send cracks in several directions, penetrating the surface at the center.	60%
CRACKED When the glass is split through one or more layers, caused by a blow, a change in temperature, or stress in the glass at the time of manufacture. This is the first stage of deterioration, leading to eventual destruction. Value is seriously affected.	50%
BROKEN An article is broken when it is in two pieces, even though one of the pieces may only be the tip of a scallop, or the corner of a base, or the peg of a lamp font. If one piece must be glued back in order to make the article whole, the article is broken and its value must be reduced accordingly.	25%

PRESSED TABLEWARE

Most glass produced in Sandwich factories was clear, so expect the price of colored articles to be high. Reproductions issued by museum gift shops have contaminated the antiques market. Learn where the "repros" were signed. Inspect for damage that may indicate the removal of a museum "logo".

Photo No.		Clear	Clambroth (Alabaster)	Opaque White	Canary	Amber	Blue	Amethyst	Green	Unusual Color
1001	a	100								
	b	100								
1002	a	100					350			
	b	100					350			
	c	125					475			
1003		450								
1004		100								
1005		45								
1006	a	45								
	b	285								
1007		550								
1008		300								
1009		200								
1010		475								
1011	a	400								
	b	—								
1012		900								
1013		4000								
1014	a	125								
	b	60								
1015		45					175			
1016		60					350			
1017	a	125								
	b	80								
1018	a	550								
	b	80								
1019		700								
1020		38								
1021		125						625 pale		
1022		210								
1023		225								
1024		325								
1025		45								
1026	a	900								
	b	40								
1027		900								
1028		2500					4500			
1029		3800					6500			
1030	a	1000								
	b	—								
1031		1500			11,000		14,000	11,000		
1032		1400								
1033	a	40			200		200	275	200	
	b	40			200		200	275	200	
1034		40			200		200	275	200	
1035		175								
1036		1800								
1037	a	45								
	b	38								

Photo No.	Clear	Clambroth (Alabaster)	Opaque White	Canary	Amber	Blue	Amethyst	Green	Unusual Color
1038	38					175	200	300	
1039 a	550								
b	75	350 fiery opalescent					350		
1040	500			1200		3000	3000		15,000+
1041	450	2750 fiery opalescent							
1042	500		1200			1750 opaque	2000		
1043	500					4800			6000
1044	650								
1045	90								
1046	300	700 fiery opalescent							
1047	4000								
1048	1200								
1049	1500					5500			
1050	375	1600	500			2000	2800	6500	
1051	5200			15,000		12,000			
1052	6500			20,000					
1053	700			3200		3600			
1054	650								
1055	90					800			
1056	235	1400 fiery opalescent	525			1600			
1057	38	110	110	210	450	375	375	450	550
1058 a	38	110	110	210	450	375	375	450	550
b	500			900		1100		2400	
1059 a	38			210		375		450	
b	450			1100		1200			
1060	42								
1061 a	900								
b	250								
1062	7500								
1063	7500								
1064	650					6000			
1065	750								
1066	475								
1067	45			250 pale					
1068 a	750								
b	85								
1069	110								
1070	85 / 1100 silver nitrate								
1071	135			1800		2500			
1072	185								
1073	—								

Photo No.	Clear	Clambroth (Alabaster)	Opaque White	Canary	Amber	Blue	Amethyst	Green	Unusual Color
1074	125								
1075 a	550								
b	600								
1076	135								
1077	1100								
1078	2400								
1079	375					4000			
1080	525								
1081	4800								
1082	625								
1083	525					2100			
1084	235	1000	900	1200		1400	1800		
1085	35			250		300	325		
1086 a	185					875			
b	—								
1087	375			2000		3200			
1088	210						500 pale		
1089	210								
1090	285								
1091	140								
1092	120								
1093	900								
1094	130								
1095	185								
1096	875								
1097	140					300			
1098	35								
1099	175								
1100	1250								
1101	110 1800 silver nitrate								
1102	225							750	
1103	575								
1104	150								
1105	150								
1106 a	250								
b	195								
1107	80	450 fiery opalescent							
1108	80								
1109	65	150 fiery opalescent				300	400		
1110 a	80	210 fiery opalescent				400	500		
b	35	125 fiery opalescent						100 pale	
1111 a	1100								

Photo No.	Clear	Clambroth (Alabaster)	Opaque White	Canary	Amber	Blue	Amethyst	Green	Unusual Color
b	90	250 fiery opalescent							
1112	55					400			
1113 a	125			900					
b	50			875					
1114	140								
1115 a	185								
b	110								
1116	65 / 85 gilded								
1117	110			1100		1500			
1118	110								
1119 a	95			400		500			
b	65								
1120	150			450					
1121	500								
1122	150								
1123	150								
1124	235								
1125	1600								
1126	1600	10,000 fiery opalescent					12,000	20,000	16,000+
1127	25			95		135			
1128	25						125		
1129 a	28					75			
b	25						125		
1130	110				450	375			
1131	65								
1132 a	65								
b	20					120			
1133	1750			4200		6500			
1134	40			650		725		850 peacock	
1135	110			900		1400			
1136 a	45			625	1050	850	950	1050	
b	45			625	1050	850	950	1050	
1137	60			625					
1138	55								
1139	65								
1140	35						185		
1141	235			3200		7500	7500		
1142 a	35			275		450			
b	—								
1143	95	575 fiery opalescent		2200		2400 peacock			
1144	185			2000		2500			
1145	15			85					
1146	235					2500			
1147	185			2000			3000		
1148	265						3000		

Photo No.	Clear	Clambroth (Alabaster)	Opaque White	Canary	Amber	Blue	Amethyst	Green	Unusual Color
1149	265			2000					
1150	95			600					
1151	375	6500 fiery opalescent		4000			6500		
1152 a	250			1600					
b	—								
1153	235			3200		7500	8000		
1154	35 ea.								
1155	110			1200					
1156	95	375 fiery opalescent							
1157	150	600 fiery opalescent							
1158	75	350 fiery opalescent					350		
1159	50 ea.			875 ea.					
1160	300 pr.								
1161	165								
1162	195								
1163 a	55			350			750		
b	60			350			750		
1164	60 ea.			350 ea.			750 ea.		
1165 a	95								
b	50								
1166	95		250	400		600			
1167	85			1400					
1168	225			1400					
1169	285			3200					
1170	100			900					
1171	475								
1172	600								
1173	110			1050					
1174	650								
1175	525			5400		6500	7500		
1176	1500			10,000		15,000	18,000		25,000+
1177	85								
1178	110			1200					
1179	85 ea.	1100 ea. fiery opalescent	775 ea.	1400 ea.		1500 ea.			
1180	95			700			750		
1181 a	110			850			1400		
b	85					900			
1182 a	110								
b	55								
1183	28								
1184	165		400						
1185	135	1200 fiery opalescent							

Photo No.	Clear	Clambroth (Alabaster)	Opaque White	Canary	Amber	Blue	Amethyst	Green	Unusual Color
1186 a	75								
b	75								
1187 a	125	900 fiery opalescent				1500			
b	400								
1188	165			650		1000			
1189	325						1200 light		
1190 a	—								
b	18								
1191 a	235								
b	285								
1192	55								
1193	55								
1194	50	400 fiery opalescent							
1195	95		185			525			
1196 a	110								
b	110								
1197	75					325			
1198 a	55								
b	—								
1199	—								
1200 a	65 / 80 engraved								
b	15 ea. / 18 ea. engraved								
1201	30 / 40 engraved								
1202 a	40								
b	—								
1203 a	70								
b	75								
c	55								
d	125								
1204 a	125								
b	60 without cover	225 without cover	300 without cover	550 without cover		550 without cover		750 without cover	
c	75								
1205	100								
1206 a	75								
b	70								
c	75								
1207	35 ea. without cover	235 ea. without cover fiery opalescent							

Photo No.	Clear	Clambroth (Alabaster)	Opaque White	Canary	Amber	Blue	Amethyst	Green	Unusual Color
1208 a	40					140			
b	—								
1209	—								
1210	85 engraved								
1211 a	18			100	160	120	120	175	
b	28			125	175	150	150	200	
c	185						575		
1212 a	150								
b	185								
1213	55								
1214	550		750						
1215	45					1800			
1216 a	55								
b	195		575						
1217	—								
1218	275								
1219	55								
1220	45								
1221	325								
1222 a	65								
b	375		575						
1223 a	95								
b	185								
1224 a	35								
b	95								
1225 a	95								
b	145								
1226	75								
1227	50								
1228	95								
1229	55	325 375 gilded				1100 1250 gilded		1300 1450 gilded	
1230	225								
1231 a	125								
b	160								
1232 a	50								
b	40								
1233	325 pr. 500 pr. engraved								
1234 a	135								
b	160								
1235	95								
1236	115 265 decorated			300				575	
1237 a	525								
b	475								
1238	525								
1239	110								
1240 a	85								
b	—								

Photo No.	Clear	Clambroth (Alabaster)	Opaque White	Canary	Amber	Blue	Amethyst	Green	Unusual Color
1241	18								
1242	55								
1243 a	90								
b	115								
1244	295 the set								
1245	40								
1246	40								
1247	65								
1248	30								
1249	35								
1250 a	12 15 gilded								
b	28 35 gilded								
1251	135 165 gilded								
1252 a			115						
b			65						

FREE-BLOWN AND BLOWN MOLDED TABLEWARE

Most glass produced in Sandwich factories was clear, so expect the price of colored articles to be high. Blown objects have been heavily reproduced. It is difficult to find originals on the open market. Pieces accompanied by family documentation are worth up to three times more.

Photo No.	Clear	Clambroth (Alabaster)	Opaque White	Canary	Amber	Blue	Amethyst	Green	Unusual Color
1253	400								
1254	125					525	525		
1255	180 with stopper								
1256 a	140			750		900	900		
b	80			700		850	850		
1257	400								
1258	18								120
1259	18 ea.			25 ea.	45 ea.	30 ea.			
1260	18 ea.			25 ea.	45 ea.	30 ea.			
1261		45 opal decorated							
1262	225								
1263	325								
1264	125								
1265	390					1500			
1266	750								
1267	700								
1268	4800								
1269	4600								

Photo No.	Clear	Clambroth (Alabaster)	Opaque White	Canary	Amber	Blue	Amethyst	Green	Unusual Color
1270	—								
1271	3200								
1272	3800								
1273	110					325			
1274 a	45 with stopper								
b	—								
c	45 with cap								
1275	180					450	475		
1276	35					235	250		
1277	70								
1278 a	235								
b	—								
1279	180 ea.					450 ea.	475 ea.		
1280 a	180					450	475		
b	180					450	475		
1281 a	235								
b	110								
c	100								
1282 a	70								
b	70								
1283	—								
1284	475 the set								
1285	—								
1286	235 with cap								
1287	—								
1288	90					325			
1289	125								
1290	125							150 pale	
1291	250								
1292	150					375			
1293 a	150					375			
b	185					750			
1294	275								
1295	425								
1296	200								
1297	175								
1298	165								
1299	600								
1300	1500					2200			
1301	600								
1302	900								
1303	235								
1304	325								
1305 a	150								
b	25								
1306 a	225								
b	225								
1307	275								
1308	325								

Photo No.	Clear	Clambroth (Alabaster)	Opaque White	Canary	Amber	Blue	Amethyst	Green	Unusual Color
1309	4200					6000			
1310	235								
1311	875								
1312	325								
1313	275								
1314	400								
1315	125								
1316 a	220								
b	275								
1317	325								
1318	275								
1319 a	275								
b	25								
1320 a	190								
b	225								
1321	600								
1322	275								
1323 a	150					600			
b	1200								
1324	800								
1325	575					2200	3000		
1326	600					3200			
1327	235								
1328	115								
1329	275								
1330	300								
1331	235 ea.								
1332	1200 the set								
1333	775					4000	3800		
1334 a	235					900			
b	250					1000	1200		
1335	875					4000			
1336	550								
1337	140 without stopper								
1338 a	250								
b	550								
1339 a	2100								
b	900								

PRESSED CUP PLATES

A cup plate with a pontil mark is a base that was broken away from a lamp or a candlestick. It should not be highly valued. The invention of the cap ring allowed the number and shape of rim scallops to vary on the same pattern cup plate. This variation does not indicate a rare example and does not affect value of a given cup plate pattern. Value is not affected by slight changes in pattern due to handwork by the mold maker. Prices given for unrecorded colors may be for variants.

Photo No.	Clear	Clambroth (Alabaster)	Fiery Opalescent	Opaque White	Amber	Blue	Amethyst	Green	Unusual Color
1340 a	52								
b	—								

Photo No.	Clear	Clambroth (Alabaster)	Fiery Opalescent	Opaque White	Amber	Blue	Amethyst	Green	Unusual Color
c	35					400			
d	35								
1341	55								175 pale pink
1342 a	32					900			
b	35								
1343 a	110								
b	35								
c	38					750			
d	32					900			
1344 a	35								
b	40								
c	48								
1345	45				225				
1346	42								
1347	48		175					235 pale	
1348	60		235						
1349	75						650		850 black
1350	30								
1351	1600								
1352	60		250 blue						
1353	50								
1354	90					1500 silver-blue			
1355	40				175	1500 silver-blue			
1356	55					1500 silver-blue			
1357	75					1600 silver-blue			
1358	—								
1359	25								
1360	45								
1361	75								
1362	75								
1363	75								
1364	35							395	
1365	40		135			180 opalescent			
1366	100					450		650	
1367	110								
1368	38								
1369	32 ea.	150 ea.							
1370	60								
1371	32					235 / 235 pale	235 / 235 pale		
1372	38					350 peacock			
1373	38								
1374	35	90		90					
1375	250								

Photo No.	Clear	Clambroth (Alabaster)	Fiery Opalescent	Opaque White	Amber	Blue	Amethyst	Green	Unusual Color
1376	—								
1377	50			110					
1378	50					390		650	
1379	65		175			600		850	
1380	32	90		110		375	375	450	
1381	35			110				275 pale	
1382	25	90					135 pale		
1383	20								
1384	35								
1385	28		90		500		375		
1386	35					175 pale			
1387	40								
1388	32								400 canary
1389	35					195			
1390	20								
1391	20								
1392	25	85						375	
1393	18								
1394	22								400 canary
1395	60					1000	450 light	1000	
1396	48					250		1000	
1397	55					350	650		
1398	22					400		875	875 canary
1399 a	32						550		
b	28	190				250		350	
1400	28								1000 opaque green
1401	28						500	850	
1402	25	110							
1403	22								
1404	35					500			
1405	22				275	375 / 325 peacock	175 light	375 / 325 peacock	
1406	22	90		90	400 red-amber		250		
1407	30					300 / 250 pale		450 / 425 pale	375 yellow-green
1408	22	250							
1409	40								
1410	35					500			
1411	30		175						
1412	350								
1413	35					225		375 pale	

Photo No.	Clear	Clambroth (Alabaster)	Fiery Opalescent	Opaque White	Amber	Blue	Amethyst	Green	Unusual Color
1414	50		325						
1415	50				400	425			1000 citron
1416	100								
1417	75				450				
1418	100	90				375 / 400 peacock		210 pale	
1419	75	250				325			
1420 a	800 silver nitrate center								
b	2000 silver nitrate border								
1421	2000 silver nitrate								
1422	100					325		1400	
1423	100					1200			
1424	40					500			750 canary
1425	50							2500	
1426	100					1000		3500	
1427	55								
1428	80								

OPEN AND SHAKER SALTS

Plain, heavy open salts made during the first decade of production do not command the prices of intricately molded Lacy pieces. An intense color is worth more than a pale color. Expect to pay more for shakers with patented devices that break up the salt. A slight variation in a mold due to handwork by a mold maker does not affect value. Prices given for unrecorded colors may be for variants.

Photo No.	Clear	Clambroth (Alabaster)	Fiery Opalescent	Canary	Amber	Blue	Amethyst	Green	Unusual Color
1429	35						750		
1430	350								
1431	125					600			
1432	400					600			
1433	400 without cover					600 without cover			
1434 a	400 without cover					600 without cover			
b	400					600			
1435	150					600			
1436	60							375	
1437 a	40								
b	—								

Photo No.	Clear	Clambroth (Alabaster)	Fiery Opalescent	Canary	Amber	Blue	Amethyst	Green	Unusual Color
1438 a	30								
b	—								
1439	85				450	450		550 yellow-green	700
1440	85					450		550	700
1441	85					450			700
1442 a	60								
b						750			
1443	150	300	300			500 / 900 silver-blue			
1444	80	450	450			700			875
1445	60					750 / 1000 silver-blue			
1446	40							350 light	
1447	125	225	225	600		500		875	1000
1448	150 without cover	225 without cover				350 without cover	450 without cover		600 without cover
1449	900	1200				1400	1600		
1450	135					575			700
1451 a	900		900			1400	1600		
b	—								
1452	175								
1453	200		750		875			1000	
1454	375							450 pale	
1455		225							
1456	35				150	175	200		200
1457	110				300	275			
1458	150								
1459	100				400	250		375	400
1460 a	185					900 silver-blue			
b	150					500			
1461	75					1000 silver-blue			400 opaque white
1462	75					375 pale			
1463	300	575				900			
1464 a	300					1100 silver-blue 1100 opalescent			
b			1500			900			
1465	125	575	575			575	650		750
1466	110					475		575	
1467	150					900			
1468	150					900			
1469 a	300					1500			
b	300		1100			1500			

Photo No.	Clear	Clambroth (Alabaster)	Fiery Opalescent	Canary	Amber	Blue	Amethyst	Green	Unusual Color
1470 a	300								
b	—								
1471	125				300			575	2000 black
					750 red-amber				
1472	25				150	140	185		
1473	25				150	140	185		
1474 a	35								
b	—								
1475 a	25								
b	—								
1476	35 ea.					185 ea.			
1477	60								
1478 a	28					500			
b	225								
1479 a	28					500			
b	60								
1480	32			125		225			
1481	175								
1482	65								
	85 frosted								
1483	75								
1484	110								
1485	75 ea.		150 ea.	235 ea.		425 ea.			
1486	2 ea.	8 ea.			8 ea.	8 ea.			
	1000 twelve with box								
1487 a	35					90	110		
b	—								
1488 a	35	60 opaque				90	110		
b	—								
1489	32					90	110		
1490 a	—								
b	3	8 opaque				8			
1491	65 ea.								
1492	65								
1493	90 silvered engraved								
1494	90 silvered engraved								
1495 a	15	35 opal		90	140	200	275	250	400 ruby
b	15	35 opal		90	140	200 250 peacock	275	250	400 ruby
c	150 stand								

Photo No.	Clear	Clambroth (Alabaster)	Fiery Opalescent	Canary	Amber	Blue	Amethyst	Green	Unusual Color
1496	180 the set	200 opal the set		300 the set	450 the set	500 the set	650 the set	600 the set	1000 ruby the set
1497	40	60		115	165	225 275 peacock	300	275	425 ruby
1498		110 ea. opal decorated							
1499 a	35				175	175	325	325	
b	55				200	200	375	375	
1500 a		85 opal decorated							
b		40 opal decorated							
1501		90 ea. opal decorated							
1502		450 opal decorated the set							
1503		235 pr. opal decorated							
1504						150 spangle			